THE WOMEN'S MOSQUE OF AMERICA

The Women's Mosque of America

Authority and Community in US Islam

Tazeen M. Ali

NEW YORK UNIVERSITY PRESS

New York

NEW YORK UNIVERSITY PRESS
New York
www.nyupress.org

References to Internet websites (URLs) were accurate at the time of writing. Neither the author nor New York University Press is responsible for URLs that may have expired or changed since the manuscript was prepared.

Library of Congress Cataloging-in-Publication Data
Names: Ali, Tazeen M., author.
Title: The women's mosque of America : authority and community in US Islam / Tazeen M. Ali.
Description: New York : New York University Press, 2022. | Includes bibliographical references and index.
Identifiers: LCCN 2022006324 | ISBN 9781479811298 (hardback) | ISBN 9781479811304 (paperback) | ISBN 9781479811311 (ebook other) | ISBN 9781479811281 (ebook)
Subjects: LCSH: Muslim women—United States. | Women in Islam. | Muslim women—Religious life—United States. | Women's rights—Religious aspects—Islam.
Classification: LCC BP173.4 .A4765 2022 | DDC 297.5/7082—dc23/eng/20220404
LC record available at https://lccn.loc.gov/2022006324

New York University Press books are printed on acid-free paper, and their binding materials are chosen for strength and durability. We strive to use environmentally responsible suppliers and materials to the greatest extent possible in publishing our books.

Manufactured in the United States of America

10 9 8 7 6 5 4 3 2 1

Also available as an ebook

For Maa and Baba, with gratitude

CONTENTS

NOTE ON TRANSLITERATION

This book uses simplified, anglicized spellings of all Arabic words (Qur'an, Muhammad, *Jummah*, *khutbah*, *khateebah*, etc.) rather than follow academic conventions for Arabic transliterations in English. This both reflects how my interlocutors commonly rendered key Arabic terms in English and facilitates reading for non–Arabic speakers. For example, while I use ' to signify an internal *ayn* and ' to signify an internal *hamza*, I exclude the external *ayn* and *hamza* (e.g., *ulama*). There are also instances where a *ta marbuta* is signified by either an "a" or an "ah" depending on how the word is most commonly rendered in English (e.g., *ijaza*, Shi'a, Sunnah, *surah*). Lastly, when I quote from other sources, I maintain the spelling of the original source.

Introduction

Reimagining the US Mosque

What were the wives of the Prophet told to do by Allah?
They were to recite the signs of Allah in his wisdom! . . . We
know that four of the wives were *hafidhah*—that means they
knew the Qur'an by heart. . . . Seven of the wives gave legal
decisions and were judges and scholars, not just for women
but to the entire community.
—Gail Kennard, from her August 2015 *khutbah* (sermon),
"The 12 Female Disciples of the Prophet Muhammad"

On Friday, August 28, 2015, Gail Kennard stood before a congregation
of Muslim women and their interfaith allies in downtown Los Angeles
and, in her characteristic soft-spoken but firm tone, detailed the ways
that the twelve wives of the Prophet Muhammad were role models for
all Muslim women. She noted that Muhammad's wives embodied religious knowledge, authority, and moral excellence. Kennard, an African
American Muslim in her mid-sixties, was the designated *khateebah*
(female preacher) at the Women's Mosque of America (WMA) that
month. A former journalist, she served as the president of the oldest and
one of the largest African American architectural firms in LA, which
had been founded by her late father in 1957.[1] Her remarks on Muhammad's wives made up the *khutbah* (sermon) that she delivered prior to
leading *Jummah* (Friday prayer). This was eight months into the tenure
of the WMA, an emergent multiracial women-only mosque in LA that
hosts monthly Jummah for Muslim and non-Muslim women, girls, and
boys under age twelve. After each Jummah, the khateebah sits together
with the congregants in a circle and answers their questions about the
khutbah, before entering into a general dialogue with them about topics
usually related to Islam and women.

The khutbah, congregational prayer, and post-Jummah discussion circle are all designed to be intimate communal experiences that mark the Women's Mosque of America as a safe space for women. All those who participate, including the khateebah, are encouraged to share their vulnerabilities and anxieties with each other. Modeling this intimacy, before delving into how the Prophet Muhammad's wives are moral exemplars for Muslim women everywhere, Kennard confided in the congregation her visceral discomfort at the Prophet's polygynous marriages. Expressing her unease about it, Kennard described how while Muhammad had been in a monogamous twenty-five-year marriage with his first wife, Khadijah, after her death he married multiple women in succession, totaling twelve.[2] This troubled Kennard because she, like many other Muslims invested in gender justice, believed polygyny to be inherently oppressive to women, and these multiple marriages therefore disrupted her understanding of Muhammad as a morally exemplar husband.

To address her ethical concerns about the Prophet Muhammad's polygyny, Kennard detailed to the WMA congregation how she turned to the Qur'an, the sacred Islamic scripture that Muslims consider to be the revealed word of God, for answers. After searching within the scripture, she came to understand Muhammad's wives as divinely ordained to speak as religious authorities in the early Muslim community.[3] Elaborating on her Qur'anic reflections before the congregation, Kennard cast the twelve wives[4] of Muhammad as his disciples, chosen by God to disseminate his teachings. To her, the wives' task of spreading God's message was especially noteworthy because this role had historically only ever been delegated to men, and she cited the twelve disciples of Jesus and Jacob's twelve sons as examples. By reflecting on how marriage was the only way for Muhammad to legitimize his close access to the women who had been chosen by God to be his disciples, given the social mores of seventh-century Arabia, she came to terms with his polygynous practices.[5]

To Kennard, the fact that none of Muhammad's wives after Khadijah bore him any children who survived past infancy further confirmed that there was a higher, divine purpose to their marriages. Furthermore, she stated that in the Qur'an, God speaks directly to the wives, asking them to recite Muhammad's teachings and referring to them as the "Mothers of the Believers." At the beginning of her khutbah, Kennard described how she had previously only considered Muhammad's first wife, Khadijah—a successful businesswoman fifteen years his senior who proposed marriage to him—as an empowering role model for Muslim women. By the end, she extended this categorization to all of his wives: "Let us embrace all of them, not just Khadijah. Their spirit is reaching across the centuries to remind us that we can do more than we think is possible. If they could do what they did in their time, why not us and why not now?"[6] Kennard concluded by calling on congregants to draw inspiration from Muhammad's wives to speak up and assert their voices in matters of faith. She identified the WMA as a space where Muslim women could carry on the legacy of Muhammad's wives, using their own voices to spread religious knowledge and serve as community leaders.

The Women's Mosque of America was indeed conceived as a space to elevate Muslim women's voices. Its services officially began in January 2015, when it held its inaugural Jummah for an all-female congregation at the Pico Union Project near downtown LA.[7] At the service, one woman called the *adhan* (call to prayer) while another delivered the khutbah and led prayer. Over one hundred supporters attended. Today, the WMA continues to host women's monthly Jummahs as a part of its broader aim to empower women and girls through access to Islamic knowledge and leadership opportunities.[8] In media interviews, its founder, M. Hasna Maznavi, a comedy writer, and then co-president Sana Muttalib, an international law attorney—both South Asian American women—described it as the first women's mosque in the US.[9]

The WMA's emergence fills a need in a US mosque culture that systematically yet unevenly marginalizes women in a variety of ways, including through inadequate prayer spaces, exclusion from leadership roles, and limited access to religious learning.[10] Given that US mosques vary greatly with respect to physical space, size of the congregation, internal layout, and social norms, patterns of women's marginalization are neither uniform nor universal. Yet broadly speaking, men and women's respective worship spaces within conventional mosques across the country are both separate and unequal. Women's quarters are usually smaller and inferior, though a 2011 survey found that African American–led mosques and Shi'i mosques are typically more inclusive of women than Sunni mosques with South Asian, Arab, or other ethnic majorities. This mosque survey also revealed that over 60 percent of US mosques used physical barriers to mark off women's prayer space from the main space reserved for men.[11]

In cases where women do not pray directly behind men and a physical partition, they are usually consigned to a poorly ventilated and dimly lit basement or other marginal space. As such, women often do not have access to the imam (the prayer leader) and in many cases are not even able to hear the khutbah. Those in the WMA community, including board members, khateebahs, and congregants, implicitly critique the various factors that contribute to women's subordinate status within US mosques. To be clear, patriarchal mosque culture is not unique to US Muslim communities. Around the globe, the mosque represents "a spatial expression of a patriarchal ethos," where men occupy its main spaces and assume leadership roles.[12] The WMA seeks to provide an alternative to this patriarchal ethos by creating space for women to worship and opportunities for them to cultivate religious authority. In so doing, the American Muslim women at the WMA collectively reimagine what a mosque is and what it should be.

Both the form and function of mosques have evolved over the course of Islamic history and differ across geographical region, Islamic sect, and individual Muslim communities. Moreover, for centuries, Muslim historians and contemporary scholars of religion and architecture alike have contested the criteria that properly constitute a mosque.[13] *Masjid*, the Arabic term for mosque found in the Qur'an, signifies a place for prostration and could therefore broadly apply to a range of locations, temporary or purpose-built, within a private home or in an open space. Among Muslim historians, the Prophet Muhammad's house in Medina has been widely understood to be a mosque, in which ritual worship, religious instruction, and communal gatherings all took place.

As Islamic studies specialist Simonetta Calderini has shown, the criteria and distinct architectural features for a mosque became increasingly specialized in the centuries following Muhammad's death, with emerging restrictions around access that prohibited the entry of non-Muslims and those who did not meet ritual purity standards. She summarizes: "the meaning of the term 'mosque,' its physical shape and functions, are open to interpretation. These underwent changes over time which reflected diverse contexts, from an informal and multifunctional place of gathering at specific times of prostration, to the material space which reflected and asserted the ruler's political authority and legitimacy."[14] That mosques have never been fixed in meaning in either Muslim-majority or -minority contexts allows us to situate the WMA within a global and historical Islamic context. When WMA members raise questions about the right configurations and criteria for a mosque, they are partaking in debates that have been occurring for centuries.

In other words, the women in the WMA community are not breaking with the Islamic past by raising questions about right religious practices and contesting gendered marginalization in existing US mosques. Muslims have been voicing similar concerns since the early centuries of Islam. Rather, the WMA, as a living community of Muslim women and an emerging Islamic institution, legitimizes different existing configurations of Islamic authority and combines them to promote the notion that mosques should be gender-inclusive spaces where women lead prayer, interpret the Qur'an, foreground their experiences in exegesis, commit to multiracial and intrafaith inclusivity, and build interfaith community.

This book uses the WMA to illuminate significant trends and tensions relating to Muslim women's religious authority within and beyond the US context. Muslim women around the globe occupy various positions of authority across different religious networks, including as educators at Islamic institutions, board members at mosques, Sufi shaykhas, khateebahs, and prayer leaders. Shifts in Muslim women's religious authority proceed from uneven global processes of privatization and individualization of religion, which has resulted in the decentralization of established religious authorities. In the global Islamic context, scholars describe this process as a fragmentation of authority previously monopolized by the *ulama*, the Muslim scholarly elite, and its expansion to a wide range of lay actors.[15] In the US context, this privatization of religion shapes religious congregations as civic institutions through which religious actors acculturate to American norms, including women's increased participation in public religious life and engagements in interfaith dialogue.[16] Therefore, to understand the WMA, it is necessary to attend to both the global processes of Islamic authority and the privatization of religion in the US context. Analyzing how these contexts converge further illuminates global Islamic debates on the fragmentation of religious authority and the racialized criteria by which religions become Americanized.

In their constructions of Islamic authority, American Muslim women must negotiate their marginalization in their patriarchal religious communities while also navigating the Islamophobia prevalent in mainstream US society. The WMA provides a platform for Muslim women, particularly those without any formal Islamic training, to navigate both of these terrains; it creates space for them to cultivate forms of Islamic authority that are based on the Qur'an, center women, and also speak to the sociopolitical climate of the US. These forms include ritual authority to lead prayer and deliver khutbahs (explored in chapter 1), and interpretive authority to engage in oral exegesis in those khutbahs, based on English translations of the Qur'an (chapter 2). In their oral exegeses, khateebahs draw on their experiences as women to interpret sacred texts (chapter 3), and often also use their khutbahs to engage contemporary social justice issues and promote building multiracial (chapter 4), intrafaith, and interfaith community (chapter 5).

Gail Kennard's khutbah on the wives of Muhammad provides an introduction to the WMA's model of Islamic authority, illuminating especially the central role that the Qur'an plays in it, while also exemplifying the significance that the WMA community places on approaching scriptural interpretations *as women*. For example, to address her concerns about polygyny, Kennard turned to particular Qur'anic verses[17] about Muhammad's wives to posit that they were divinely ordained to act as religious authorities. The Qur'an provided the basis for her argument that the wives of Muhammad are better understood as his disciples. Moreover, it was her discomfort, as a woman, with Muhammad's polygynous marriages that drove her exegetical inquiry into the roles of his wives in the first place, offering an example of the kind of unique contribution, according to the WMA ethos, that women can make in their approaches to Qur'anic interpretation.

Kennard cites the examples of the wives of Muhammad to encourage women in the WMA congregation to seek roles of religious authority. She explains that in seeking more information about them, she learned that four of Muhammad's twelve wives had the entirety of the Qur'an memorized, seven had been known to act as legal arbiters, and the early Muslim community had regarded all of them as authority figures. By drawing on Islamic scriptures and the legacies of prominent Muslim historical figures like the wives of the Prophet to argue that American

Muslim women, like those in the congregation, should take up similar roles, Kennard situates the WMA project within Islamic history. Additionally, by referring to Muhammad's wives as his twelve disciples, Kennard adopts a Christian framework recalling the disciples of Jesus. She also draws connections with the Jewish patriarch and Islamic Prophet Jacob and his twelve sons, demonstrating her sense of a shared religious history. These references are not only meaningful to Muslims but also work to welcome the WMA's Jewish and Christian congregants.

Two years later, when I was conducting my fieldwork interviews at the WMA, congregants repeatedly cited Kennard's khutbah on Muhammad's wives as his disciples as among their favorites. In particular, they appreciated hearing a woman's perspective on female figures in Islamic history. Broadly speaking, congregants sought female exegetical voices, increased Islamic knowledge, spiritual community, and adequate worship space in their religious lives, and were compelled by the WMA's potential to provide all of these things. As an institution, the WMA produces new ways for women to cultivate Islamic authority that bypass the requirements of formal religious training, which creates more opportunities for women's exegeses. In the absence of formal Islamic training, women's embodied experiences, their community activism, and their professional credentials grant them religious authority. For example, Kennard, who has been a WMA khateebah multiple times, was also a prominent member of various other Muslim communities in Southern California.[18] Her respected position within different LA circles contributed to her religious authority within the WMA community.

The WMA community is diverse in age, race, and religiosity, and the size of the congregation has fluctuated over the years. The numbers have shifted from seventy to a hundred women every month in 2015 to approximately thirty to fifty women in attendance in subsequent years, with select months in 2018 and 2019 attracting up to seventy-five congregants. Attendance dipped to a dozen or so each month during the COVID-19 pandemic, during which the WMA shifted its services to a virtual format over Zoom, although online views of khutbahs on Facebook and YouTube consistently hit several hundred views.[19] The WMA runs on donations, and membership is voluntary and does not entail formal fees, though congregants are encouraged to contribute five dollars a month if they are able.

Figure I.1. Gail Kennard delivers her khutbah "The 12 Female Disciples of the Prophet Muhammad" at the Women's Mosque of America (August 28, 2015). Source: Faezeh Fathizadeh, the Pluralism Project at Harvard University

Amid fluctuations in congregant numbers, there is a core constituency of African American Muslim women over the age of sixty, like Kennard, whom other congregants describe as the heart of the community. There are also white Christian and Jewish women in the same age range who come as interfaith allies. An ethnically diverse group of younger women in their twenties and thirties—Black, South Asian, white, Arab, East Asian, and Latina—are also in regular attendance. This racial and ethnic diversity itself is consistent with the majority of US mosques. A 2020 study confirms that mosques in America are among the most ethnically diverse religious bodies in the country, especially during Friday congregational prayers. However, this diversity is not evenly distributed and 75 percent of American mosques have one dominant ethnic group, with the number of African American mosque attendees declining between 2010 and 2020.[20] By contrast, no single ethnic group at the WMA dominates the congregation. Moreover, given that African Americans make up approximately one-fifth of US Muslims, the WMA's diversity more accurately reflects the overall demographics of Muslims in America than do the majority of American mosques.

Through its analysis of the WMA, this book offers insights into the dynamism of Islam and the American Muslim women who interpret it, who approach the Qur'an as a tool to resist social hierarchies and empower themselves. It demonstrates how WMA khateebahs assert themselves as meaningful religious actors in the US and beyond, by intervening in debates about Islamic authority as the intersections of gender, religious space, and national belonging. The WMA's model of authority fits into a discernible American Muslim pattern of treating the English language as a Muslim vernacular, as scholars of Islam in America Mucahit Bilici, Justine Howe, and Timur Yuskaev have all shown.[21] In its turn toward lay interpretive authority, the WMA also fits within global revivalist trends that emphasize individual interpretation of the Qur'an. While still a part of ongoing US and global Islamic trends, the WMA produces a distinctive model of authority through its khutbahs and the interactions between khateebahs, congregants, and board members. This model of authority combines new and existing trends that assert women's right to lead prayer, engage English translations to interpret the Qur'an, and center women's experiences and social justice issues in exegesis, as well as forge multiracial and intra- and interfaith solidarity. Authority, through the lens of the WMA, then, offers us an alternative to hegemonic models of authority that are rooted in maleness, Arabic language expertise, and formal Islamic credentials.

Religious Authority at the WMA

Authority, both how it is cultivated and the ways in which it is contested, has long been of interest in the study of religion. Historian of religion Bruce Lincoln defines authority as an "effect" produced when the actions of a given actor align with an audience's historically and culturally specific expectations.[22] The relationship between WMA khateebahs and congregants reflects this dynamic. Supporters of the WMA share key assumptions about the patriarchal nature of US mosques and women's subordinate status within them. In other words, WMA members—broadly defined as khateebahs, board members, volunteers, and congregants, including those from interfaith backgrounds—all believe that Muslim women belong in positions of religious authority. This shared belief predisposes them to "attitudes of trust, respect, docility, acceptance, even reverence" toward WMA khateebahs, and therefore meets the conditions to produce religious authority.[23] In other words, WMA members do not need to be persuaded to take khateebahs' authority seriously since they arrive at the WMA already convinced of the merit they bring to the role. Likewise, their own self-professed commitments to social and racial justice inform their expectations of what makes a speaker authoritative, and they are receptive when khateebahs address subjects that are meaningful to them.

Thinking specifically about women's religious authority, it is useful to consider gendered patterns of authoritative claim making across modern American history. Scholar of religion and Africana studies Anthea Butler helps us to think about how women have subverted patriarchal authority within religious institutions through both their selective acquiescence and resistance to male power. Butler shows that early twentieth-century Pentecostal African American women in the Church of God in Christ, in their negotiations for spiritual authority, upheld men's exclusive right to preach while simultaneously eroding male influence by taking up alternative roles such as teaching in the church.[24] Women at the WMA are similarly judicious with which patriarchal norms they set out to contest, and as a result, they subvert male modes of authority by formulating new ones, even as they appear to defer to or tolerate male authority in some respects.

Women throughout American religious history have also cultivated their authority by developing auxiliary networks and institutions outside of their faith communities. Here, historian of religion Judith Weisenfeld provides a way to understand how women have carved out their own spaces outside of the formal structure of the church to exert influence and authority.[25] Weisenfeld's research on African American women's Christian activism in twentieth-century New York City illuminates how women's venues created at the margins of the church, like the Young Women's Christian Association, serve as rich sites for understanding the extent of women's authority in and beyond their religious communities.[26] The WMA can be understood through this lens as an alternative space created outside preexisting LA mosques that operates exclusively under the authority of women.

These late nineteenth- and early twentieth-century examples of African American women within the various Protestant congregations that make up the institution of the Black church provide useful ways to think about some of the moves that US Muslim women make in their own claims to Islamic authority. As African American Protestant women contested patriarchal power within their churches, they were simultaneously working toward Black liberation and faced intersectional marginalization on account of their racial and gender identities. Contemporary US Muslim women, many of whom are African American and other women of color, similarly exist in a space of "double liminality" as they challenge male power while also combatting anti-Muslim racism.[27]

The WMA offers ways for lay Muslim women without formal Islamic training from religious institutions in the US or overseas to cultivate religious authority. The notion of religious authority based on criteria other than educational credentials can be traced back to women during the time of the Prophet Muhammad. Female followers of Muhammad—those among his Companions, members of the *Sahabah* who had personal contact with him during his lifetime—served as transmitters and narrators of the Hadith, records of Prophetic sayings that Muslims consider the most authoritative source of Islamic law and norms after the Qur'an. Reflecting the literacy norms of the time, these female Companions were not required to be educated.[28] Rather, the prerequisite for transmission was proximity to Muhammad.[29] As Muslim scholars began to formulate Islamic law and canonize the Hadith in the early centuries following Muhammad's death, an important form of authoritative claim making was to position the Companions of Muhammad as Islamic authority figures.[30] In this view, being a Companion of Muhammad was the primary qualification for authority rather than formal education or gender, and female religious authorities were afforded the same legitimacy as their male counterparts.[31] However, the privilege of proximity to the Prophet was gendered. The wives of Muhammad, above all of his other Companions, male and female, were uniquely positioned to authoritatively narrate hadith traditions about his personal habits, including hygiene and conduct within the household. This helps us to better understand WMA khateebah Gail Kennard's remarks that Muhammad's polygynous marriages were necessary to legitimize his access to certain female disciples who then disseminated religious knowledge as authority figures in their communities.

Beyond the Prophet Muhammad's lifetime up until the present day, Muslim women have continued to inhabit various positions of authority in the global context without formal credentials. As Hilary Kalmbach shows, throughout Muslim societies prior to the late twentieth century, women were largely precluded from acquiring scholarly authority because only men had access to formal education.[32] Muslim women therefore cultivated authority through other means in alternative sites. In Sufi lodges, for example, female leaders were spiritually equal to their male counterparts and could achieve sainthood and confer *baraka* (spiritual blessings) on their followers. Muslim women have also served as religious teachers in informal settings, where their authority was based on "reputation, teaching experience and personal style," rather than on formal education.[33] Women were also Islamic scholars, Hadith transmitters, prayer leaders, khateebahs, or teachers in informal study circles as well as in madrasas, Islamic schools that teach on subjects such as the Qur'an and the Hadith.

Kalmbach also notes that those who possess Islamic knowledge do not exist as authorities in a vacuum devoid of community, but that "amassing legitimacy requires a multi-dimensional interaction in which the speech, dress, and conduct of the authority both influence and are influenced by those witnessing the performance, be they peers, students, or the general public."[34] At the WMA, interactions between those in leadership positions and those in the congregation together produce religious authority. Religious authority does not simply trickle down from religious leaders into worship communities for congregants to passively receive. Rather, authority is layered and produced through dynamic interactions between different religious actors. While there is indeed hierarchy at the WMA, knowledge and authority are not disseminated from religious leaders to congregants, but shift and flow between and among them, much like the process Kalmbach describes above. The multidimensional interactions between Muslim leaders and congregations render a fluctuating relationship between formal religious credentials and Islamic authority at the community level.

The WMA promotes an explicitly gendered model of religious authority based on women's lived experiences that does not replicate existing forms of male authority. For example, WMA policies for khateebahs encourage them to share vulnerabilities and offer advice on how to overcome personal struggles using the Qur'an and other scriptural sources.[35] Furthermore, on the basis of my field interviews, in the eyes of congregants, khateebahs' experiences as women lent credence to their authority and qualified them to speak on particular subjects that, in their view, men could not meaningfully engage in a similar fashion.

WMA khateebahs center women's embodied experiences as a fruitful site of inquiry into the Qur'an and its meaning. Here, scholar of religious studies Debra Majeed's Black Muslim womanist theological reflections provide a frame to analyze their activities. Her womanist framework privileges African American Muslim women's lived experiences as they relate to a racist and patriarchal US context. Based on this framework, she argues for a Qur'anic interpretive method that is grounded "in the nuances of black struggles for survival, in quests for Islamic legitimacy, the adaptability of the Qur'an, Islam's emphasis on justice and equity, and in the social activism of African American Muslim women."[36] Majeed's emphasis on activism accords with the values at the WMA, where racial injustices in general and anti-Black racism in particular are collective concerns of the community. Accordingly, some khutbahs put Islamic scriptures in direct conversations with US social movements such as Black Lives Matter. Given that African American women form a core part of the WMA congregation, their institutional attention to anti-Black racism in the US again exemplifies their attention to lived experiences.

At the WMA, Muslim women are active mediators of the Islamic tradition. I draw on cultural anthropologist Talal Asad's concept of Islam as a discursive tradition to theorize Islamic authority as historically contingent and embodied within interpretive communities. The emergent model of authority that I conceptualize here relates to the past, but does not seek to comprehensively imitate it.[37] I consider how WMA members' interpretive activities fit into academic debates about the "crisis" of authority. Scholars characterize the crisis of Islamic authority as the fragmentation of authority previously monopolized by the ulama, the Muslim scholarly elite, and its expansion to a range of lay actors since the onset of modernity.[38] As historical anthropologist Zareena Grewal has shown, some US Muslims seek authority through formal credentials: studying Arabic and acquiring *ijazas* (Islamic certifications) on particular subjects, or attending an Islamic educational institution in the Middle East, Africa, or South Asia. In the process, they construct transnational moral geographies that link their religious identities to a global Muslim community.[39] These US Muslims place Islamic authenticity in a "sacred East."

Attitudes that equate Islamic authenticity with the "foreign" East situate the US at the periphery of the Islamic tradition and undermine certain American Muslims as legitimate religious actors and potential mediators of the tradition. Islamic studies scholar Aysha Hidayatullah shows that critics discredit a substantial body of feminist exegeses of the Qur'an, produced by Muslims in the secular US academy, as inauthentic based on their "Western" influences. She situates these feminist exegeses at the "edge" of the Islamic tradition, "a place of animated change and the avowal and disavowal of tradition."[40] The WMA arises from precisely this place of animated change, growing from elements of the genre of Muslim feminist exegesis.

Yet it should be noted that the WMA does not brand itself as a feminist space, and indeed has carefully avoided this label. The feminist label, as we will see, is polarizing across many US Muslim communities. It is perceived by some as not authentically Islamic but a product of "Western influence," despite how Islamic feminists, in their scholarship and activism, have carefully documented the ways that they draw on their Islamic religious teachings and native cultures to frame their projects.[41] Part of the WMA's avoidance of identifying as feminist then, has to do with appealing to mainstream US Muslim communities, or at least attempting not to alienate them. Even despite the WMA's institutional evasion, many congregants and khateebahs happily identify themselves as feminist. At the same time, there is also a broader reluctance among self-identifying US Muslim feminists themselves to identify with other US feminists, especially those who are white, because of anxieties that their own projects might be co-opted by both conservative and liberal imperialist narratives that denigrate Islam. For this reason, Black feminist and womanist scholarship that incorporates intersectionality as a way to work toward women's liberation while also combatting white supremacy provides a useful frame to think about the "feminist" moves of WMA actors, while still acknowledging the broader ambivalence many of them may have toward a feminist label.

Recognizing how the WMA emerges from the genre of US Muslim feminist exegesis and using Black feminist and womanist frameworks to situate their interpretive activities provides an opportunity to analyze the US as at the center rather than the periphery of debates over Islamic authority. Emphasizing the US as an integral site for Islamic studies debates over authority allows us to take seriously American Muslims' engagements with their religious tradition. It also allows us to recognize American Muslims, particularly women, as legitimate religious actors in the fabric of US society. Therefore, this book contributes to a deeper understanding of authority within both the global Islamic and the American religious landscapes.

Moreover, since the 2016 presidential election, white nationalism, misogyny, and Islamophobia have returned to the public sphere in full force. Alongside these trends, the stereotype of the subjugated Muslim woman has reemerged in American public discourse. Earlier scholarship on Islam and women focused on dismantling this trope through nuanced accounts of Muslim women exercising agency.[42] Recent studies have gone even further to show the complexities of gender debates in US Muslim communities.[43] There is also a growing body of literature on transnational networks of authority and Muslim women's roles within them, as well as work on Islam in America that analyzes race and identity.[44] However, there is still insufficient scholarship exploring new developments in Muslim women's religious authority against a backdrop of patriarchal and racialized trends in the US context. Despite the public attention garnered by Muslim women increasingly taking up public roles in Islamic scholarship, leadership, and institution building in the US and Europe, academic scholarship on the subject remains scarce. As a result, scholarship in both US religions and Islamic studies overlooks American Muslim women's dynamism as religious actors who both shape and are shaped by the US context.

The WMA draws attention to new ways that American Muslim women are constructing religious authority by renegotiating normative assumptions around women's roles in their communities. American Muslim women who take issue with the marginal status of women in their religious communities are in a particularly tenuous position as they must negotiate change within their communities against the precipitous rise of Islamophobia in the US. Here scholar of critical race theory and law professor Kimberlé Crenshaw and religious studies scholar Sa'diyya Shaikh provide models to engage with internal critiques of sexism within Muslim communities, while keeping in mind the global imperial context in which ideas of Islam, women, and identity circulate.[45] Crenshaw, who coined the theory of intersectionality, notes that single-issue frameworks do not account for the multidimensional experiences of women, particularly in communities of color.[46] In other words, the different women featured in this book do not face discrimination based only on their gender, their race or ethnicity, or their religious identities;

rather, combinations of these factors and more shape their daily experiences and inform how they are treated and perceived by others. Advocating for an intersectional approach in the study of gender and Islam, Shaikh advances the utility of the multiple critique method, which simultaneously accounts for a multiplicity of inequalities and their interactions with one another—e.g., race, class, colonial status, sexuality.

Employing Shaikh's multiple critique method allows us to understand the contours of American Muslim women's marginalizing experiences. Applying such an intersectional approach enables us to account for how a Black Muslim woman's experiences would differ from a South Asian or white Muslim woman's experiences due to rampant anti-Black racism within US mosque communities, despite their shared identity as Muslim women. Likewise, while anti-Muslim racism and discrimination may create a shared experience in US Muslim communities across genders, women and LGBTQI Muslims are subjected to distinct forms of gendered Islamophobic violence that differentiate their experiences from those of cis-gendered men.

Taking seriously American Muslim women's recent engagements in cultivating religious authority provides an important scholarly opportunity to advance the study of Islam and gender beyond simply advocating for national belonging or dispelling negative stereotypes. In this book, I treat members of the WMA as meaningful actors within the fabric of American religious life rather than as exemplars meant to validate the broader Muslim presence in liberal societies. In so doing, I show how women at the WMA legitimize specific ways of being American Muslims. Furthermore, since the WMA is a multiracial community, I also examine the internal dynamics of historically tense relationships between Black and immigrant Muslims (including those of first and subsequent generations) in the US. As religious minorities in the US, Muslims are racialized as political others, and congregations develop in relation to hegemonic whiteness, which in turn has a profound effect on the relationships among Muslims of different racial and ethnic backgrounds. In debates over religious pluralism, then, this book attends to the uneven balance of power that affords some religious groups positions of power in interfaith dialogue while marginalizing others.

To be clear, this book does not suggest that the WMA creates a *new* sui generis form of religious authority. As we saw earlier, members of the WMA cultivate authority in ways that resemble earlier precedents from non-Muslim and Muslim contexts both in the US and globally. The WMA also shares a common orientation with contemporary US Muslim third spaces, which typically function as replacements for, or complements to, established mosques that do not meet the needs of all of their community members. Third spaces differ from first and second spaces, like home and school respectively, or in this case, home and the mosque, by adopting hybrid spatiality between the practical everyday and more formalized knowledge.[47] As Justine Howe shows, Muslim third spaces can transform modes of pious practices in US Islam by questioning existing modes of authority. She categorizes Muslim third spaces as sites structured by alternate modes of authority, textual engagements, and ritual expression.[48] By these criteria, the WMA would be considered a third space; however, in its own narrative, it identifies as a mosque. By branding itself as a mosque rather than as a third space, the WMA attempts to redefine what a mosque community should look like.

For example, while the majority of US mosques boast ethnically diverse congregations as we have seen above, many of them along with other US Muslim institutions reproduce, in anthropologist Su'ad Abdul Khabeer's terms, the "ethnoreligious hegemony" of immigrant Islam. Ethnoreligious hegemony refers to how, in particular, Arab and South Asian Muslims in the US monopolize defining the parameters of authoritative and authentic Islamic identity and practice over Black Muslims.[49] Many Arab and South Asian Muslims claim this monopoly based on their proximity to the Islamic East through their cultural heritage and infantilize Black Muslims in the process, often assuming religious authority over them even when they have less technical expertise in, say, Qur'anic recitation or knowledge of the Islamic legal tradition.[50] The WMA attempts to build a multiracial mosque that could offset the hegemony of immigrant Islam, beyond simply having a diverse congregation that continues to perpetuate anti-Blackness. It is certainly not the first space to challenge this ethnoreligious hegemony, as American Muslims operating outside of the structure of conventional mosques have routinely done so. For example, Khabeer's ethnography of young Muslims in Chicago shows how working and volunteering at a Muslim nonprofit dedicated to the arts and community activism helps build solidarity between non-Black and Black Muslims, and combats Arab and South

Asian hegemony by recognizing Black Muslim practices and customs as authoritative.[51]

In fact, the individual features of the WMA—a place where women lead prayer, use English translations to interpret scriptures, draw on experiences as a key exegetical method, build multiracial Muslim solidarity rooted in social justice concerns, and cultivate interfaith ties—are not new or unique on their own. Yet the combination of these features represents a form of authority that is indeed distinctive. The particular constellation of features of authority at the WMA continually shifts and adapts to new challenges and community pressures. The WMA therefore provides us with the potential to think about new directions in Islamic authority, in which English translations and women's experiences are valued in Qur'anic exegesis over Arabic language expertise and formal credentials; and where social justice activism is prioritized as a moral imperative, and interfaith relationships are cultivated as a result of, but also to combat, a broader climate of Islamophobia. In other words, women at the WMA make conceivable a kind of lay American Islamic authority that is an alternative to hegemonic models of authority rooted in maleness, Arabic language expertise, and formal credentials.

However, in its promotion of lay authority, the WMA is not anti-clerical. For instance, the WMA's model of lay authority does not discredit Arabic language expertise or formal credentials—or even maleness for that matter—as individually problematic or as an ill-suited basis for authority. Rather, the WMA illuminates how the combination of such criteria for Islamic authority precludes gender inclusive interpretations of scripture, and by extension inclusive religious communities. In so doing, the American Muslim women at the WMA enable us to think about alternative modes of authority that decenter Arabic language expertise and formal Islamic credentialization, and instead foreground gender-inclusive community norms.

Encountering the WMA

I first learned about the WMA through the media buzz and the intra-Muslim controversy that surrounded its early moments in 2015 while I was living on the other end of the country in Boston, Massachusetts. At that time my understanding of the WMA was framed by the social media debates surrounding the legal validity of woman-led Jummah and non-Muslim media narratives about Muslim women "fighting back" against patriarchy by carving out their own religious spaces. Both the American Muslim and non-Muslim narratives about the WMA assumed the radical nature of the space, and so I had imagined that WMA congregants were likely united by their negative experiences in mosques and looking to revolutionize the status quo. This was not the case, and I would learn that, for many of its members, the WMA was but one of multiple mosques in LA where they were active participants. I had also assumed that interfaith allies only occasionally participated in solidarity, before observing that, in fact, they regularly attended the WMA every month. There was also a constant stream of occasional participants. These were floating members from the greater Southern California area who attended when their schedules permitted, as well as out-of-town-visitors who, while passing through LA, sought out the WMA as something of a pilgrimage site.

While the WMA is a living religious community of dynamic actors who shape new religious practices and debate established norms, it is also engaged in an ongoing discursive project to produce and publish women's khutbahs. These khutbahs are meant to be consumed by a community beyond the WMA congregation in LA, signaled by their publication online and, since June 2018, through livestreaming on Facebook. By analyzing a selection of WMA khutbahs from the years 2015–21, I show how khateebahs interpret scriptures through their experiences, producing malleable, embodied, and local readings of texts. As an ethnographic field of study, the WMA contributes to our understanding of debates over gender and authority within and beyond the American Muslim landscape. Over the course of four months in 2017, I engaged in participant observation at monthly WMA Jummahs and its annual co-ed iftar (fast-breaking meal in Ramadan) and Qiyam (supererogatory night prayers in Ramadan) event. I also attended other Muslim community events in LA hosted by various organizations that WMA members often belonged to as well. During my time attending WMA Jummahs, I met visitors from Oregon, Massachusetts, North Carolina, and even the United Kingdom. So while the heart of this book is based on my textual analysis of WMA khutbahs, which are all published online, the ethnographic material provides a more complete picture of this interpretive community at large.

I conducted twenty-three ethnographic supplemental interviews with members of the WMA between May and September 2017 in LA. These interviews, unlike those in other ethnographies, focus solely on my interlocutors' relationships to the WMA and their reflections on its khutbahs, rather than on their personal lives as well. The ethnographic portions of the book therefore provide only brief glimpses into who these women are as individual people and offers instead their specific insights into the experiment in American Islamic authority that is the WMA. In other words, this is a book about an emergent model of lay Islamic authority cultivated in community that incorporates conversations with a sample of American Muslim women in Southern California who are its key authors. This book does not attempt to present a full portrait of these individual Muslim women, laying bare their personal triumphs or struggles, which might help to render them more sympathetic, or even simply more legible, to US readers, both Muslim and non-Muslim, who all operate within a climate of gendered Islamophobia. Instead, I ask that readers take for granted that Muslim women are complicated and diverse religious actors with storied histories, and understand the ethnographic elements of this book as a way to analyze the WMA's religious and cultural productions more fully.

Of my twenty-three interlocutors at the WMA, eight had served as khateebahs prior to our interviews, three were board members at the time of the interviews, and twelve were regular congregants who had not been formally involved in leadership. They occupied a diverse age range and came from different racial and ethnic backgrounds. Three were in their mid- to late twenties, nine were in the thirties, five were in their forties, and six were in their fifties or sixties. All of them identified as American. Eight were of South Asian descent, including from Indian, Pakistani, Bangladeshi, and Afghan backgrounds. Six were African Americans, five were white, two were Latina, two were East Asian, and one was Arab. All names have been changed to maintain anonymity and any identifiable information has been omitted, except for one who wished to be identified by her real name to defy the erasure of Black women's voices. I also spoke with founder M. Hasna Maznavi and a few WMA khateebahs explicitly about their khutbahs. In these instances, I use their real names since I refer to information that is already public either through the online publication of khutbahs or media interviews.

I used different approaches to recruit conversation partners for this study. A number of WMA khateebahs are public figures in their own right, and I sought out introductions to those whom I encountered at different community events or those whose khutbahs I was particularly drawn to from listening to them online. After providing background information about my research project, I would ask them if they had the time and inclination to sit down with me for a conversational interview about their experiences at the WMA. By contrast, with WMA congregants, I did not recruit specific individuals but let connections form organically. Over the course of various Ramadan social events, I had gradually started to recognize and be recognized by some faces from my WMA Jummah attendance. I would mostly seek interviews with those who had struck up conversations with me as a fellow congregant and expressed interest in my research after I had explained what brought me to the WMA. These recruits made excellent conversation partners who were happy to share their views on the topics I had prepared, and also on aspects of the WMA and other Muslim communities that I had not previously considered. These introductory conversations usually occurred when the discussion circles held after Jummah wrapped up, or afterward when congregants socialized outside of the venue by a halal food truck, whose proceeds went toward the WMA. I made one formal attempt to solicit participants to interview during the July 2017 Jummah, when I stacked a handful of flyers with my contact information on a table placed in front of the entryway to prayer area; I gained two interviewees through this method. I conducted most of my interviews at various coffee shops and cafes around LA and some at the Islamic Center of Southern California, one of the largest mosques in the area, conveniently located near downtown, where a number of WMA members were also congregants, and which also had parking spots readily available outside of prayer times, a major consideration when determining a meeting place.

In making such contacts, I felt acutely aware that my Muslimness and Bangladeshi American background facilitated the process of gaining conversation partners. While all self-identifying women, regardless of their religious affiliation or lack thereof, are welcome at the WMA, my being Muslim and of South Asian heritage likely made congregants more amenable to sharing their time with me. Nearly two decades of constant surveillance and state-orchestrated harassment of American

Muslims since 9/11, coupled with the anti-Muslim hostility sanctioned by the Trump administration, have made many American Muslim communities more guarded with outsiders. Spies and informants, planted by federal and state agencies to collect personal information on community members, have become commonplace in Muslim communities across the nation. As a result, many American Muslims are suspicious of outsiders to their worship communities who solicit information from them. There is also a more generalized suspicion of journalists and academics, myself included, who may have particular agendas in soliciting interviews. While my own background as an American Muslim woman granted me access to participate in the WMA Jummahs, it also requires a theorization of insider-outsider status. In many ways, my experiences that summer as a WMA participant mirrored those of the other women in my age group. I would often hear from interviewees in their twenties and thirties that they felt that the WMA community was a very nurturing space, particularly because of the elder African American women who, as regular congregants, continually made them feel supported. I felt similarly welcomed when I attended my first WMA Jummah in May 2017. I remember nervously making my way into the Pico Union Project, the interfaith facility near downtown LA that hosted the WMA for its first two and a half years, when I was immediately approached by Malika, a middle-aged African American woman, dressed in a black abaya and a brightly colored hijab, who was walking in at the same time. Malika had recognized that I was a newcomer to the WMA, and she warmly introduced herself and welcomed me with a hug.

Malika, I would soon learn, was a WMA regular who would often deliver the adhan for the congregation, and later that summer she shared her experiences with me for this book. I briefly mentioned my research to her during our chat, and Malika then took it upon herself to walk me around the prayer hall and introduce me to other women to whom she thought I should speak. As I situated myself in LA and its Muslim communities, I gradually gained conversation partners over the course of the next few months. Throughout that time, especially with respect to the six older Black women featured in this book, I would have the distinct feeling of being taken in by them, the way someone might guide a mentee or a younger sister. Through this particular dynamic, I would continue to reflect on my own experiences as a floating member of the WMA.

This book examines how gender is continually constructed and performed.[52] I employ the concept of gender as a meaningful category of analysis to investigate the WMA's own assumptions about gender and sexuality.[53] Given the racial and ethnic diversity of the WMA preachers and congregants, as well as its emphasis on social justice, I take seriously in my analysis the categories of both gender and race, which never operate separately. Moreover, I see Islamophobia, which is particularly gendered and racialized in the US, as an important context against which members of the WMA justify their decisions. I argue that the WMA produces a distinct model of Islamic authority that is informed by the US context but also speaks to global Islamic trends. The first chapter details the formation of the WMA, focusing on the community debates that it generated on ritual authority. It analyzes critics' fixation with contesting the Islamic legality of woman-led prayer. I argue here that WMA members do not share the same level of concern as their critics with legal debates over women's ritual authority, and I unpack their various motivations, values, and perspectives that draw them to the WMA.

Drawing on the history of women's Qur'anic interpretations in the US, chapter 2 argues that the WMA reimagines the criteria necessary for interpretive authority. By inviting "everyday" women rather than religious scholars to serve as khateebahs, the WMA provides a platform for them to contribute to Qur'anic exegesis. Khateebahs promote individual relationships to scripture and the use of English-language translations of the Qur'an, contesting American Muslim norms that uphold Arabic as the sole language of God. Chapter 3 introduces the concept of embodied authority based on women's experiences, drawing on Sa'diyya Shaikh's *tafsir* (exegesis) of praxis, Black feminist epistemology, and Muslim womanist thought. Here, I demonstrate how the WMA community confers authority on its khateebahs by viewing them as in a privileged position to comment on particular subjects in sacred texts on the basis of their experiences as women. These subjects include, but are not limited to, motherhood, grief, and gender violence. Women at the WMA view its khateebahs as particularly authoritative because of their gendered experiences, not in spite of them. In so doing, the WMA promotes a feminine model of authority.

Chapter 4 investigates the WMA's commitment to social justice activism and building multiracial solidarity. Islamophobia and the racialization of Muslims motivate WMA khateebahs to put Islamic scriptures in conversation with social justice causes. Khateebahs thereby cultivate activist authority by using sacred texts to connect with social movements such as Black Lives Matter. In the eyes of its members, the WMA's engagement with contemporary American social issues like structural racism, environmental degradation, and gender discrimination bolster its religious authority. Nevertheless, despite the WMA's institutional engagements with confronting anti-Blackness, congregants come away with varied experiences of interracial solidarity.

The final chapter examines points of overlap and divergence among American Muslim, Jewish, and Christian women in their negotiations of religious authority. As a Muslim site of interfaith engagement, the WMA participates in an emergent trend of forging intersectional interfaith alliances and cultivating intrafaith inclusivity as a means to combat religious bigotry in post-2016 America.[54] While the WMA's intrafaith inclusivity offers a powerful corrective to discriminatory and often racist trends within Muslim communities, its interfaith relationships can have more complicated implications. Interfaith engagements, despite their merits, are for US Muslims often a part of a broader bid for national belonging, and the larger climate of Islamophobia can compel them to seek such alliances. In this way, the WMA's embrace of interfaith engagement is continuous with the post-9/11 trends in US communities to promote interreligious dialogue among the Abrahamic traditions. The WMA cultivates interfaith solidarity as a central part of its aims as a community, but there are challenges and limitations to these relationships.

Overall, the WMA offers ways for Muslim women, particularly those without formal Islamic training, to cultivate religious authority. It allows them to become active mediators of Islam as a discursive tradition, in which norms of authority are historically contingent and embodied within interpretive communities, on the basis of their own gendered experiences. As a product of the margins of the Islamic tradition, the WMA demonstrates the dynamism of Islam and the women who interpret it, who approach the Qur'an as a tool to resist social hierarchies, build community, and empower themselves. And as a result, the American Muslim women at the WMA make conceivable a model of lay Islamic authority that challenges patriarchal and other marginalizing trends in Muslim communities.

1

Ritual Authority

Beyond Legal Debates on Woman-Led Prayer

I love new things. I love things that turn things we know on
their side—not on its head, but on its side a little. It's what
I love best [about the WMA]. . . . It's when you take something you know really well and put it on its side, so that you
get to experience it in a new way. Like, I've heard a gazillion
adhans [call to prayer], heard a gazillion khutbahs, but the
fact that it is just being done by a woman instead of a man,
you just get to encounter it from a fresh perspective.
—Amal, white, in her forties

In the weeks leading up to its first Jummah on January 30, 2015, and
thereafter, Muslim responses to the WMA ranged from enthusiasm and
support to criticism and condemnation. The WMA also garnered attention from mainstream US media outlets such as the *Huffington Post* and
the *Wall Street Journal*, whose reception was positive, even celebratory.[1]
Many American Muslims, both leaders and community members alike,
were less congratulatory, and debates on the WMA's religious legitimacy
quickly emerged across social media and the Muslim blogosphere. As
Islamic studies scholar Juliane Hammer observes, these internal Muslim debates operate in the "public gaze" of the non-Muslim public. In
other words, American Muslims who participate in debates about the
WMA are acutely aware of the broader scrutiny of their intra-religious
discussions.[2] As a woman-only congregation, the WMA has managed to
mostly circumvent contentious debates over ritual leadership in mixed-
gender settings; yet as we will see, it has still been met with spirited
criticism from other American Muslims.

Two aspects of the WMA caused particular controversy. Primarily,
critics of the WMA contested the Islamic legal validity of a woman-led

Jummah, arguing that it lacked historical precedent from the time of the Prophet Muhammad and therefore did not conform to the *fiqh*, Islamic jurisprudential, tradition.[3] Jummah prayer is a two-unit prayer performed in congregation on Friday afternoons, and it replaces the regular four-unit midday prayer, *dhuhr*, which is obligatory for Muslims to perform individually or in congregation during the rest of the week. Citing a lack of historical precedent, the WMA's critics contend that the majority of Sunni legal schools permit women to lead other women in standard daily ritual prayer, but not Jummah. For their part, WMA leaders accommodate congregants who might share the view that woman-led Jummah is legally invalid by allotting time for them to perform the dhuhr prayer.

Secondarily, some critics claimed that the WMA's exclusion of men was divisive and abandoned the principles of *ummah* (Muslim community). These critics lamented the WMA's potential to fragment "already fragile" American Muslim communities.[4] Public concerns over the state of the American Muslim ummah demonstrate how the WMA catalyzed a national conversation on mosques and gender roles within them, in some ways continuing an earlier conversation from 2005. In 2005, Indian American author Asra Nomani organized a Jummah event in New York City in which amina wadud, a pioneering scholar of Islam and gender, led a mixed-gender congregation in prayer.[5] Nomani's 2005 event, for which she courted significant media attention, generated debates and often-hostile criticism regarding women's ritual authority, their visibility in the public sphere of the mosque, and the general state of the American ummah among Muslims around the world. Responses to the WMA represent a recirculation of these same gender debates.

Within the first five months of the WMA's tenure, its leaders offered official responses to both of the critiques above. Just three months after their inaugural event, to alleviate concerns about the legal validity of woman-led Jummah, they incorporated into their official program a time slot for an optional congregational dhuhr, the standard midday prayer. The addition of an optional dhuhr meant that those concerned about potentially missing a required prayer could still meet their obligation. To address concerns about the WMA's divisiveness, in May 2015, founder Maznavi intervened in community debates by penning a nine-point list of facts about her institution in the *Huffington Post*.[6] One of these points emphasized that the WMA complements rather than competes with existing mosques. Maznavi's article ostensibly spoke to non-Muslim audiences eager to learn about the WMA, but she also sought to sway Muslims who objected to the idea of a woman-led mosque.[7] Elsewhere, she has also explicitly stated: "we want women to come here, gain inspiration, and go back to their mosques with that inspiration."[8] According to its institutional narrative, then, the WMA does not challenge other mosques, but aspires to work together with them.

As for WMA congregants, many do belong to other worship communities, indeed treating it as a complementary space. Moreover, early supporters, who would later become regular congregants, did not perceive the WMA as some kind of radical space that would revolutionize the status quo of US mosques. Many did not anticipate that their participation in the WMA would be considered so controversial among other Muslims. For this reason, Amal's statement above provides a particularly apt image of how many supporters perceived the WMA as new and different, but not altogether unfamiliar. She understood its differences from other mosques as subtle rather than pronounced, declaring that the WMA turns well-known concepts on their side rather than upside down. Likewise, for Mariyah, a South Asian American in her thirties, the formation of the WMA felt "normal," or organic.[9] To her, the level of controversy that ensued felt unwarranted and even silly. Amal's and Mariyah's respective characterizations of the WMA cohere with the general sentiment among the congregants I spoke with, since none of the women in this study articulated a desire to bring about sweeping changes to American Muslim communities through their involvement in the WMA. This is despite the mainstream media coverage that pronounced the WMA a catalyst for monumental change across US Muslim communities.[10]

This chapter investigates how critics' fixation with the legal debates on ritual prayer compares with WMA members' own priorities. I situate the WMA in the broader milieu of the institutions and leaders that shape the major debates and practices in American Muslim communities. Moreover, I posit that the various narratives that academics, journalists, and religious leaders consume about American Muslim women are heavily informed by three factors: American Muslims' internal anxieties about religious authority, external anxieties fueled by Islamophobic debates on their national belonging, and lastly, the cultures of patriarchy that pervade both Muslim and non-Muslim American communities. Due to these three factors, I contend that in light of new institutional developments like the WMA, lay commentators, Muslim leaders, and academics alike overstate American Muslim women's investment in ritual authority.

To be sure, the WMA is undeniably interested in women's ritual authority, but its overall impact as a Muslim institution extends beyond the assertion of women's right to lead prayer. This chapter lays the groundwork for understanding the WMA's broader impact by analyzing how it fits into preexisting debates in American Muslim communities on gender and religious authority, first by describing the formation of the WMA, the key players involved, and the considerations of its organizers during its nascent stages. The chapter then delineates the particularities of Islamic legal debates on woman-led prayer, highlighting how the "radical" 2005 mixed-gender Jummah and the WMA's 2015 inaugural Jummah elicited surprisingly similar responses from American Muslim public figures. The last section turns to WMA supporters as individuals and as members of a community, unpacking their motivations and values on their own terms and in comparison to their critics' claims. The chapter ultimately argues that the WMA is invested in ritual leadership as only one avenue among many other, arguably more significant, avenues for women to cultivate religious authority.

The Formation of the WMA

People were just very afraid because all they had to use as an example was the amina wadud model that caused so much controversy.
—Seher, South Asian American, in her thirties

On August 23, 2014, Maznavi held the first public town hall meeting at a friend's apartment to discuss the launch of the WMA. She had announced it on her personal Facebook page a month prior, inviting all interested parties to attend in order to find out how they could get involved as organizers or in other leadership roles.[11] Between thirty and forty people showed up, many of whom were Maznavi's friends lending their support. Seher, a South Asian American woman who was in attendance that day, later described the attendees of the town hall as a "diverse assortment of men and women of different ages, races, and backgrounds" who were all enthusiastic about Maznavi's vision.[12] According to Seher, the purpose of the town hall was to educate people and clarify the WMA's aims. In particular, attendees discussed the woman-only aspect of the WMA at length. Seher recounted that during the town hall, Maznavi was adamant that supporters should know that the WMA was, and would always remain, a woman-only mosque.[13] Their discussions that day made explicitly clear that even if particular WMA supporters or Maznavi herself ever felt that a mixed-gender mosque would fit their personal spiritual needs, the WMA would never be that mosque. Seher welcomed this commitment, as she had never felt fully comfortable attending mixed-gender mosques. "I always kind of shrink into myself as a woman in the mosque," she explained. "I just don't feel relaxed or comfortable or natural in my community because I just think of all the shaming of women that's been done from a young age."[14] A female-only space promised Seher and other women like her a chance to finally feel more at home in a mosque setting.

From a public relations perspective, Seher explained, emphasizing the woman-only aspect of the WMA was crucial in securing allies from within the Southern California Muslim scholarly community.[15] She described how some of the Muslim communities in Southern California had reservations about the WMA: "people were just very afraid because all they had to use as an example was the amina wadud model that caused so much controversy. And I don't really know too much about it because I wasn't there . . . but that was a kind of controversial example, so people were hesitant."[16] The "amina wadud model," as Seher and other WMA members referred to it, was the highly publicized 2005 prayer event in New York City described above. This 2005 event appeared to be at the forefront of LA Muslim communities' concerns in discussions about the WMA. As such, after the initial planning meeting, Maznavi, Sana Muttalib (the WMA's co-president for much of 2015), and other lead organizers were careful to explain to others how their project differed from the 2005 event. Despite some initial hesitancy, local mosques in southern California did eventually pledge their support. According to Maznavi, some even offered to host the WMA, but given that these mosques also host their own Jummah prayers, coordinating logistics, particularly with regard to parking, has not been possible.[17]

Ultimately, the WMA held its inaugural Jummah in January 2015 at the Pico Union Project, a multifaith center near downtown LA that was controversial in its own right. Founded by Jewish musician Craig Taubman in 2013, the Pico Union Project was designed as a cultural arts center and worship space that now permanently houses a Korean Christian church, an Evangelical Pentecostal church, a Methodist Episcopal ministry, and a Jewish synagogue; the latter two of these congregations have a female pastor and rabbi, respectively. It has also routinely rented out space to religious groups like the WMA and Victoria Outreach, a global Latinx ministry. The building itself, a designated Historic-Cultural Monument since 1977, was originally built as a synagogue in 1909, making it the oldest synagogue in LA. It was then converted into a Welsh Presbyterian church in 1924 before Taubman bought it in 2012.[18] It derives its name from its location in the Pico-Union neighborhood in central LA, an area that borders Koreatown, East Hollywood, and downtown, and houses mostly Latinx and Korean immigrants. Taubman's vision for the Pico Union Project as an inclusive multicultural, multifaith, and LGBTQ-friendly community reflects the cultural diversity of its neighborhood. However, his pluralistic approach to the space drew criticism and alienated him from some conservative Jewish communities in LA who had previously supported him as a Jewish leader.[19] Just as Taubman's idea of religious community challenges prevailing views of Jewish community, so too does the WMA challenge hegemonic conceptions of Muslim community, making it a natural fit with the Pico Union Project.

The WMA hosted Jummah in the Pico Union Project's multipurpose room on the main floor from January 2015 to May 2017. During these Jummahs, the multipurpose room would be decorated with two large dark rectangular banners with golden-yellow lettering that hung behind the minbar (pulpit). The first banner was adorned with Arabic calligraphy that read "Allah" with the Qur'anic quote "And when my servants ask about me, then truly, I am near" emblazoned in English underneath. In parallel fashion, the Arabic calligraphy on the second banner read "Muhammad" followed by a hadith in English stating "I have only been sent to perfect your good manners." When describing their initial impressions of the WMA, almost all of the women I spoke with mentioned these banners in some capacity, describing how they lent the prayer space a beautiful and welcoming aesthetic. I attended my first WMA Jummah in May 2017, the final month that it would be housed at the Pico Union Project before moving locations due to rising rent costs. It first moved to the Church of Jesus Christ of Latter-day Saints in nearby Koreatown, and finally to the First Unitarian Church in the same area in August 2017, where it continues to be housed. Since the duration of my fieldwork coincided with the WMA's transitional period, I was able to attend Jummah at all three of its locations. The decorative banners and other furnishings, owned by the WMA, moved from space to space, lending a consistent aesthetic to each of its host venues.

Despite the fact that only Judeo-Christian spaces have hosted the WMA thus far, its status as a mosque, and not a Muslim women's center or an interfaith organization, is central to its institutional narrative. The interfaith elements of the WMA are also crucial to its overall narrative, but are ultimately secondary to its function as an American mosque. The WMA's strong relationships with Judeo-Christian institutions do not undermine its relationship to the Islamic tradition. From the very start of the project, Maznavi has explicitly stated that her vision for the WMA is rooted in Muslim history. In media interviews, she has cited the legacy of Muslim women's leadership and scholarly contributions throughout history, and the existence of women-only mosques all over the world, such as in India, Syria, and China, as her inspiration.[20] This information is also included on the WMA's official website, and Edina Lekovic, the first khateebah, also mentioned it in her inaugural khutbah.[21] Despite WMA actors' frequent reference to women's mosques around the world, they do not explore these global precedents in much depth, nor do they attend to the vast differences among them. Instead, their references to women's mosques in Syria or China are presumably meant to emphasize that the WMA is not breaking from the Islamic tradition, but following it. Comparably, in her own media engagements, Muttalib, the WMA's former co-president, credits the Qur'an for her understanding of Islam as a gender-egalitarian religious tradition and her motivations for being a part of the WMA, as opposed to crediting sources outside of the Islamic tradition.[22]

Prior to starting the WMA, Maznavi studied under Shaykha Reima Yosif, a traditionally trained American Muslim female scholar, for a year, and continues to regard her as a teacher and spiritual mentor.[23] Yosif exemplifies one of the various ways that Muslim women occupy positions of religious authority in the US: at neo-traditional[24] and revivalist Islamic educational institutions, secular academic institutions, and within transnational Sufi networks. At institutions like the neo-traditional Zaytuna College in Berkeley,[25] the Sufi-leaning Al-Madina Institute in the DC metro area,[26] and the Salafi-leaning AlMaghrib Institute based in Houston,[27] instructors, both male and female, typically have formal religious credentials from Islamic institutions in the Middle East and South Asia (some of which are state-sponsored), or through ijazas. An ijaza is an Islamic certification through which a well-reputed scholar transmits his or her authority on a particular text or subject to a student, who is then authorized to teach it to others.[28] For her part, Yosif has multiple ijazas in Qur'anic recitation and exegetical texts, and is a *hafidhah*, a Muslim who has memorized the Qur'an in its entirety. She has also been affiliated with the Al-Madina Institute in the past. She additionally founded the Al-Rawiya Foundation and college in New Jersey, which aims to teach American Muslims about the tradition of female scholarship in Islamic history.[29] Through Al-Rawiya, Yosif hosts a yearly "Shaykha Fest," a platform featuring diverse female speakers from Shi'i, Sunni, traditionalist, and modernist backgrounds, including neo-traditional scholars of Islam, academics, performance artists, and activists from around the world.[30] Shaykha Fest creates a platform to revive female scholarship in Islam both by honoring its legacy in the historical tradition and promoting the works of contemporary female scholars.[31] Taking account of Maznavi's relationship with Yosif helps to illuminate the often overlapping threads of American Muslim institutions and the different forms of Islamic authority that they represent.

Yosif, based in New Jersey, was originally slated to be the WMA's first khateebah, but ultimately could not travel to LA due to health reasons. Nevertheless, her scholarship still authenticated the WMA as a legitimate Muslim institution. In fact, she published an hour-long video on the subject of woman-led prayer on her YouTube page the same day as the WMA's inaugural Jummah, January 30, 2015. In her video, Yosif did not specifically focus on the WMA but spoke more broadly on the subject of woman-led prayer and women's mosques. She divided her legal discussion of women's prayer leadership into four categories: women leading other women in prayer, women leading mixed-gender congregations in prayer, women leading Jummah, and women giving a khutbah. Encouraging viewers to look into the opinions of the ulama that she cites in her video lecture for themselves, Yosif detailed the process by which these Islamic jurists make legal decisions, explaining that first they refer to the Qur'an, second to the Hadith, and then to the *ijtihad* (independent reasoning) of scholars.[32]

Yosif began her lecture by asserting that there was no Qur'anic evidence denying the legitimacy of woman-led prayer in any of its forms. She then presented a hadith that prohibited women from leading others in prayer, but contested its accuracy, stating that several respected "heavyweight" ulama, including the fifteenth-century Islamic scholar Ibn Hajar Al-Asqalani categorized this particular hadith as unreliable, with a weak chain of transmission (*isnad*).[33] She also provided textual evidence of women leading other women in obligatory prayer, citing the example of the wives of Muhammad. Throughout her lecture, Yosif presented several Islamic legal sources that argued for and against the permissibility of woman-led prayer, demonstrating that debates over the legitimacy of woman-led prayer were not a new or contemporary phenomenon, but rather a subject that classical Islamic jurists discussed at length.[34]

Additionally, while Yosif stated that she herself would not be comfortable leading men in prayer, she also cited the hadith of Umm Waraqa[35] as an example of Muhammad appointing a woman to lead a mixed-gender congregational prayer. There are multiple interpretations of this hadith, which narrates that Muhammad was observed to have appointed one of his female Companions, Umm Waraqa, to lead her household or community in prayer, but it is often cited by supporters of woman-led mixed-gender prayer as evidence of legal validity. Yosif's interpretation of this hadith about mixed-gender prayer, alongside her citation of other hadiths affirming that women during the time of Muhammad routinely led other women in prayer, signals her view that these were not radical or reformist practices. Her lecture ultimately affirmed the value of women's spaces, and encouraged Muslims to work together toward building community.

During the first few months at the WMA, Maznavi recounted that some attendees would raise concerns about the Islamic legality of woman-led Jummah during the discussion circles that were held after

Jummah. In response, Maznavi would refer these women to Yosif's video: "Whenever people ask us [about the legitimacy of woman-led Jummah], we're like, 'Hey, there's this [Shaykha Reima Yosif's] opinion, you know, this is what we're following and we invite you to look at it.'"[36] Maznavi's rhetoric is important here, because it reflects her understanding of the Islamic legal tradition as pluralistic. Her choice of words presents the WMA's legal stance on woman-led Jummah as one of many possible valid legal opinions, not the only option. Furthermore, she invites those who are uncomfortable or who might disagree with woman-led Jummah to research the scholarly arguments that inform the WMA's decision-making processes and make their own judgments, rather than insist that they accept its validity.

WMA leaders support the validity of women's prayer leadership as a core value, given that its main service as an institution is to provide woman-led Jummah once a month, even as they accommodate legal differences of opinion by including an optional dhuhr prayer to the program. The board's decision to add optional dhuhr to its program was the result of ongoing debates in the LA Muslim community that began one day prior to its official launch. On January 29, 2015, Shaykha Muslema Purmul, a Southern California–based Islamic scholar, took to her public Facebook page to share her concerns about the WMA's scheduled Jummah, while notably also expressing support for the project as a whole. In fact, her 586-word Facebook post is bookended by supportive sentiments toward the women involved in the WMA. The beginning of her post reads: "A lot of people have been asking me about the all women's Jumuah that is supposed to be held tomorrow in Los Angeles. As someone who has been actively involved in teaching and mentoring Muslims at the grassroots level in mainstream Muslim institutions for over 10 years, I understand and support the idea of creating an all women's space." Here, Purmul cites her decade of experience as a female religious leader as the basis for her opinion that all-women's spaces are a welcome addition within the milieu of Muslim institutions in the US. Her receptive attitude to the women-only aspect of the WMA reflects a heightened understanding of the gendered dynamics within mainstream US Muslim spaces. For this reason, her subsequent critique stands apart from those of the WMA's chorus of critics who interpreted its gender exclusivity as divisive and antithetical to the concept of Muslim community.

Only after expressing support for the WMA as a women-only space does Purmul proceed with her critique: deeply held reservations about the legal validity of an all-women's Jummah. She states: "There is no opinion in any of the *madhahib* [Islamic legal schools] which recognizes the legal validity of such a prayer [an all-women's Jummah]. However, women can lead women in the five daily congregational prayers." In contrast to Reima Yosif's legal opinions outlined above, Purmul declares that women's Jummah is invalid according to the major Sunni legal schools. Yet it is worth noting that their respective arguments are not necessarily contradictory. While Yosif contends that there is no Qur'anic evidence *denying* the legitimacy of woman-led prayer, focusing on the silences and gaps in Islamic texts, Purmul emphasizes that, within the popular Sunni legal schools, there is no explicit recognition of all-women's Jummah. Despite the similarities in their religious training, these female scholars come to distinct conclusions. Indeed, Muslim thinkers since the earliest centuries of Islam have always been debating what constitutes right Islamic practice, often reading the same sources to different ends. Understanding how Yosif's and Purmul's respective positions on women's prayer leadership are derived from the same scriptural sources helps us to understand the dynamism of the Islamic legal tradition through which religious scholars can interpret texts differently.

In the remainder of her post, Purmul's critique of the WMA's planned Jummah manifests as concern for the congregation, and she accordingly offers her advice as a religious scholar and leader:

My advice to the organizers is either ask everyone to pray Dhuhr afterwards, or simply have the female imam lead the other women in four rakahs of Dhuhr prayer. I say this not to destroy the energy or creativity of the organizers, because I support the idea of all women's programming and spaces. My main concern is that 200 women will be praying tomorrow and may miss the obligation of Dhuhr because they think an all women's Jumuah will take its place. . . . I have immense respect for the organizers and for Sis. Edina Lekovic who will be leading this effort, though it is legally invalid insofar as it counting as a fard [obligatory] prayer. . . . As an American Muslim Azhariyyah from the College of Shariah I state that an all women's Jumuah is legally invalid according to all the opinions I know about. . . . That being said, I love the sisters behind this for Allah

and would love the opportunity to better understand where they are coming from. I hope everyone understands this is not a condemnation. This
is an invitation. Let's engage.[37]

Purmul's engagement with the WMA in her Facebook post is multilayered: she draws on her Islamic legal training to, in no uncertain terms,
authoritatively deny the legitimacy of woman-led Jummah. Her chief
concern is that the women who attend the WMA Jummah will be missing out on their obligatory dhuhr prayer by mistakenly, in her view,
believing their Jummah to be valid. Yet she simultaneously expresses
an enthusiasm for the WMA by affirming the need for women-only
religious spaces. Furthermore, Purmul publicizes her respect for WMA
organizers and Edina Lekovic, the first khateebah, and invites them to
have a community discussion on the matter. She does not warn women
against going, or even discourage them. Rather, she advises the WMA
organizers to lead a congregational dhuhr instead of, or in addition to,
Jummah. She then advises participants to take it upon themselves to
pray dhuhr individually even if the WMA organizers do not make official arrangements.

Purmul's Facebook post was also published in its entirety as an article
on a Muslim blog titled "Guarding the Validity of the Prayer: Women's
Mosque of America" the following day.[38] Purmul, known as Shaykha
Muslema to her community members, is an American-educated,
Azhari-trained Islamic scholar who has served in various leadership
roles within Muslim communities in Southern California, and she has
spoken as an Islamic law expert in religious venues all over the world.
Additionally, she and her husband cofounded the Safa Center for Research and Education, an online platform to share her work with the
public, and she currently serves as a chaplain for students at USC and
UCLA. All that is to say, she is a well-regarded scholarly Islamic authority figure among Muslims—especially women—in the LA context
in which both she and the WMA primarily operate. Her measured criticism of the WMA marks a departure from community reactions to the
2005 prayer event, despite the similarities in the substance of their critiques that contest the legal validity of woman-led Jummah. The mostly
male critics of the 2005 prayer event condemned the prayer as a *fitnah*,
a disruption and source of chaos in the community.

Ultimately, Maznavi and the rest of the WMA executive board, which then comprised nine members, both male and female, reached a unanimous decision to add an optional dhuhr prayer to their program. In this compromise, Maznavi recalls the precision that she employed with her choice of language, opting to use the qualifier "optional" when introducing dhuhr into their program:

> I wrote specific language to introduce the concept. It's the reason we include the optional dhuhr prayer, deliberately using the word "optional," deliberately using the word "include," to specify that this is extra. . . . When we first started, a lot of new Muslims and people who weren't Muslim, who were just joining us, they would just pray it because they thought it was required part of the service. I deliberately put in the word "optional" to be more inclusive of people with a difference of opinion on the matter. That way, it's very clear.[39]

Maznavi's attention to language here functions in two ways. Firstly, it preserves the integrity of her own belief in the validity of woman-led Jummah, which is rooted in a scholarly engagement of scriptural sources. Secondly, it creates a respectful space for those who reject, or are unsure about, the legitimacy of woman-led prayer. Beyond that, Maznavi and the rest of the board intended the language of the optional prayer policy to communicate to new congregants that the WMA's official stance did not include dhuhr in the main prayer service.

Internal debates among WMA members on woman-led Jummah and whether they should pray the additional dhuhr demonstrate the spectrum of legal opinions held by American Muslims even within a very localized context. Purmul and Yosif's differing legal opinions on woman-led Jummah hint at this spectrum, since they are ostensibly similar authority figures: both are traditional Muslim scholars with Islamic legal training and both have had a profound influence on the shape of the WMA through their respective legal opinions. Purmul influenced WMA organizers to take seriously some Muslims' concerns that they might be missing an obligatory prayer by participating in woman-led Jummah. According to some of the early WMA supporters I spoke to, Purmul's social media ruling against woman-led Jummah injected doubt in people's minds about the legitimacy of the space. Before Purmul's

Facebook post, the WMA did not have plans to implement an optional dhuhr into its program. Ultimately, according to the women I interviewed, only about five to seven women would participate in the optional dhuhr during any given month. However, WMA board members mentioned that many of the female speakers that they were interested in inviting as khateebahs were hesitant to accept until Purmul officially approved of the space, or until she herself agreed to give a khutbah. While to date Purmul has not served as khateebah or led Jummah, she did accept the WMA's invitation to serve as a speaker at its Mother's Day high tea event in May 2016.

Notably, Yosif supported the idea of woman-led prayer. And as a mentor and teacher to Maznavi, she also legitimized the WMA beyond offering an affirmative legal position on woman-led prayer. The emphasis in Yosif's own work on reviving female voices in the Islamic tradition paved the way for the emergence of institutions like the WMA. Moreover, Yosif's scholarly and activist interventions affirmed the WMA's goals of expanding women's religious leadership. In their conflicting views, both shaykhas delivered nuanced and measured responses. Even as Purmul declared woman-led Jummah invalid, she shared her support for the WMA and her subsequent appearance at the WMA to deliver a special Mother's Day lecture quelled local concerns about the WMA's legitimacy. The WMA's relationship to both of these traditional female scholars demonstrates its aim as an institution to honor women's voices. Its organizers take seriously both Yosif's and Purmul's scholarly opinions, and adjust their programming accordingly, while also staying firm in their belief in the validity of woman-led Jummah.

The impact of Yosif's and Purmul's respective legal opinions on woman-led Jummah in the local LA Muslim context indicates the broader relevance of Islamic law in American Muslim communities. Enough women were concerned about the legal validity of the WMA in the early months of its tenure to warrant a response from its organizers. WMA members' concern with Islamic legal legitimacy occurs within a broader history of Muslims using Islamic legal argumentation to authenticate religious practice. Hammer suggests that the existence of legal opinions on woman-led prayer from as early as the ninth century indicates that this was also a concern for early Muslims.[40] This means that the community debates over women's ritual authority that have come about in the wake of the WMA's inception are not new and do not even represent distinctly American Muslim concerns. Rather, American Muslims are actually participating in a conversation about women-led prayer that has been ongoing for centuries, and they draw on premodern legal opinions to produce multilayered and even conflicting opinions of their own.

WMA practices reflect a legal diversity among its khateebahs and congregants. As Hammer contends, the debate over women's prayer leadership is not simply a "dichotomy between those who support women leading prayers and those who do not."[41] Instead, interpreters debate the particularities of ritual authority, including if, how, what, and who to lead.[42] At the WMA, the majority of members believe in the validity of woman-led Jummah, but this can be expressed differently from one khateebah to the next. Some lead prayer from in front of the congregation, while others prefer to stand in the first row and lead prayer from within the congregation. The practice of women leading prayer from the first row is rooted in three of the major Sunni legal schools, which stipulate that a woman may lead other women in some prayers provided that she stands in their ranks and not in front of them. Notably, these three legal schools—Hanafi, Shafi'i, and Hanbali—do not permit women to lead Jummah, though they do not require women to participate in Jummah either. The Maliki school by contrast does not permit women to lead prayer under any circumstances. The fact that some WMA khateebahs choose to lead from the first row rather than from in front of the congregation, thereby adhering to the rules of particular legal schools that arguably also deny them the right to lead Jummah in the first place, demonstrates their layered relationships with the Islamic legal tradition. Other WMA members consider women's Jummah leadership to be invalid, and participate as a part of the congregation but then pray dhuhr afterward. Because the WMA equates the roles of khateebah and prayer leader, any WMA member who does not believe in the legal validity of woman-led Jummah is not permitted to deliver a khutbah or lead prayer. Instead, these women are invited to give a pre-khutbah *bayan*, or talk, and lead dhuhr instead.[43]

The WMA also creates space for diverse opinions on menstruation and prayer—though not prayer leadership—within its congregation. Across the major Islamic legal schools, menstruation renders invalid

of ritual cleanliness required for prayer, fasting, and circum-
ating the Kaaba during Hajj, the obligatory pilgrimage to Mecca
all Muslims physically and financially able. As communications
pecialist in gender and Islam Krista Riley argues, the stigma around
menstruation in Muslim communities extends beyond exclusion from
certain ritual acts to also include ideas about women's contamination
and inferiority.[44] As a result, menstruating women are sometimes prohibited from entering mosques or touching the Qur'an, and shamed for
spreading their "contamination." Riley spotlights three feminist Muslim
bloggers who have challenged stigmatizing norms around menstruation
with their virtual Muslim communities in part by highlighting hadith
that narrate how Muhammad dealt with the subject openly and without
ascribing to it any cultural taboos. While all three of these bloggers acknowledge that not all Muslims interpret the legal rulings on menstruation to explicitly prohibit women from praying while menstruating, only
one openly declares that she prays during her period.[45] The other two,
while appearing to conform to the mainstream Islamic legal practice
of not praying during menstruation, still contest its social taboos and
reject ideas about contamination. WMA policies similarly reject the notion of menstruation as contamination and recognize that some Muslim
women choose to pray while having their periods, but do not challenge
legal prohibitions on prayer.

By acknowledging that women on their periods may choose to pray,
the WMA effectively welcomes them into the prayer space and prohibits
its members from policing congregants' bodies. At the same time, WMA
leaders do indeed police khateebahs' bodies, requiring that they schedule their khutbahs and prayer leadership on a day when they will not
be menstruating. They otherwise have the option to give a pre-khutbah
bayan and not lead prayer. According to WMA guidelines for khateebahs, the rule against permitting women on their menstrual periods
to lead prayer is rooted in concern for congregants who feel that their
prayer would be invalidated.[46] Yet this level of intimate scrutiny of their
bodies can feel profoundly intrusive and alienating, and some women
have told me that they declined the invitation to serve as a WMA khateebah for this reason. Their feelings of alienation are perhaps exacerbated
by the fact that male khateebs at conventional mosques are typically
never asked about their state of ritual purity when they are scheduled to

lead prayer. That some women may interpret the WMA's policy on khateebahs and menstruation as egregious purity policing gestures at the
complex tensions that exist among Muslims who identify with the aims
of the WMA and agree that there is a need for more female authorities.
These tensions arise from inevitable differences in opinion regarding to
what extent the WMA should conform to, overlook, or challenge Islamic
legal norms. Overall, the particularities of the relationship between
menstruation, prayer, and prayer leadership at the WMA demonstrate a
layered and complicated relationship to Islamic law.

At the WMA, then, women navigate questions of ritual leadership for
members and khateebahs in complex and individual ways. Their layered
relationships with the Islamic legal tradition exemplify Islamic studies
scholar Kecia Ali's assertion that Muslims mostly engage Islamic sources
to approach ethico-legal questions as individuals, rather than looking
to particular authority figures.[47] This individualized focus accounts for
the WMA's accommodation of multiple perspectives and its organizers' willingness to compromise with other Muslim community leaders
and members. I read their accommodation of multiple perspectives on
prayer leadership as pragmatic because it illustrates their broader refusal
to succumb to a controversial narrative characterized by a sole fixation
on women's prayer leadership. In fact, some WMA members themselves
make direct comparisons to the 2005 mixed-gender prayer to measure
the relative success of community reception of the WMA. Therefore,
while debates over ritual authority are not central to my analysis of the
WMA, they are nevertheless an important part of its overall narrative.
Ritual authority is particularly important for understanding the Islamic
legal debates on woman-led prayer that reentered American Muslim consciousness following the emergence of the WMA and similar initiatives.

From 2005 to 2015: American Muslim Legal Debates on Woman-Led Prayer

I talk about it [the WMA] as a success and a point of progress especially in light of the amina wadud co-ed mixed
prayer, that was ten years before or something like that . . .
and how badly all of that went for multiple reasons. But the
reception that the Women's Mosque got was vastly improved

and for the most part some conservative *shuyukh* [plural of shaykh] on social media even said basically, "I don't like it but it should be a wake-up call for us in the community."[48]
—Edina Lekovic, the WMA's first khateebah

When amina wadud led prayer at a mixed-gender Jummah in New York City in 2005, the negative backlash was swift and intense. wadud received death threats and shouldered much of the hostility directed at the event, even though she had not organized it and had merely led the prayer. Such animosity often manifested in both misogynistic and racially charged ways.[49] A decade later, despite eliciting its fair share of criticism, the WMA managed to avoid the same level of hostility by being a women-only space. Where those involved in the 2005 mixed-gender Jummah were met with blatant misogyny, the WMA faced paternalistic condescension.

Yasir Qadhi's social media statement on woman-led spaces was one such example of this paternalism. Qadhi, a popular American Muslim preacher with both religious and secular training in Islamic studies, has served as the dean of academic affairs at the Islamic Seminary of America since 2019. Prior to this, he was the face of the AlMaghrib Institute, a global institution that offers courses and seminars on Islam online and in cities around the world. Qadhi and the AlMaghrib Institute tend to espouse socially conservative views on gender norms that uphold the heterosexual nuclear family structure wherein Muslim men occupy the religious public sphere and are financial providers for the household, while women are caregivers who primarily operate in the private realm.[50] Qadhi responded to the WMA's emergence in a widely shared public Facebook post on February 2, 2015, just three days after its first Jummah. In his post, Qadhi never explicitly referred to the WMA by name or stated whether he deemed it legally valid. Rather he directed his audience to acknowledge the conditions that gave rise to Muslim women taking "matters into their own hands."[51] Some Muslims read the absence of an explicit condemnation as his conditional approval of the WMA, or at least, as a sign of his willingness to address women's marginalization in conventional mosques.

In fact, many Muslim women on Facebook expressed their gratitude to Qadhi for his public recognition of the poor conditions they faced in

US mosques. To them, his response validated their negative experiences of exclusion. And in our conversation excerpted above, Edina Lekovic, the WMA's first khateebah, and a community leader in her own right, explained to me that responses like Qadhi's demonstrated progress in Muslim communities. To her, his acknowledgement demonstrated the extent to which the WMA served as a wake-up call for "conservative" Muslim leaders to confront the reality of women's systemic marginalization in the mosque. She commented on his post at the time, writing: "Thank you for taking this stand. Mosques need to pay attention & make immediate changes now. I look fwd to working on this issue with you."[52] Notably, Lekovic uses the term "conservative" to describe Qadhi as do I above. Labels like "conservative," "moderate," or "liberal" can be reductive and problematic, not least because they are deployed in the War on Terror discourse in nefarious ways. Within this discourse, "conservative" typically signifies a "bad" religious Muslim prone to violence and "liberal" signifies a "good," less overtly religious or non-religious Muslim amenable to assimilation and uncritical of the US military-industrial complex.[53] Yet US Muslims still employ such labels especially within intra-Muslim conversations like the one between Lekovic and myself that operate within the shared understanding that "conservative" need not have a negative connotation as per War on Terror discourse. I take Lekovic's use of the term "conservative" to gesture at attitudes toward Muslim women's public presence in mosques that range from ambivalence to explicit discomfort. If we consider Qadhi's general conservatism to be a benchmark for many US Muslims, then his non-condemnatory response to the WMA indicates how community sensibilities had shifted between 2005 and 2015 to become more amenable to recognizing gender inequality in mosques as an issue.

Yet it is worth lingering on how Qadhi's response to the WMA falls short of signaling any meaningful commitment toward improving the deplorable conditions for women in US mosques. His lack of direct engagement with the WMA, in legal terms or otherwise, signals a refusal to take it seriously. Qadhi appears to understand the WMA and other initiatives like it as unfortunate products of our times, when women roam freely and can amass the resources to initiate such "counter-reactions."[54] In his post, Qadhi unequivocally calls for more equitable spaces for women in US mosques, yet never affirms that there is any inherent value in women participating in public religious life. His post also lacks any reference to Muslim women's ongoing initiatives to promote equitable changes in mosque culture.[55] Rather, Qadhi's call for gender equality in the mosque is framed by his observation of women's visibility in all public spheres in the US: "In a day and age where our sisters are going everywhere, visible everywhere, active everywhere, the BEST place for them to be is in the masjid."[56] He therefore argues that men should support women in going to mosques, because it is better than "going shopping or watching a movie."[57] Qadhi seems to advocate for women's improved conditions in mosques because the alternative—expecting them to stay home—is not tenable in contemporary US society. Therefore, while he tacitly advocates for women in mosques, he stops short of recognizing women as contributors to public religious life on their own terms. Moreover, it is hard not to imagine that Qadhi is nostalgic for a former "day and age"[58] when it would have been feasible to demand that women stay in the home.

Given the equivocal nature of Muslim responses of "support" for the WMA from figures like Qadhi and even Purmul, coupled with the more overtly critical voices, it is clear that even with key differences in their forms and aims, the 2005 mixed-gender Jummah and the first WMA Jummah represent two very similar moments in American Muslim history. Just as the 2005 Jummah was not an isolated event but rather an organic culmination of preexisting debates on Muslim women's authority, the WMA is likewise the result of many conversations about the scope and nature of female leadership within Muslim communities.[59] As such, the WMA and other comparable institutions that have emerged afterward[60] are both continuous with the 2005 mixed-gender Jummah and distinct from it.[61] WMA organizers consciously distinguished themselves from the 2005 event in both subtle and explicit ways in a move to prevent a similar backlash that might overshadow its broader aims.

Despite WMA organizers' best efforts to brand themselves as different from the "amina wadud model," the same scholarly refutations of woman-led prayer that American Muslim leaders leveled against the 2005 prayer organizers were reappropriated against them. Among the prominent scholarly voices that argued against the legitimacy of the 2005 prayer event were Muslim scholars and community leaders Zaid Shakir and Ingrid Mattson. Shakir, an African American Muslim scholar with a degree in the Islamic sciences from Abu Nour University in Syria,

RITUAL AUTHORITY | 45

co-founded the Zaytuna Institute in Berkeley in 1996. In 2008, Zaytuna became the first accredited Muslim undergraduate college in the US. Mattson, a white Canadian scholar with a PhD in Islamic studies from the University of Chicago, notably served as the first female president of the Islamic Society of North America (ISNA) between 2006 and 2010. ISNA is the largest umbrella Muslim organization in North America, and it provides a platform for various social, civic, and community programming efforts. Founded in 1982, ISNA grew out of the first Muslim Student Association (MSA) formed in the 1960s. ISNA hosts an annual convention that tens of thousands of Muslims attend, featuring scholarly lectures, comedy, artistic performances, matchmaking services, and hundreds of book, food, and clothing stalls. I consider Shakir's and Mattson's views to be representative of a significant constituency of American Muslims as they are both popular Islamic authority figures in the US.

Shakir argued against the legitimacy of the mixed-gender Jummah in a public essay published in 2005.[62] In January 2015, Purmul shared a link to this essay in her Facebook post referenced earlier, demonstrating its continued relevance to discussions of the WMA. In his 2005 essay, Shakir positioned himself as representative of a so-called Islamic orthodoxy, rooted in the Sunni legal tradition, which he argued remains highly influential in how Muslims engage their faith in the contemporary world.[63] Through this lens of traditional Sunni jurisprudence, Shakir offered his reading of the hadith of Umm Waraqa, which, as we saw in Reima Yosif's supportive stance on the WMA, is often used as the basis for supporting woman-led prayer. Shakir cited the hadith as: "The Prophet (peace be upon him) commanded Umm Waraqah, a woman who had collected the Qur'an, to lead the people of her area in prayer. She had her own *mu'adhdhin* [person who performs the call to prayers]."[64] Shakir first agreed that the Umm Waraqa hadith is found in multiple hadith compilations and holds widespread scholarly acceptance. However, he ultimately contested its reliability, based on his view that the hadith has a weak chain of transmission. For Shakir, this weakness rendered the hadith inadequate to establish the Islamic legal validity of woman-led prayer.[65]

Shakir further argued that even if the Umm Waraqa hadith were sound, or authentic according to Muslim tradition, then its actual content still failed to provide adequate basis for the permissibility of women leading men in prayer. In his view, Umm Waraqa was granted permission from Muhammad to lead her private household in prayer. Shakir assumed that Umm Waraqa's "household" was all female, citing a different narration of this hadith that explicitly uses the term "her women" rather than "her household." In Shakir's view, this latter narration, which implies that Umm Waraqa was instructed to lead her women in prayer, was more consistent with his readings of other hadith narrations that confirm that the wives of Muhammad, including Aisha and Umm Salama, led all-women congregations in ritual prayer.[66] Shakir claimed that the notion that there were men present in Umm Waraqa's congregation, in her household, or in her neighborhood, was purely speculative, and he therefore rejected the hadith as proof of a historical precedent of a woman leading mixed-gender prayer.

In Mattson's response to the 2005 mixed-gender Jummah, she also rejected the validity of unprohibited women's ritual leadership.[67] However, Mattson argued for shifting the focus away from the singular issue of the validity of women leading men in prayer (which she opposed) to thinking about religious authority more broadly. She asserted that many Muslim women experience Islamic authority in a negative way, making her sympathetic to the conditions that gave rise to the 2005 Jummah. Mattson recognized women's limited access to Islamic knowledge and the benefits that Muslim institutions promised to bestow. However, she proposed that rather than pursue ritual leadership, women should take up other leadership roles on mosque boards, or as youth directors, for example. This, in her view, would enable Muslim communities to better represent the needs of Muslim women. Mattson urged American Muslims to include women in the leadership of Muslim communities in ways that address the specific needs of the community, rather than focusing on the role of prayer leadership. While Shakir also acknowledged the inequitable conditions in mosques for women, unlike Mattson he did not provide any solutions to address this gender inequity. Mattson also expressed full support for women's right to lead other women in congregational prayer (but not Jummah) and for women leading men in family congregations and optional prayers provided they were the most qualified to lead.[68]

To these two views, Laury Silvers, a white Muslim activist and secularly trained Islamic studies scholar (like Mattson), offered an alternative argument in the 2005 debates on woman-led prayer in a blog post. In her response, she explored new approaches to the question of woman-led prayer and asserted that Muslims should support woman-led prayer in solidarity, as an act of civil disobedience even in the absence of a sound legal argument. She identified the prohibition of women's unrestricted prayer leadership as a form of gender injustice and an indication of the broader issue of Muslim women's marginalization in their own communities.[69] Furthermore, Silvers argued that women's alienation from the mosque ran counter to the intended objective of social cohesion that congregational prayer is meant to achieve. She stated: "if one of the goals of the congregational prayer is to bring about social cohesion . . . then the present order of the mosque works against an important purpose of the congregational prayer."[70] She further attested to the social benefits that would ensue with women taking up authoritative positions in Muslim communities, stating that the increased visibility of women in leadership roles would create a broader culture of respecting women.

Silvers also highlighted that Islamic jurisprudence is not a divine enterprise but rather a human engagement with sacred sources, critiquing religious scholars and leaders who sanctify the Islamic legal system by refusing to question it in light of gender inequality and even other social wrongs such as slavery. Silvers's essay therefore challenged Muslim leaders and scholars of Islamic jurisprudence to find a way to permit woman-led mixed-gender prayer. She also contested Shakir's characterization of woman-led prayer as disruptive to Muslim community. Moreover, she claimed that such debates would open the door to "a greater discussion of women's role in the community in general, not just the desirability of women leading the congregational prayer in particular."[71] Ultimately, Silvers argued for the symbolic importance of ritual leadership in opening other avenues for Muslim women to assume public roles in their religious communities.

Later, in a 2011 academic journal article, Silvers and her co-author, Ahmed Elewa, attribute disrespect for Muslim women to their invisibility in the religious public, a connection that Qadhi fails to make in his 2015 response to the WMA.[72] In their article, Elewa and Silvers express respect for a range of legal opinions on woman-led prayer as legally valid, but they also argue for the validity of unrestricted female prayer leadership in communities that wish to practice it.[73] Drawing attention to Islamic legal scholars who emphasize the lack of a clear prohibition of woman-led mixed-gender prayer, they interpret this as permissibility, given that the community in question agreed to it. I highlight Silvers's arguments here not only as an example of an eloquent rebuttal of both Shakir's and Mattson's views on the impermissibility of women's prayer leadership, but also because of the authority she holds among certain Muslims based on her activism and academic training in early Islam and Sufism. Silvers has been an influential voice in North American progressive Muslim circles for decades, serving as a board member of the now defunct Progressive Muslim Union, and later cofounding the El-Tawhid Juma Circle in 2009, an LGBTQI-affirming mosque in Toronto.

Nevertheless, it is worth noting that Silvers wields less influence than either Mattson or Shakir, who are better known among US Muslims on the basis of their respective affiliations with ISNA and Zaytuna. By way of example, in 2022, Mattson and Shakir had approximately 57,700 and 121,500 Twitter followers respectively, in comparison to Silvers's 6,740. Yet discrepancies in levels of popularity between figures like Shakir, Mattson, Yosif, Purmul, Silvers, or wadud among American Muslims does not undermine the importance of the debates between them or the significance of voices on the so-called margins. Given that the WMA itself exists on the "edges" of the Islamic tradition even as it brands itself as a "middle ground space,"[74] the scholars, leaders, and activists who most shape the trajectory of the WMA (tacitly or explicitly) obviously would not represent the views most prevalent across US Muslim communities, especially with respect to women's prayer leadership. It is true that a small fraction of congregants pray the additional dhuhr, indicating that their views might indeed conform to the opinions of folks like Shakir and Mattson. However, in not praying dhuhr, the majority of WMA members appear to believe in the validity of woman-led Jummah. I highlight the kinds of scholarly arguments that rebut the arguably more popular views on the limits of Muslim women's ritual authority to draw attention to the kinds of rich, and often contentious, debates occurring within mainstream Muslim circles that are generated by edge cases like the WMA. In other words, despite their locations on the edge, their relatively small numbers, and their branding by popular figures as violating the principles of Islamic jurisprudence, spaces like the WMA do indeed shape the trajectory of community conversations on Islamic authority and more broadly on the form and function of mosques in meaningful ways.

Additionally, in 2015, Muslims were not the only people debating the presence and character of the WMA. As internal Muslim debates on the WMA played out, some of the non-Muslim public vocalized their concerns over its women-only nature in their own online discussions. A cursory glance at the online comments sections of otherwise positive mainstream media articles on the subject of the launch of the WMA reveals hostile views from non-Muslims. The responses to one *Wall Street Journal* article included remarks such as: "Gender apartheid. How lovely, 'inclusive' . . . and predictable" and "the women's only mosque follows the tried-and-failed approach of curing segregation with more segregation. This is a non-starter and sets back the Muslim's public image in the U.S. by exposing their backwards policies."[75] Bearing in mind that the Internet is replete with toxic comments on any given subject and we should avoid ascribing too much value to them in thinking about the non-Muslim reception of the WMA, the frequency of hostile responses by non-Muslims reflects the culture of casual, gendered Islamophobia that had become normalized by the first few years of the WMA's existence. These Islamophobic remarks unironically express in tandem an apparent commitment to gender equality with a clear disdain for Muslim women. Comments on the *WSJ* article ranged from the flippant, such as "Cool! Now they can oppress themselves!" to the more charged, "The muslim religion treats dogs better than women. What woman would continue in such a religion, other than those that like being doormats."

Muslim commenters, both male and female, also chimed in. "I am an American Muslim and this is so wrong and I would never accept praying in [a] mosque like this," wrote one. "I have lived all over the Middle East and all the imams I know say this is Bida [heretical innovation]."[76] Across Muslim media sites that covered the WMA launch, some commenters lamented the loosening standards of modesty in American Muslim society and warned against adopting "feminist" values.[77] It is evident here that some American Muslims and non-Muslims had a shared scorn for the development of the WMA, which is at least partially rooted in the same misogynistic disapproval of women in positions of authority. However, anonymous trolls across the Internet were not the only ones lamenting Muslim women who adopted "feminist" values. In their articulations against women-led prayer initiatives, some popular US Muslim leaders with institutional platforms and large social media followings perpetuated the claim that developments such as the WMA were dangerous.

On April 24, 2017, aboutislam.net, a confessional North American website founded in 2016, published the views of one such public figure, Yasmin Mogahed, an Egyptian American woman, respected by many American Muslims as an authoritative figure despite her lack of scholarly training in Islamic studies. In a fatwa (Islamic legal opinion) style response to an online query about whether it was a step toward liberation, Mogahed decried women-led Jummah prayer.[78] Stating that women should not aspire to lead prayer, Mogahed characterized any desire to disrupt the status quo as Muslims falling prey to the principles of godless Western feminism.[79] "But as Western feminism erases God from the scene, there is no standard left—except men," Mogahed opined, claiming that "Western feminism" dictated that women should be exactly like men in order to have equality.[80] In her view, since Muslim women were already upheld as equals in Islam, they did themselves harm by trying to "emulate men"—by which she not only meant pursuing ritual leadership, but also having careers or wearing short hair.[81] These women, according to Mogahed, used men as standard bearers for equality and therefore fundamentally misunderstood and rejected the concept of "dignity through distinctiveness" that Islam granted women.

Mogahed's response was originally written as a post on her personal blog[82] in May 2005 in reference to wadud's leading the mixed-gender Jummah two months prior, but it enjoyed new life in April 2017, when it was republished on the heels of the first Jummah prayer at the then newly founded Qal'bu Maryam Mosque (QMM) in Berkeley.[83] Following the aboutislam.net 2017 republication of Mogahed's response, this article was shared widely on social media. The QMM describes itself as a woman-led, inclusive prayer and community space, and notably counted amina wadud among its board members in its early months. I read the timing of aboutislam.net's renewed interest in Mogahed's original reflection as a response to the phenomenon of women-led mosques more generally.[84] It is worth noting here that between the establishment of the WMA in 2015 and the QMM in 2017 other women-led mosque initiatives had emerged, including the Maryam Mosque in Copenhagen (2016), Masjid al-Rabia in Chicago (2016), the women-run mosque in Bradford, UK (2016), and the Ibn Rushd-Goethe mosque in Berlin (2017). This was in addition to inclusive initiatives such as the afore-mentioned El-Tawhid Juma Circle mosques in Toronto, established in 2009, and the Inclusive Mosque Initiative in London from 2012, which are queer-affirming, gender-egalitarian mosques.[85]

In the original posting of the aboutislam.net article, its editors leveraged two major inaccuracies to bolster its authoritativeness to American Muslim audiences. First, they erroneously claimed that wadud had since reconsidered her position on women leading mixed-gender prayer, and had expressed regret at her participation in the 2005 event, characterizing it as a "mistake."[86] In so doing, the editors at aboutislam.net attempted to delegitimize a significant moment in the history of debates about women-led prayer. The second inaccuracy was attributing this claim to Mogahed, a fellow female Muslim public figure. The website later issued a retraction after wadud herself contested their claim on her own public social media. Mogahed then issued a statement on her public Facebook page on April 28, 2017, clarifying that she had not authored the sentence about wadud regretting her role in the 2005 prayer event and that it had been tacked on to her response. Mogahed added that the editors at aboutislam.net also failed to inform her that they would be republishing her post.[87] Aside from this clarification, she otherwise reaffirmed her previous views on the 2005 event.[88] The fact that islamonline.net did not seek Mogahed's permission to republish her post illustrates one of the ways that prominent female figures are appropriated and weaponized in debates over Islam, gender, and authority. There are layers of significance to Mogahed's reflection on woman-led Jummah and its subsequent piracy by a website that counts only male scholars among its expert consultants[89] as it relates to broader debates over Muslim women's authority. Though Mogahed has the platform to set the record straight with no damage to her brand, the website still tokenized her to make a statement about Muslim women's authority.

The gendered and racialized criteria that contribute to Mogahed's status as an authoritative female voice across Muslim communities in the first place are worth examining. Her reflection on wadud and the 2005 mixed-gender prayer epitomizes the power dynamics that contribute to the former's prominence in many US Muslim communities and explains why the latter is polarizing in these same communities. Mogahed, an Arab Muslim with neither secular nor religious credentials in Islamic studies, articulates views of gender roles that conform with patriarchal understandings of the family to discredit wadud. wadud, who is African American, has both religious and secular Islamic studies credentials, with a PhD in Islamic studies as well as training in Arabic, Qur'anic studies, exegesis, and philosophy from Cairo University and al-Azhar. As a Qur'anic exegete, she writes authoritatively about gender and Islam, while Mogahed, trained in psychology, journalism, and mass communications, is a creative writer whose essays are primarily on spirituality and personal development. In the process of critiquing her leading of a mixed-gender Jummah, Mogahed makes a series of assumptions about wadud and her views on motherhood, career choice, and the concepts of compassion versus rationality. In these assumptions, Mogahed ignores wadud's publications, which clearly delineate her perspectives on motherhood and compassion.[90] Mogahed instead reduces the issue of woman-led prayer to a choice that women make between prioritizing worldly leadership and heaven. Moreover, Mogahed posits a stark dichotomy between the West and Islam, effectively precluding African American Muslims like wadud, who can only be both Western and Muslim.[91] Furthermore, her Arabness is deployed against wadud's Blackness in her contestation over the 2005 prayer event in a way that highlights the ethnoreligious hegemony of Arab Islam over Black Islam.

The disparate receptions of Mogahed and wadud in Muslim communities based on race demonstrate the incoherent relationship between Islamic authority and the idea of a classical Islamic tradition in lived practice. Despite her lack of scholarly training, Mogahed is upheld as a popular voice of authority among Muslims in North America and beyond (for reference, she has over half a million Twitter followers in comparison to wadud's seven and a half thousand). Conversely, for her critics, wadud's credentials are evidently insufficient to take her seriously. Just as Mogahed's femaleness makes her vulnerable to being republished without consultation, wadud's Black womanhood negates her scholarly credentials and denies her the basic respect that those same credentials might otherwise confer upon her male counterparts. Reflecting on the often inconsistent relationship between Islamic authority and formal training, Kecia Ali notes that many who claim authenticity typically have a "selective and often incoherent relationship to law and scripture interpretations. . . . Yet because their views are congruent with conventional wisdom about what is 'Islamic'—or because their maleness and ethnic background give them an air of authority—their pronouncements are not questioned."[92] Accordingly, Mogahed's authority in the community is derived from both her Arab background and the content of what she is promoting because it aligns with sensibilities committed to protecting male privilege. While wadud has become a polarizing name in Muslim communities across the world since the 2005 mixed-gender prayer, Mogahed is a regular invitee on the speaker circuit of MSA talks around the country, a stark demonstration of ethnoreligious hegemony in US culture whereby Arab heritage constitutes religious authority even in the absence of formal Islamic training. She also teaches at the AlMaghrib Institute, the Islamic educational institution referenced earlier that was affiliated with conservative American preacher Yasir Qadhi. Furthermore, the discrepancies in their respective treatments highlight how anti-Black racism informs community sensibilities on Islamic authority and authenticity in the US.

Reflections on Ritual Authority and Women-Only Spaces

Nobody's out here hurting anyone, so I hate when people make a big deal of things like that. It's like, oh my god, get over it. I'm glad they have the two prayers, because now what are people going to complain about?[93]
—Yasmin, South Asian American, in her twenties

Yasmin was a relatively new congregant at the WMA when I met her there in May 2017; she had started attending just a couple of months earlier. She was therefore not present during the initial controversy over woman-led prayer that surrounded the WMA's early months. The debates over ritual authority came up over the course of our conversation when she asked me whether I knew why they had two separate prayers during the Jummah service. I shared what I knew about the contestations over the validity of woman-led Jummah in the local LA context and in American Muslim communities more widely, and how the WMA board had decided to include an optional dhuhr prayer in response to these debates. Yasmin responded that, although she did not realize woman-led Jummah was even an issue for some Muslims, she had even more respect for the WMA leaders for including an optional prayer because it made the environment more inclusive.[94] Furthermore, Yasmin felt that the WMA's willingness to compromise on this matter would shield it from unnecessary criticism. Her own reasons for participating in the WMA included its supportive community of women, the content of its khutbahs, and the discussion circle, which provides congregants direct access to khateebahs.

When I asked other WMA members to share their views on the debates over the legitimacy of woman-led prayer and on the WMA's optional dhuhr prayer, they held a range of views. Some prayed the optional dhuhr while others did not. Overall, among those I interviewed, it seemed clear that legal debates over ritual legitimacy were not particularly important to WMA members. Tina, an African American in her sixties, was one of the staunchest supporters of the WMA, and had been since its earliest days. Of all the women I spoke to at the WMA, she was also the most vocal critic of the addition of dhuhr into the program:

> I get frustrated with it, but the reason I don't participate is because I want to take a stand and the stand is: "I've just finished Jummah, I don't know what the hell you're talking about. . . . Why come if you're not going to go ahead in there?" But I respect the policies, I understand the policies and so that's my personal opinion and you probably won't hear me say it out loud too many places. . . . Now, if you really believe in it, then [I have] to support it whether [I] believe it or not. But if it's because your imam told you or your husband told you or . . . [but] who am I to be like, "Why you doing that?"[95]

Tina expressed her annoyance at the "man-made" issue of the legality of woman-led prayer, which she suspected might be born from external male judgment and control. She had her suspicions about where concerns about the invalidity of prayer originated, and wondered whether women who prayed dhuhr genuinely believed the claim that woman-led Jummah did not "count" or whether their religious leaders or family members were pressuring them to believe that. Nevertheless, Tina did not see it as her role to question her fellow congregants' intentions or decision-making processes and accordingly stated that she understood the WMA's adoption of dhuhr. Ultimately, Tina's personal disagreement on the addition of dhuhr did not detract from her enthusiasm as a WMA congregant, and she described herself as the WMA's "ultimate fan."[96]

Yasmin, as I highlighted above, was not previously aware of the Muslim debates on the legitimacy of woman-led Jummah, and accordingly did not pray the optional dhuhr. At the opposite end of the spectrum, Mariyah, a South Asian American in her thirties, who was an active member of multiple mosque communities in LA and a WMA supporter from its very first Jummah, had been aware of the controversies over the validity of woman-led Jummah. However, like Yasmin, she had no issue with it, stating, "I had never heard of the idea that women could not lead Jummah before, so for me, I had no hang-ups about going at all."[97] Neither Yasmin nor Mariyah prayed the optional dhuhr; they both, like Tina, asserted the validity of woman-led Jummah, but were also not particularly bothered by or invested in the debates. Yasmin was happy with the addition of the optional dhuhr because she felt it gave critics less to disparage, while Mariyah simply expressed that it was not an issue for her.

Tina's critical position on the WMA's addition of dhuhr demonstrates how Muslim women experience religious community differently across race. African American Muslim women like Tina tend to have greater leadership roles in their own mosques in comparison to their Arab and South Asian counterparts[98] and this shapes their expectations for women's participation in religious community. Tina was frustrated at the addition of dhuhr because she read it as accommodating male critics of woman-led prayer. This fits into Tina's overall perception that Arab and South Asian women face greater gender barriers than African American women in Muslim communities and need to be less timid and more "in your face."[99] While Yasmin and Mariyah, both South Asian, also do not pray dhuhr, neither was particularly concerned with its addition to the WMA program. Since Mariyah regularly took on leadership roles in interfaith spaces and participated in many other Arab- and South Asian-dominated Muslim spaces in LA, I imagine she picks her battles carefully and genuinely was not interested in debates on the legitimacy of prayer. For Yasmin, who had stopped going to mosques altogether for an extended period of time because of her negative experiences of feeling undervalued as a woman, I suspect that the controversies did not surprise her. As someone only recently reentering Muslim spaces, Yasmin had come to expect that "people make a big deal" over small matters, perhaps making her more inclined to accept the addition of dhuhr. Tina, on the other hand, had higher expectations of other Muslims and less tolerance for what she perceived as women's efforts being silenced and discredited. Her expectations were likely based on the public roles and spaces she and her fellow African American Muslim women had already carved out for themselves in their own Muslim communities.

Like Yasmin and Mariyah, Rana, another South Asian American in her early thirties, explained that she was not concerned about debates on the legality of woman-led Jummah. She does pray dhuhr, but did not appear to feel strongly about the matter either way. Rana did, however, seem aware of the legal arguments against woman-led prayer as she asserted that extenuating circumstances such as those currently facing American Muslim women's marginalization in mosques could sufficiently warrant new legal rules. She states:

> There's no harm in doing this extra prayer, but I wasn't that concerned. To me it's just so clear, throughout anything I've learned about the Prophet *sallallahu alayhi wasallam* [peace be upon him] and Islam, when a situation is unfair or there's an injustice happening or a system is not working how it's supposed to—there are exceptions made that allow you to go outside what would normally be the law because if mosques are not being run the way they're supposed to, and women are being treated badly, then my understanding is that God's not going to fault the women who have tried to create an alternative. He's going to fault those that didn't create the right situation. So to me, it was the bigger, broader intention and not the technicalities.[100]

Rana confidently articulates that based on the circumstances that give rise to a space like the WMA, "God's not going to fault" those who have implemented woman-led Jummah, even if it is outside of "what would normally be the law." While she is clearly aware of the legal debates on Jummah across Muslim communities, Rana states that she does not get caught up in the technicalities of what constitutes valid prayer. To her, the larger issue is that women are facing the injustice of poor treatment in mosques. She implies that if mosques were being run "the way they're supposed to" then these debates about the legality of prayer would not even emerge in the first place. Her attitude toward praying the optional dhuhr, then, is rooted not in the worry that woman-led Jummah might be invalid, but rather in the logic that there was "no harm" in doing it anyway.

Seher, the South Asian American in her thirties mentioned earlier, also prays dhuhr. She did not take a clear position on the Islamic legality of woman-led Jummah, but expressed a stronger sense of uncertainty in comparison to someone like Rana. On the addition of dhuhr into the WMA program, Seher shared: "I was going to do it [pray dhuhr] myself anyways so it's nice. . . . I wouldn't take a definitive position because I'm not a scholar. For me personally, it just kind of feels like I'm checking off all my options of doing both."[101] Foregrounding her lack of scholarly expertise, Seher suggested that she does not have enough knowledge to have a clear position for or against the validity of woman-led Jummah. She is overall appreciative that the WMA added it into the program, since as she states, she was "going to do it myself anyways." Seher's comment suggests that she sees praying dhuhr as a way to feel that she has covered all of her bases, which is not all that dissimilar from Rana stating that there is no harm in performing the prayer. However, their articulations appear distinct, since Rana described dhuhr as an "extra" prayer and affirms that God would accept woman-led Jummah, while Seher stated clearly that she does not know whether woman-led prayer is valid.

Sarah, a white American in her twenties, was forthcoming about her doubts about the legal validity of woman-led Jummah. Like Seher, she positioned herself as "personally unsure" about it, "even if it is just for other women. I'm glad that they have that option because it appeals to people who might be unsure or firmly believe that women shouldn't lead Jummah."[102] To Sarah, the addition of dhuhr into the WMA's official program made it a more welcoming and inclusive space to women who did not believe in the validity of women's Jummah or otherwise harbored doubts. Her qualification of "even if it is just for other women" indicates that she is well aware of the different argumentations on either side for and against woman-led Jummah. Accordingly, Sarah appreciates that the WMA creates a space for women like her, by not forcing them to justify their position or definitively take a stance either way. Rana, Seher, and Sarah all pray dhuhr after Jummah, but each has her own reasons for doing so that do not reflect the same position on the validity of women's Jummah.

During my time at the WMA, I observed that about five to seven congregants out of approximately thirty to forty would participate in the dhuhr prayer. I also asked other WMA members if this proportion was typical, and they confirmed that it was more or less consistent from month to month. Those who abstain had distinct reasons for their non-participation but their attitudes toward the extra dhuhr did not define their relationship to the WMA. None of these women seemed particularly concerned about whether their views perfectly aligned with those of others in the congregation, and it was clear that debates over female-led Jummah did not feature centrally in their engagement with the WMA. In fact, I suspect that the subject of ritual authority would not have figured into many of my conversations with WMA members, unless they were involved in leadership, had I not brought it up myself. If women at the WMA are largely unconcerned with staking a claim in the legal debates over women's ritual authority and broadly disinterested in the legal acceptability of prayer, what, then, motivates them to participate in a space such as the WMA in the first place? If congregation members are not fully invested in participating in legal debates over ritual authority, then their broader objectives must lie outside of these debates. When speaking to WMA members, it was unclear how relevant the Islamic legal tradition was in terms of their lived experiences in American Muslim communities. This raises the question about how both WMA members and the mosque's critics determine the criteria for religious authority.

When recounting their motivations for attending its first Jummah, many women described the WMA as a way for them to simply be with other Muslim women, feel empowered in their faith, or broaden their knowledge of Islam. Mariyah was one such congregant. Self-identifying as a "masjid-hopper" who prays at mosques all over Southern California and is a regular at two of them, Mariyah enthusiastically attended the inaugural WMA Jummah and has continued to come monthly since. She describes her initial interest in the WMA as a result of how women-only gatherings and spaces had been spiritually and emotionally nurturing for her in the past.[103] She therefore welcomed the idea of the WMA, in which a community of Muslim and non-Muslim women would gather together and pray. In addition to Mariyah, many other WMA members expressed similar sentiments about the value of women-only spaces. Sarah shared the following reflection:

> What drew me to it? Just that it's an all-women's space, I think that's so important in religious settings and in normal life settings since I went to a women's college . . . so I know just how valuable they [women-only spaces] are, and how hard they can be to find sometimes. . . . This is such a patriarchal world we live in, it's so important for marginalized people, any marginalized people to have their own spaces that focus on them. . . . And then Muslim women also face being marginalized as Muslims. In the US they face marginalization for being Muslims, as women, and even within the Muslim community, women are often treated as second-class citizens, so to have a space for just Muslim women and interfaith allies is really important.[104]

Sarah attests to the necessity for marginalized groups to have their own spaces, separate from public spaces in the mainstream patriarchal societies in which their lives are already immersed. She further describes how spaces for Muslim women are particularly valuable based on the marginalization they already feel as Muslims in America, and as women in both non-Muslim and Muslim communities.

Leila, an Arab American Muslim in her thirties, was also drawn to the WMA on the basis of its women-only nature. She, like Sarah, had a deep appreciation for women-only spaces, especially because gender-segregated spaces were the norm within her Arab American upbringing. She stated: "I was feeling like I am never in female-only spaces anymore and it's something that I grew up used to, just like the gender segregation in a lot of mosques and in Arab societies . . . so I was feeling the lack of that. The fact that it was women-only and the fact that it was very unapologetically progressive are the two things that drew me."[105] Leila elaborated on how her married adult life in LA, where many of the people in her inner circle happened to be men, was very different from the gender-segregated Arab culture that she grew up in. Because of this sharp contrast, Leila missed being around more women in her day-to-day life and explicitly extolled the culture of gender segregation of her childhood. It seemed to me that, having grown up around them, Leila had taken women-only spaces for granted and in adulthood suddenly felt their absence. Sarah, a white American, presumably did not grow up around gender-segregated spaces but came to value them through experiences such as attending a women's college.

Yasmin simultaneously expressed criticism of gender-segregated mosque culture and an appreciation for the women-only aspect of the WMA. She shared that, prior to becoming a member of the WMA, she had not set foot inside a mosque since she was about thirteen years old:

> [In] mosques generally, women are separated from men, and I hate it. Not because I feel that I need to be around guys all the time, but I just feel like why are we separate? What's the big deal? Are they better than us? How come they get to sit in the front and why are the women in the back? Like why do we have to worry about guys looking at us when we're all there or should be there for the same reason. So I hate that about traditional mosques, so much. Like, the women I feel have to be hidden. You know? ... I remember when I finally kind of realized, that's just the way it is. I was like eff this, I don't wanna go, I don't care about it anymore.[106]

Yasmin felt that the gender segregation in conventional mosques compels women to hide. I asked her then how she felt about the WMA as a women-only space. Yasmin responded that women-only spaces were distinct from gender-segregated spaces in that women were not hidden "because there's no one to hide from."[107] She continued that, in women-only spaces, women can be comfortable without feeling judged by men. To further illustrate her point, Yasmin, who is South Asian, compared women's spaces to Black-only groups:

> They [Muslim men] have plenty of other places to go. It's the same as with race issues. When white people complain that there are Black-only groups or things like that, they make a big deal of it. But they [white people] are able to go anywhere, so if you can let a group have a space where they feel safe, where they can talk about issues that really relate to them, I like that. I think it [the WMA] should stay a women's mosque ... because most mosques are only men anyway.[108]

Unlike Leila, who was nostalgic for the gender-segregated spaces of her upbringing, Yasmin's childhood memories of gender segregation were negative, and the reason why she had stopped attending mosques. Nevertheless, Yasmin, like Leila, Sarah, and Mariyah, ultimately appreciates the safe space of a women-only congregation, because she sees it as a space exclusively catering to the needs of women, rather than a measure to keep women hidden. To Yasmin, women-only spaces offer a corrective to the status quo of patriarchal spaces and cannot possibly be discriminatory toward Muslim men, who "have plenty of other places to go." To her, the fact that women are marginalized in "most mosques" justifies the existence of exclusive spaces for women and enhances their value. Given their wider marginalization in mosques across the US, Yasmin rejects the notion that spaces exclusively designed for women are a step backward for gender equality, instead seeing them as safe spaces where women can openly discuss particular issues. Here, she compares the WMA's women-only aspect to Black-only groups in the US and explains that while "white people complain" about them, they are necessary safe spaces for Black Americans as they navigate the status quo of white supremacy ("white people are allowed to go anywhere"). Yasmin's framing here helps us to understand why so many WMA congregants celebrated its women-only nature on its own terms rather than seeing it as a compromise with critics who take issue with woman-led mixed-gender prayer. In fact, far from understanding its women-only aspect as acquiescence to Muslim critics or to a particular interpretation of the Islamic legal tradition, many congregants were drawn to the WMA precisely because it was exclusively for women.

Rana also expressed gratitude for the community of women at the WMA. However, unlike the others who were specifically drawn to the WMA because it is a women-only congregation, Rana was caught off guard by her enjoyment of the women-only space. After attending her first WMA Jummah in the fall of 2016, Rana recalled sharing with her husband that she did not realize how much she needed the WMA until after she had experienced it. She was struck by how moving it had felt to hear a woman preach, describing it as "even more powerful than I realized."[109] She further stated, "You feel a stronger sense of community because you know there's a common experience that everyone there has, which is true in a sense of any congregation—we're all here because we're Muslim—but I think there's a stronger bond, and a stronger sense of community and shared experience and identity because we're all women."[110] The heightened sense of community that Rana felt in the WMA contrasted with her previous mosque-going experiences. This feeling of camaraderie surprised her, as she had been a regular mosque-goer her whole life, and did not feel marginalized. Many of my other interlocutors, particularly those who were active members of other mosques like Rana, expressed a similar sentiment about feeling caught off guard by how emotionally affective attending the WMA was to them. These were the members who generally supported the aims of the WMA insofar as they addressed the marginalization of women in mosques, but did not consider themselves to be lacking in spiritual community due to their generally positive experiences in other mosques. After experiencing the WMA, though, they were particularly moved by the women-only community.

However, those who support the WMA as a women-only space are not necessarily supportive of gender segregation more broadly. For example, women like Yasmin, who clearly articulated her distaste for gender segregation and cited it as the primary reason why she stopped attending mosques as a teenager, considered the women-only nature of the WMA to be one of its strongest assets. She differentiated between gender segregation in conventional mosques and the WMA, where she felt that in the absence of men, women were not segregated from them. Furthermore, while the WMA avoids labels such as "feminist" or "progressive," many congregants do self-identify in these terms and may, in turn, project their values on the space. For example, Leila proudly characterizes the WMA as an "unapologetically progressive" space that is meant for women only.[111] Tina also commends the WMA as a space independent from male control.[112] By contrast Celeste, another African American congregant in her sixties, shared that she was initially hesitant to get on board with the WMA because she felt that the exclusion of men did not seem like a step toward gender equality, but later had a change of heart after experiencing the community.[113] Ultimately, the women I spoke with did not seem to experience a tension between the WMA's women-only nature and their broader commitments to gender equality.

I highlight congregants' appreciation for the women-only aspect of the WMA to think about the WMA on its own terms rather than in comparison to community responses, legal debates, or connections to the 2005 mixed-gender Jummah. Earlier I noted that some WMA members and organizers felt acutely aware of the backlash of the 2005 mixed-gender prayer event and were determined to avoid the same volatile reaction. While this is certainly the case, the WMA's women-only aspect is more than a pragmatic compromise; it should not be reduced to a move designed to quell the concerns of voices that would contest mixed-gender prayer. Rather, many members of the WMA community view having a women-only congregation as particularly valuable because it provides an alternative to male-dominated spaces. Despite the ways WMA leaders are attuned to gendered marginalization in mosques, it is worth noting that their reliance on a binary division of gender excludes individuals who do not identify as either male or female, even as they welcome trans-women by stating that it is a mosque for all self-identifying women. Individual congregants are likely to have a range of views about the fact the WMA does not, at the time of this writing, officially embrace nonbinary Muslims (or interfaith supporters), but their support for the WMA is undergirded by an implicit critique of patriarchy and a white supremacist culture that marginalizes Muslim women in US society. Irrespective of whether every WMA member identifies as feminist or not, congregants all actively participate in the feminist critique that mainstream configurations of social and religious spaces are not doing enough for women.

In fact, because so many mosques across North America fail to provide women with religious community, access to hearing the khutbah, seeing the imam, and on the most basic level, adequate space to pray, women are increasingly seeking alternative spaces. Here Krista Riley's work on the significance of virtual spaces through blogs, Tumblr, and other social media in enabling Muslim women to forge religious community is again instructive. Riley shows how online spaces that draw attention to gender inequality in mosques can elevate women's individual grievances from "a matter of private concern" to "being of public importance."[114] Moreover, she observes that Muslim women continually "find ways to challenge the physical spaces in which they find themselves and to harness creative ideas for building new communities."[115] The WMA is one such new community, and although it is a physical space, its online presence and its courtship of mainstream media in its first years enable it to have the kind of broader impact on Muslim debates to which

Riley refers. The WMA's established online presence is also what perhaps facilitated its shift to virtual Jummah services in 2020 during the COVID-19 pandemic, since, for example, it had already been livestreaming its Jummah services on Facebook since mid-2018. Even prior to that, by posting their khutbahs on Soundcloud and YouTube since the very first Jummah, the WMA has always tried to appeal to a virtual community beyond those who could participate in its physical space. Indeed, as Islamic studies scholar Robert Rozehnal argues, throughout the twenty-first century Muslims across the US and around the world have increasingly utilized the Internet "as a vital alternative space for Muslim self-imagining and social networking, piety and performance, politics and polemics."[116] In particular, for North American Muslim women and nonbinary people, turning to virtual religious communities and networks as a place to forge social connections and cultivate piety is sometimes the only available option. So when the COVID-19 pandemic compelled mosques around the US to physically shut down in 2020 to shift to virtual services and many Muslim men began to lament their sudden spiritual isolation, the Muslims for whom conventional mosques had already been inaccessible—women, nonbinary, queer—were already accustomed to participating in virtual communities.

For its congregants, the WMA represents a new kind of community: a women-only safe space that is an alternative to existing mosques. As an institution, the WMA also considers itself as a transitional space that complements rather than replaces other mosques. The long-term plans of the WMA include offering co-ed classes that promote Qur'anic literacy in English and teaching female perspectives on Islamic knowledge. Maznavi and her team think of the WMA as a place to help women cultivate authority to interpret sacred texts and then take up leadership positions in their co-ed mosques. Until these long-term plans come to fruition, it is too early to speculate on how the WMA will function as a transitional space that prepares its congregants to (re)enter conventional, co-ed mosques. In fact, the WMA may even have the reverse effect of putting women off conventional mosques after introducing them to a worship community where they feel valued, respected, and spiritually rejuvenated. Indeed, Seher, who is South Asian and in her thirties, mentioned in passing that, since being a part of the WMA, she has felt less motivated to attend her regular mosque as often as she used to because it was not as satisfying or enriching an experience. However, as it stands, a number of congregants are already active members in their mosques, while some have no desire to be a part of another Muslim community outside the WMA. Some congregants are particularly drawn to the WMA's inclusive mission statement and share the general view that women should have more access to religious knowledge. Still others come out of curiosity for the kind of community that the WMA promises to build, especially when their conventional mosques fail to deliver on those promises.

Overall then, WMA congregants are drawn to participating in a women-only community that feels both nurturing and empowering for them, and like a refreshing departure from the male-dominated spaces that characterize other aspects of their lives. Congregants did not appear fixated on community debates over women's ritual authority and their right to lead Jummah, and likewise neither did WMA leaders. In the WMA executive board's willingness to adopt an optional dhuhr prayer, I read them as refusing to subject themselves to the sorts of communal criticism that would overshadow their broader aims as an institution. Wider American Muslim contestations over ritual authority do not reflect members' own concerns and objectives. Many WMA supporters are simply unmoved or unmotivated by legal debates over ritual prayer; they fail to grasp the urgency with which critics voice their concerns about the validity of woman-led prayer. This is not to say that they do not have views on the matter; indeed the majority of them support woman-led Jummah. However, congregants are not returning to the WMA every month out of a desire to continually assert women's ritual authority; they return for the sense of spiritual community that many of them have not experienced elsewhere.

In some ways, the portrait presented here about how women in the WMA community navigate the external Muslim criticism and debates over ritual authority might give the impression that it is a conflict-free community where congregants', khateebahs', and board members' interests all align. While there is a certain level of alignment between these different actors, this is not to say that all those who are sympathetic to the aims of the WMA have no criticisms of it. We saw with congregants like Tina, who was unhappy with the addition of dhuhr prayer into the WMA program, that there are those who would make different leadership decisions than Maznavi and her team. However, women like Tina who have certain criticisms but opt to continue being a part of the community ultimately choose to focus on the elements of the WMA that they agree with. In other words, these women are more invested in the success of the WMA than they are in their critiques of it, ultimately accepting it for what it is rather than what they as individuals imagine it should be. Their acceptance in many ways translates into support for and loyalty to Maznavi and her personal vision for the WMA.

Conversely, Muslims invested in increased opportunities for women's religious authority who are critical enough of the WMA to be put off by it opt not to participate. These are the women who decline invitations to serve as khateebah, or who might decide to participate only once in a while as a congregant. These women include those who have anecdotally shared with me how the WMA's policies on khateebahs and menstruation, or the requirement to submit a khutbah for Maznavi and her team's approval in advance, were deal breakers for them. While the voices of such women could enrich the analysis here of the different ways that American Muslim women seek to take up Islamic authority through interventions perhaps considered more "radical" than the WMA, interviewing Muslims outside of the WMA is beyond the scope of this book. For this reason, the voices highlighted in this chapter, and in this book more broadly, necessarily skew toward those who reflect appreciatively on the WMA's stance on ritual authority and the way that it accommodates critiques of woman-led prayer since they identify as a part of the community.

The WMA's accommodation of multiple perspectives is strategic to be sure, and can be interpreted as acquiescence to patriarchal demands in American Muslim communities. Nevertheless, by not fixating on ritual leadership the WMA opens up new spaces for gradually rethinking women's religious authority in more substantial ways. Maznavi and her team demonstrate that they are not concerned with indoctrinating their congregants with particular perspectives on ritual. Rather, they are committed to encouraging as many women as possible to participate in interpreting scripture and engaging social issues in their communities. Congregants are receptive to this attitude, and many appreciate that WMA leaders are not single-mindedly focused on the ideological battle for women's right to lead Jummah.

Regardless of how WMA leaders and khateebahs might compare themselves to the organizers of the 2005 mixed-gender prayer event in NYC, their careful navigation of prayer leadership indicates that they are not interested in confining their goals to ritual authority. Put another way, the WMA's disinterest in taking a more "radical" 2005-style stance (beyond also asserting a Muslim woman's right to lead Jummah) on gender and ritual leadership allows them to focus on other interventions in authority—like its discursive production of women's khutbahs. In the next chapter, we explore how, by producing women's khutbahs, the WMA enables women to cultivate interpretive authority in ways that both adhere to and depart from how other global and US Muslim communities engage the Qur'an in Arabic and in English translations.

2

Interpretive Authority

Reading the Qur'an in English

Why would anybody repeat something and not know what they're saying? . . . If I don't know what I'm saying, I'm not comfortable saying it. That's been my experience with every African American that I know. . . . Of course, you have to practice just to be able to say the words, the sounds [in Arabic], but invariably, I know what I'm saying. By the time I've mastered these sounds, I also have mastered what I'm saying. I couldn't imagine any other way to do it. . . . [It is] surprising to discover that so many eastern Muslims—immigrant Muslims—did not actually understand the Qur'an.
—Zahara, African American, in her sixties

Classical Arabic is the language of the Qur'an, believed by Muslims to be the eternal word of God, revealed to the Prophet Muhammad through the Archangel Jibril (Gabriel) in seventh-century Arabia. It is also the liturgical language of Islamic prayer as Zahara, a regular at both the WMA and a number of other LA mosques, alludes to above: "of course, you have to practice just to be able to say the words [in Arabic]." Muslims all over the world, in their homes and mosques, engage the Qur'an as a devotional text and conduct their daily prayers in classical Arabic, whether they understand it or not, as they have done for centuries. However, beginning in the eighteenth century, Muslims around the world increasingly viewed the Qur'an as a source of practical and intellectual guidance for Muslim life.[1] The WMA as an institution and a community follows this global Islamic trend, and its members uphold the Qur'an as more than a devotional text. This is especially true of the WMA's African American congregants. For example, Zahara values the meaning of the Qur'an as much as she does its Arabic recitation in prayer, to the extent that she experienced cognitive dissonance upon learning that many of the "eastern, immigrant"—Arab and South Asian—Muslims across her LA communities did not.

In her sixties, Zahara had an ebullient personality and even as she maintained a cheerful and reflective demeanor, she always spoke frankly about her observations and experiences in Muslim communities. She could not make sense of how or why some Muslims would recite in prayer words that they did not understand. She recalled thinking: "These people have come from the Middle East, say that they're Muslim, yet don't understand the Qur'an?!"[2] Indeed, as Zahara's observations indicate, even native speakers of modern Arabic are unlikely to understand the classical Arabic of the Qur'an without formal study. However, her surprise that some Muslims from the Middle East could not understand the Qur'an reflects more than her possible conflation between classical and modern Arabic; rather, it points to her own commitment to learning the meaning of her Qur'anic recitations. She explained that in her experience, African American Muslims were accustomed to learning the meaning of the Qur'an along with its recitation. While she acknowledged the significance of mastering Arabic Qur'an recitation, or "the sounds," she simultaneously upheld the importance of knowing its meaning. Notably, she emphasized how she pursued both of these skills at the same time: "by the time I've mastered these sounds, I also have mastered what I'm saying." For Zahara, the religious significance of learning Qur'anic recitation and comprehending its meaning are inextricably linked.

Likewise, Kenyatta, an African American in her forties and a religious leader in her own right, similarly expressed the importance of understanding the meaning of the Qur'an in her own Muslim community. Describing her religious practice, she explained, "I'm not a person who just blindly follows [Islam]. It has to logically make sense for me. . . . I feel like for us [African American Muslims] it needs to come down to that very organic basis of quoting Qur'an."[3] Kenyatta attested to the importance of understanding the Qur'an, stating it must "logically make sense" to her. To be sure, neither Kenyatta's nor Zahara's respective experiences represent those of all or even most US Black or African American Muslims. These diverse communities defy generalizations and many Black Muslims in the US, including African Americans and African immigrants, also engage in the practice of learning Qur'anic recitation without memorizing meaning, in ways comparable to the South Asian and Middle Eastern Muslims who earned Zahara's shock and dismay.[4] However, Kenyatta's and Zahara's shared emphasis on understanding the meaning of the Qur'an in their native English language provides insight into the values of the WMA and its core members.

Furthermore, Kenyatta also described how her Islamic beliefs were rooted in the Qur'an rather than the Hadith, and characterized African American Muslim communities as sharing this emphasis, stating, "For African Americans or Blacks, we didn't really learn about Hadith until the nineties. It wasn't something we grew up with . . . it was just Arabic and Qur'an. That's all."[5] Kenyatta speaks from her own experiences and of course does not represent the diversity of Black American Muslims, but what is noteworthy here is that her views align with how WMA leaders also prioritize the Qur'an and its meaning over the use of the Hadith.[6] In 2015, Maznavi described reading the Qur'an in English as the "single most empowering" thing she had ever done, stating that the entire WMA executive board "agree[d] that we all need to get the Muslim ummah back to the Quran."[7] Kenyatta's emphasis on the Qur'an over the Hadith coheres with the WMA's mission of bringing the Muslim community back to the Qur'an. However, while board members shape the priorities of the institution and have power to influence the congregation, many congregants, particularly African Americans like Zahara and Kenyatta, already held similar views on the centrality of the Qur'an and its meaning.

Though Zahara and Kenyatta represent two different generations, their characterizations of the relationship between the Qur'an and their African American Muslim communities are consistent. Zahara was not brought up in a specific religious tradition; her father was from a Christian background and her mother was briefly associated with the Nation of Islam (NOI). They raised Zahara with a belief in a monotheistic God, and she formally embraced Islam when she was older: "When I read the Qur'an, I was like 'this is what I've always believed. That makes sense. That makes sense. That makes sense.'"[8] By contrast, Kenyatta was raised Muslim—her parents were members of the NOI; they later embraced Sunni Islam under the leadership of W. D. Mohammed (d. 2008), who disbanded the NOI in the 1970s. She explained that like most African American Muslims she knew, she was taught the importance of the

Qur'an. The importance that both Zahara and Kenyatta place on understanding the Qur'an coheres with the WMA's goal to promote Qur'anic literacy. They demonstrate that the WMA's emphasis on the meaning of the Qur'an has a receptive audience in its African American congregants who share their views, especially those who came up in the NOI or in W. D. Mohammed's communities like Zahara and Kenyatta. Taken together, their comments gesture at the centrality of English translations of the Qur'an not only in their own lives, but also at the WMA.

Khateebahs' interest in the meaning of the Qur'an is continuous with the global history of Qur'anic interpretation. Islamic studies scholar Johanna Pink shows how, before the eighteenth century, Muslim scholarship that focused on interpreting scriptural meaning was "an elitist endeavor" that was not directed toward facilitating lay Muslims' understanding of the Qur'an, but operated exclusively in the realm of the ulama.[9] Accordingly, in the premodern period, translations of the Qur'an were primarily tools to help readers decipher particular Arabic terms. These were either literal translations of individual words that lacked "coherent sentence[s] in the target language," or Qur'anic commentaries.[10] Pink further highlights that it was only in the first half of the twentieth century that Qur'an translations, as proper reproductions of the meaning of the text as opposed to serving only as reading aids for the original Arabic, shifted to the center of discourses on Muslim reform in West Africa, the Middle East, and South Asia.[11] This shift was the result of the rise of mass literacy coupled with the role of nation-states, from West Africa to the Middle East and South Asia, in promoting education in their national languages. Moreover, twentieth-century Muslim reformers brought the Qur'an to the fore of debates on Islamic practice as they sought to "promote rationalism, fight superstition and enable reforms" as a way to combat the authority of the religious elite class.[12] The WMA's focus on the Qur'an and its translations in English therefore fit within this broader global trajectory of shifts in Islamic authority and debates over Muslim practice. Moreover, the WMA also fits into trends in the US context wherein Muslims have negotiated the roles that English and Arabic play in their national and religious identities.[13] At the same time, in its call for Qur'anic literacy, the WMA embraces English as more than just a linguistic common ground for US Muslims, elevating it to the sacred status of Arabic.

By elevating the status of English translations of the Qur'an, the WMA encourages lay Muslims without formal religious training and Arabic expertise to cultivate interpretive authority as khateebahs. WMA leaders invite a range of Muslim women to be khateebahs, including community activists, medical doctors, local politicians, and university professors. Most are local to Southern California, though others occasionally travel from other parts of the country. With some exceptions, the majority of WMA khateebahs lack formal religious credentials and are not proficient in Arabic. Even for khateebahs with the language skills to quote from the Qur'an in Arabic in their khutbahs, the WMA board requires them to include English translations, foregrounding the meaning of the text over its recitation.[14] By inviting lay Muslim women to be khateebahs, the WMA provides a platform for them to contribute to an evolving Islamic exegetical discourse and, in the process, reimagines the criteria necessary for interpretive authority, privileging women's everyday experiences and individual readings of the Qur'an over formal credentials and Arabic expertise. These WMA actors also claim continuity with the Islamic historical tradition and see themselves as reviving the legacy of Muslim women in authoritative roles from the Prophetic era.

Seeking Authenticity

Critics and supporters alike often assume that the WMA departs from the Islamic tradition as an innovative and modern interpretation. However, those involved in leadership roles situate the WMA squarely within Islamic history. For example, in her inaugural khutbah, Edina Lekovic, the WMA's first-ever khateebah, stated:

> The beautiful truth is that today is not a departure from our tradition as Muslim women. It's a continuation of the proud legacy of Muslim women throughout fourteen-plus centuries who have participated in the spiritual life of their communities at all stages and all places—inside their mosques, inside their homes, and in their broader societies as scholars, as teachers, as leaders, and fundamentally, as partners. In fact there have been mosques by and for Muslim women in at least ten countries that we know of, so we're not the first. Alhamdulillah, praise be to God.[15]

In her remarks, Lekovic declared that Muslim women had long been taking up various roles of religious authority in public and private. Furthermore, she characterized the WMA as continuous with over fourteen centuries of Islamic history. Her khutbah highlighted that women's mosques have existed all around the world, emphasizing that the WMA was not the first. In fact, Lekovic explained that the Prophet Muhammad used to allocate one day per week exclusively for teaching women in his mosque, offering the earliest possible Islamic precedent for the WMA.[16] She explained that this measure was taken in response to complaints from the Prophet's female Companions about their marginalization.[17]

Likewise, in interviews with mainstream media throughout the WMA's first year, Maznavi repeatedly asserted that women-only mosques existed in Muslim communities all over the world, including in India, Syria, and China. She further explained that the WMA "come[s] from a long legacy of women's involvement in Islam" and that her personal inspiration for the project was "learning about the thousands of Muslim women scholars and leaders who were actively engaged in the formation and spread of Islam."[18] In no uncertain terms, Maznavi and Lekovic see themselves as reviving past practices in the Islamic tradition.

However, the very idea of what constitutes the "Islamic tradition" to American Muslims is itself contested. Grewal shows us that the Islamic tradition involves a continual process of excision and modification, wherein its various custodians—including the ulama (Muslim scholarly elite), traditionally trained scholars, and even lay American Muslims— play active roles in its transmission and transformation. She argues that although some Muslims may understand the transmission of tradition over time as a simple process of preserving the past, it is actually "a mediation process that is reflexive and selective. Elements of the past are mediated into the present by custodians, individuals in the present who decide which aspects of the past are nonessential to the tradition's future and, therefore, may be deleted or deemphasized."[19] The Islamic tradition therefore, changes over time under the evaluation of actors who choose to highlight and minimize different elements in response to particular contexts.

Grewal argues that for Muslims the Islamic tradition in its contemporary forms carries the full weight of its past authority, despite its continual change, given that its "essential elements" have not been omitted. Indeed, she states that members of the ulama and revivalists alike have already integrated expert knowledge from non-Islamic "secular" sources into the Islamic tradition. However, she challenges the idea that the Islamic tradition can simply be preserved from the past into the future in its identical form. Tradition, she argues, necessarily changes through debates about which of its parts should carry on into the future and which should be left behind.

Yet the concept of an authentic, untarnished Islamic tradition prevails in American Muslim communities, including at the WMA. While understanding tradition as adaptive creates space to situate the WMA within it as an authentic expression of Islam, these are not the terms that its organizers use to frame their project. Instead, the WMA's institutional narrative insists on its continuity with Islamic history and does not purport to be reforming Islamic practice by advocating for women as khateebahs and as prayer leaders. Rather, the WMA views itself as reviving the legacy of women's mosques and leadership from the Prophetic era and throughout Islamic history, rather than introducing any new elements based on their current circumstances—exactly as Lekovic stated in her inaugural khutbah.[20] WMA leaders are invested in understanding the Islamic tradition in what Grewal calls commonsense terms, as "a discrete body of ideas and practices" that is transmitted through preservation in order to lay claim to Islamic authenticity.

The WMA's own narrative of historical continuity is integral to understanding how its leaders conceptualize the space. It is also necessary however, to situate their narrative in the broader discourse of how contemporary Muslims frame their projects as Islamic. While claiming continuity is important for any Muslims vying for Islamic authenticity across various geographical contexts, it is especially the case that American Muslim women and gender-nonconforming individuals frame their interpretive projects in this way. Kecia Ali observes that "women accused of complicity with Western views may try especially hard to promote their views as 'natural' and transparent as part of a quest for practical influence."[21] While Ali is specifically referring to Muslim feminist exegetes who may purposely avoid contesting conventional Islamic wisdom because of the scrutiny they already encounter, her argument also applies to the WMA. Any Muslim activist project, like the WMA, that aims at catalyzing social change within existing religious communities must contend with prevailing ideas about the correlation between tradition, its continuity, and authenticity.

Grewal has shown that, especially since the 1990s, multiple generations of US Muslims have believed that "intellectual mastery over the [Sunni] tradition could be the new, universal measure of religious authority."[22] In pursuit of this universal authority, American Muslim seekers travel to the Middle East, North Africa, and South Asia to learn Arabic, *tajweed* (Qur'anic recitation), and Hadith, and to study legal texts. She shows that they are usually seeking a timeless tradition to bring back to their local American mosques, but are largely unsuccessful.[23] While US Muslim youth tend to study in "unofficial study circles" because of their suspicions about state-run religious institutions in the Middle East,[24] others prioritize institutionalized credentials.[25] As scholar of Islam and politics Alexander Thurston notes, in a milieu of "educational pluralism" where Muslims seek different types of Islamic training, either through traditional or secular institutions or informal networks, Islamic authority is polyvalent. Thurston further observes that heightened transnational interactions among Muslims "can change the structure of religious authority by adding new sources of legitimation as well as by changing the balance among different sources."[26] As Islamic credentials evolve across a transnational stage, how communities like the WMA reframe these transformations is increasingly relevant to discussions of religious authority.

The WMA implicitly acknowledges the polyvalent nature of Islamic authority since it opens up space for multiple authoritative voices: those with traditional and secular training in Islamic studies, and most importantly, those with neither. Women with a wide range of backgrounds, both scholarly and non-scholarly, may occupy the role of khateebah, and this diversity is integral to the overall branding of the WMA. The WMA presents itself as an inclusive space that deploys "rotating imams and khateebahs in order to offer diverse perspectives from a wide range of scholars" and to grant religious leadership opportunities to women previously precluded from them.[27] The WMA explicitly purports to champion the voices of everyday women who otherwise would not have opportunities to speak from a position of religious authority. Additionally, by not adhering to any legal school, the WMA allows for a plurality of Islamic practices. They provide rose petals, prayer beads, and clay tablets in the prayer hall to accommodate Shiʻi ritual prayer, and also accommodate the Hanafi tradition of a bayan, or pre-sermon talk.[28] The WMA's non-sectarian inclusivity further indicates the broad spectrum of the kinds of voices and perspectives its leaders consider authentically Islamic.

While there is no singular model of authority and authenticity in US mosques, it is nevertheless useful to consider the elevated status of Arabic expertise and traditional credentials within many of them. Throughout US mosque communities, both Arab and non-Arab Muslims have advocated for more Arabic instruction as part of and in addition to Sunday school programs.[29] Even African American Muslims committed to contesting the hegemony of Arab and South Asian Islam in their mosques have advocated for training in the Islamic sciences in the Middle East to do so.[30] W. D. Mohammed, who preached a distinctly African American Islam that empowered Black Muslims even as he transitioned his followers from the NOI into the Sunni mainstream, likewise also promoted traditional credentials. He spearheaded a program in Damascus in 2000 for his followers to learn the "Arabic sciences—Qurʾanic recitation and memorization, handwriting, grammar, morphology—and Islamic sciences—*fiqh* and *tazkiyyah* (purification of the soul)."[31] To be sure, for Mohammed and his followers, these formalized credentials were a part of a broader pursuit to "indigenize mainstream Islamic beliefs," but they nevertheless upheld the importance of Arabic training and formal credentials.[32]

Moreover, US Muslim communities' emphasis on Arabic training and formal credentials as a marker of authenticity reveals how Islamic authority is racialized. In other words, Arab ethnoreligious hegemony facilitates Arab leadership over non-Arab Muslims while also reinforcing anti-Black racism within Muslim communities. For example, native Arabic proficiency (even in colloquial Arabic as opposed to classical Qurʾanic Arabic) or expression of Arab norms in clothing can stand in for expertise where there is none.[33] As Khabeer shows, this is often at the expense of individual Black Muslims or a Black hip hop aesthetic adopted by either Black or non-Black Muslims.[34] In these cases, conforming or appealing to Arab culture (through elements like language proficiency, clothing, or music) can qualify someone as more authentically Muslim and supersede any formal expertise of Black Muslims in many communities.[35] We saw this dynamic play out in the disparate community perceptions of African American Islamic studies scholar amina wadud and the Egyptian public figure Yasmin Mogahed, who has no religious credentials. Likewise, even within women's informal study circles in the US, an Arabic speaker could assume leadership over non–Arabic speakers without any formal credentials.[36]

To be sure, Islamic authority at the WMA is also racialized, with anti-Black sentiment manifesting in ways that do not necessarily resemble the explicit anti-Black racism of other US Muslim spaces. But the larger dynamics of the WMA as a mixed-race worship community create space for combatting and correcting ethnoreligous hegemony, however imperfectly. To the extent that internal Muslim racism is rooted in the idea that Arab Islam (and some forms of South Asian Islam) is more authentic than Black forms of Islam, the WMA offers a corrective. For example, many American Muslims who seek out formal training perceive themselves as a bridge between the authentic Islam of the East and their native US where "real" Islam has yet to be established.[37] By contrast, the WMA members I interviewed reject an authenticity gap between the "Islamic East" and Muslims in the US. This creates space to consider US Black forms of Islam as authentic, and African American and other Muslims who do not appeal to Arabic expertise and Arab cultural norms, as legitimate figures of religious authority.

Moreover, as Khabeer argues, many US Muslims who are otherwise invested in the concept of an "Islamic East" from where to acquire an authentic Islam to transport to the West, overlook African countries like Senegal and Nigeria (and to some extent even Morocco and Mauritania) as legitimate sites of religious study. She argues that both Black and non-Black US Muslims do not consider these countries as sufficiently Islamic for inclusion in the broader transnational moral geographies that Grewal describes, based on their "absence from the intellectual genealogies of US American scholars who are most popular among US American Muslims."[38] This US Muslim erasure of Black African countries from the archives of the Islamic tradition illustrates how a commitment to formal training as a requirement for religious authority promotes anti-Blackness.[39] Decentering Arab sites of learning as synonymous with authentic Islam to include the US within the Islamic archive does not on its own combat anti-Blackness—after all, anti-Black racism is embedded within the very fabric of the US. However, doing so opens up pathways for the potential inclusion and recognition of different forms of Black Islam as authentic, within racially diverse American Muslim spaces as opposed to only within some Black Muslim communities.

WMA leaders appear concerned with Islamic authenticity, but do not only associate it with learning Arabic and the classical Islamic disciplines, including Hadith and jurisprudence. For them, authenticity is associated with the meaning of the Qur'an, as opposed to solely its Arabic recitation or credentials acquired overseas. The WMA's institutional emphasis on the meaning of the Qur'an opens up discursive space for more Muslim women—including Black women—to cultivate interpretive authority. While WMA actors do not invalidate authority based on traditional credentials, they open up space for its different modes that are not dependent on these credentials. In other words, WMA leaders view traditional credentials as one of many possible avenues through which to cultivate Islamic authority.

Generally speaking, modes of authority that are independent of formal training increase possibilities for women to take up Islamic authority, given their wider exclusion from traditional scholarship opportunities. Throughout Muslim societies prior to the late twentieth century, women were largely precluded from acquiring scholarly authority because only men had access to formal education.[40] Despite the expansion of educational opportunities for women at institutions such as Al-Azhar, which founded a parallel women's theological college in 1961, men continue to dominate these settings.[41] Additionally, within informal study circles, women who reach advanced levels of study are often unable to continue their education because of the dearth of female teachers and male teachers' unwillingness to take them on as students.[42] Therefore, even women who pursue traditional training cannot acquire the same level of interpretive authority as their male counterparts. Nevertheless, the increased presence of neo-traditional female scholars at US Muslim institutions in part accounts for the sophisticated responses to the WMA and woman-led prayer we saw earlier. Reima Yosif and Muslema Purmul, two female scholars with opposing views of women's prayer leadership, demonstrate that although it is still rare to see women scholars with traditional religious training, their input can foster more nuanced engagements with topics having to do with women and gender.

Given that women continue to face barriers to acquiring formal Islamic training, promoting this training as a requirement for Islamic
authority systematically marginalizes Muslim women, even if inadvertently. For example, UCLA law professor and Islamic studies scholar
Khaled Abou El Fadl critiques contemporary authoritative figures in
Saudi Arabia who favor rigid gender norms that harm women by describing their understanding of the Qur'an as incomplete, due to their
lack of traditional religious training.[43] He therefore argues that religious
authority should be cultivated "through proper training and scholarship."[44] Although Abou El Fadl's critique is aimed at Saudi male clerics,
his commitment to traditional religious training as a criterion for interpretive authority may perpetuate female exclusion. While Abou El Fadl
has secular and traditional training in Islamic studies, which bolster his
authority, his Muslim female colleagues in the US academy hold only
secular credentials that are typically insufficient to confer religious authority on them in Muslim communities.[45]

In response to this trend, Islamic studies scholar Zahra Ayubi has advocated for widening the criteria for Islamic authority to include secular
credentials because doing so would open up the interpretive enterprise
to American Muslim women for whom classical training is largely un-
available.[46] A growing number of American Muslim women have indeed
cultivated authority through the secular academy and have produced an
entire genre of feminist[47] exegesis over the course of the late twentieth and early twenty-first centuries.[48] As Juliane Hammer shows, these
scholars' works justify activist projects and confer legitimacy to new
community practices, like woman-led prayer.[49] The WMA is one such
activist project that has emerged from feminist exegeses of the Qur'an,
even as it does not identify as a feminist mosque. Specifically, the WMA
arises from elements of wadud's and other feminists' exegetical works,
in particular from their characterizations of the Qur'an as an essentially
gender-egalitarian text.[50]

Many khateebahs' interpretive methods resemble those of Muslim
feminist scholars who refer to the Qur'an as the final source of authority and selectively invoke specific hadith traditions when it is useful for
their respective agendas. They prioritize direct access to, and personal
agency in, reading the Qur'an and endorse Qur'anic literacy as a form of
women's empowerment. Where wadud and other feminist exegetes tend

to overlook the role of the Hadith in their interpretive engagements and at times even blame them for misogynistic practices in the Islamic tradition, WMA leaders similarly promote the Qur'an over the Hadith as an authoritative scriptural source.[51] They also share feminist exegetes' emphasis on ijtihad (independent reasoning) and individual accessibility of the text. Despite WMA leaders' careful efforts to disassociate themselves from wadud's high-profile example of delivering a Jummah khutbah and leading prayer in 2005, her exegetical influence is unmistakable in their approaches to the Qur'an. Even as mosque leaders and khateebahs, who together define the WMA's institutional culture, deliberately avoid the feminist label, their methods are nevertheless grounded in Muslim feminist exegesis. In other words, Muslim feminist scholars with secular academic credentials influence the way that WMA actors articulate their own religious commitments to gender-egalitarian values, whether they explicitly acknowledge it or not. Muslim feminist exegesis both validates and is validated by communities like the WMA, providing us with a small glimpse of the long-term impact of opening up the interpretive enterprise to American Muslim women.

Through community praxis, the WMA can legitimize existing Islamic discourses and prop up certain types of individuals or criteria as authoritative. Indeed, WMA leaders promote multiple voices and discourses as authoritative beyond feminist exegesis. Past khateebahs include ones with doctorates in Islamic studies from the secular academy and traditional religious training with ijazas in various subjects, as well as a *hafidhah* (one who has memorized the Qur'an) and a Sufi from the Chisti order. Significantly, however, most of the WMA khateebahs are not traditionally trained in the way that Abou El Fadl calls for; rather, they derive authority from their everyday—both personal and professional—experiences. In other words, while the WMA recognizes traditional Islamic credentials and Arabic expertise as a legitimate basis for authority in line with many other US Muslim communities, what is different here is how it creates space for other kinds of authority that are not dependent on Arabic expertise or traditional Islamic credentials.

To be sure, other US Muslim groups have also contested Islamic authority based on formal training and Arabic expertise. Justine Howe highlights ongoing debates within the Webb community, a Muslim third space in suburban Chicago, between those who advocate for more rigorous Arabic instruction and those who desire to limit Arabic to certain rituals and instead embrace English as a central part of American Muslim identity.[52] She also attests to the importance of secular university degrees as a criterion for authority among Webb members.[53] There are significant parallels here with the WMA, which likewise upholds secular degrees as authoritative and grants lay Muslim women authority. However, the women in the Webb community do not lead prayer or give the Jummah khutbah and therefore, according to Howe, "do not have the same potential to disrupt models of authoritative practices."[54] WMA khateebahs, on the other hand, present an opportunity to analyze how US Muslim women cultivate authority in the roles of preaching and leading prayer.

Additionally, Salafi or revivalist Muslims in the US who, like Muslim feminists, promote scripture over other sources in pursuit of the "real" Islam are also broadly critical of traditional training; they emphasize individual interpretation or ijtihad. Yet notably, popular US Salafi preacher Yasir Qadhi, mentioned in the last chapter, prior to pursuing an American PhD in religious studies, received degrees in Hadith and Islamic sciences and in Islamic theology from the University of Medina in Saudi Arabia.[55] Therefore, while Qadhi has described feeling empowered by accessing Islam "straight from the text of the Qur'an and hadith" and stated that "there is a sense of liberation where you're not depending on a group of clerics,"[56] his own Islamic authority is still predicated upon his traditional credentials from Medina. In fact, Grewal has highlighted that Qadhi was largely motivated to brand himself and his Texas-based AlMaghrib Institute as "orthodox" to viably compete with Hamza Yusuf, who had already successfully adopted the traditionalist label for his Bay Area–based Zaytuna Institute.[57] Qadhi and his "orthodox" brand, then, do not represent a coherent American Muslim critique of traditional training. Thus, although others have critiqued traditional models of authority, they have not necessarily contested the framework of the training itself. The WMA, though still a nascent community, already both challenges traditional training and reframes the terms of the debate on Islamic authority by inviting lay Muslim women to lead prayer and deliver khutbahs. As such, it provides a new model to think about the US as a site for authentic interpretive engagements outside of formal training and based on lay Muslim women's experiences.

Since each khateebah has a unique background, it is not possible to characterize the WMA's attitude toward the relationship between Islamic authority and formal credentials in a singular way. However, Grewal's categorizations of formalist, pragmatist, and reformist are instructive. Formalists are committed to the "licensing of expertise" and include those who seek traditional Islamic learning credentials through gaining ijazas and studying with a particular teacher.[58] By contrast, pragmatists are not as committed to the formal process of acquiring Islamic literacy, and therefore "have a less rigorous and fixed definition of Islamic expertise."[59] Pragmatists also more openly embrace their role in mediating tradition.[60] Despite the distinctions in their attitudes toward traditional forms of learning, both formalists and pragmatists are broadly committed to the preservation of the tradition. Reformists, however, do not place value on the Islamic tradition from the recent past, which they believe has been corrupted, and instead emphasize the authority of the first generations of Muslims. The WMA as a community exhibits commitments to all three of these attitudes toward traditional learning and authority.

In fact, Maznavi simultaneously expresses all of these attitudes herself. For instance, she demonstrates her commitment to formalism through the importance she places on her own credentials as a student of Shaykha Reima Yosif and the central role that her teachings played in inspiring the formation of the WMA.[61] At the same time, her WMA policies emphasize the pragmatist idea that individuals can read scripture on their own and apply its concepts to their particular contexts without formal training. Maznavi also demonstrates the reformist view that the recent Islamic tradition is a "moral departure" from its origins,[62] and Muslims should therefore engage directly with scripture. She exhibits this approach through her declaration that Qur'anic literacy is the greatest form of female empowerment, and her attribution of misogyny in the tradition to misinterpretations of the faith and to unsound, or unreliable, hadiths.[63] The complexity of Maznavi's engagement with the tradition is mirrored in the WMA as an institution that does not fit neatly into any one of Grewel's three categories mapped on a spectrum, but moves back and forth across them. The WMA board invites khateebahs who act as custodians of the tradition in different ways and hold diverse attitudes toward traditional Islamic learning. This lack of homogeneity accurately reflects the WMA's attitude toward Islamic authority.

On an institutional level, the WMA insists on its straightforward continuity with the Islamic tradition, but most khateebahs do not engage the Islamic tradition as a fixed set of pedagogical forms that require mastery. This allows them to make claims about the tradition and situate themselves within it, even as they do not all seek to "master the tradition" through formalized training. Khateebahs like Lekovic express solidarity with the past when they place the WMA in a broader narrative of fourteen centuries of Muslim women acting as spiritual authority figures, and when they associate their interpretive work as continuous with the Islamic tradition rather than a departure from it. The goals of the WMA are continuous with trends in Muslim feminist scholarship that prioritize personal agency in interpreting text and direct access to the Qur'an. Consequently, English translations of the Qur'an play a central role in the WMA's narrative since they facilitate women's direct access to reading and interpreting scripture.

Qur'anic Literacy: English as a Sacred Language

Edina Lekovic, then director of the Muslim Public Affairs Council (MPAC), had approximately two weeks to prepare a khutbah for the WMA's historic first Jummah. She had originally agreed to be the backup khateebah, the "understudy" for the inaugural event, and assumed that the responsibility was unlikely to fall on her shoulders.[64] However, as we saw earlier, Reima Yosif, the originally scheduled khateebah, the traditionally trained scholar with whom Maznavi studied and whose teachings inspired the WMA's founding,[65] was ultimately unable to participate due to illness. Lekovic, while excited by the opportunity, felt deep apprehension and self-doubt while preparing her khutbah:

> I really struggled with how to be authentic and credible, and my worst fear was being a hypocrite . . . even though I know that doctors and non-imams give sermons. Men give sermons all the time. . . . I was disqualifying myself every day as I was working on the khutbah, like, what right

do I have to give the first sermon at the Women's Mosque instead of a scholar?[66]

As Lekovic recounted her feelings of inadequacy about serving as the WMA's first khateebah, I was struck by her expressions of vulnerability. With multiple televised appearances on major news networks and high-profile speaking engagements in communities across the US, Lekovic is a well-known public representative for American Muslims and a seasoned public speaker. Yet she, and others with whom I spoke, described the unique emotional weight of the role of khateebah. To them, the unparalleled experience of addressing one's own religious community as an authoritative figure evoked a sense of gravity and even insecurity. Drawing on her own vulnerabilities, Lekovic used her khutbah to call on Muslim women to find and claim their voices, and encourage them to become empowered in faith through Islamic knowledge.

Khutbahs, particularly in the US Muslim context, are an important site of oral exegesis. As Timur Yuskaev argues, informally produced, spoken exegeses in khutbahs demonstrate how the Qur'an has been communicated to broader audiences in different communities. It is through khutbahs that the Qur'an is transformed into a "spoken text" that believers can relate to, as is evident in the examples of US preachers W. D. Mohammed, amina wadud, and Hamza Yusuf.[67] As the WMA's first khateebah, despite her internal apprehension, Lekovic set the tone for the shape of future khutbahs. WMA members, including khateebahs and congregants, continue to look to her as a model and a source of inspiration. Accordingly, her khutbah offers insight into the broader ethos of the WMA and its developing ideology of religious authority. In it, Lekovic emphasized how important it was for women to serve as religious leaders to normalize their visibility for young girls, adding that she ultimately stepped up as khateebah because of her then five-month-old daughter, in whose lifetime women's mosques will be a "truth that can never be unwritten."[68]

In our conversation, Lekovic explained that her insecurities about taking on a position of religious authority were rooted in the question of Qur'anic literacy and knowing the meaning of the text rather than just how to recite the requisite verses for prayer:

This is one of the reasons I almost said no to giving the khutbah—I have really struggled with knowing the meaning of what I am reciting over the years, even though I can do it musically. But not feeling a connection to the words turn the ritual into just ritual and mechanics, and I fell out of love with prayer. . . . In the last few years I really circled back to the idea of language and knowing what I'm saying, and I've gone back to learn how to say the Fatiha in English . . . so that even if in my prayer I'm reciting in Arabic I have a connection to the meaning. . . . It goes back to religious literacy. Even when we think we're taught Islam, we are taught the rituals and the culture and the sound of it in Arabic . . . more than what's the personal connection to the faith.[69]

As a Bosnian American and non–Arabic speaker, Lekovic has not always felt connected to Qur'anic recitation. As a result of this disconnect, she struggled to achieve meaningful daily prayer until she learned the English meaning of her Qur'anic recitations. When I asked Lekovic to reflect on this English emphasis, she described the importance of language to her, given her professional background in media and communications. Further elaborating on themes that she touched upon in her khutbah—struggling with Arabic, and by extension struggling to feel connected to ritual—Lekovic explained that learning the English translations of the *surahs* (chapters of the Qur'an) that she already knew in Arabic helped her feel grounded in ritual prayer. In other words, English translations rendered her ritual prayer meaningful because they granted her access to the content of the text. For Lekovic, understanding and reflecting on the meaning of the Qur'an is central to faith. In her view, rituals without comprehension of the words being recited are reduced to only "mechanics." In her own life, then, she has prioritized the meaning of the Qur'an over its mere Arabic recitation in ritual practice.

Broadly speaking, English translations of the Qur'an[70] play a central role in the WMA's engagements with interpretive authority.[71] Throughout her inaugural khutbah, Lekovic explicitly challenged the interpretive monopoly of the Qur'an in Arabic by legitimizing and promoting its English translations. For many Muslims, only the Arabic Qur'an has sacred status, and translations are considered to be a human rather than divine endeavor. This is why ritual prayer is performed in Arabic. As I highlighted above, the WMA does not contest the sacred status of the Qur'an in Arabic and indeed maintains the use of Arabic in ritual practice. At the same time, however, the WMA elevates the status of English translations in Muslim life by emphasizing how important it is for Muslims to engage the meaning of the Qur'an. For example, in her khutbah, Lekovic highlighted the Qur'anic concept of *tadabbur*, which she defined as thinking, rethinking, and reflecting. She stated, "To reflect about the meaning and the relevance of the Qur'an, is what the Qur'an, what God asks us to do, to think over and over again so that we can continue to remain relevant to our time and place."[72] Here Lekovic characterizes the act of reflecting on the meaning of the Qur'an as a Qur'anic mandate. Moreover, her directive for Muslims to cultivate a personal connection to the Qur'an draws from American Protestantism, which also privileges individual relationships to scripture.

Not only does Lekovic promote Qur'an translations as a way to access its meaning, but she also elevates English to having ritual currency. In her khutbah, Lekovic recited Surah Fatiha, the opening chapter of the Qur'an, and immediately challenged congregants to recite it in English with the sincerity typically associated with its Arabic recitation, before doing so herself.[73] The general notion of using English translations of the Qur'an in khutbahs is not novel, as this already happens in most mosques in the US.[74] Mucahit Bilici demonstrates that Muslim attitudes toward English have evolved from "defensive suspicion" in the colonial period to "an appropriative embrace" in contemporary life, as such discussions reflect tensions between Islamic authenticity and Americanness.[75] Other US communities view English primarily as the language of community, reserving Arabic for ritual.[76] At the WMA, English is not merely a concession to accommodate an ethnically diverse congregation, but a valuable contribution to Islamic practice. When Lekovic enjoins the congregation to recite the Fatiha in English, English is extended to a form of ritual and presented in its particular capacity to empower American Muslim women. While Lekovic attests to performing daily prayer in Arabic, she affirms that the English translation imbues the Arabic ritual prayer with a significance that is not inherently there. Engaging with the meaning of the Qur'an necessitates for her as a non–Arabic speaker, and presumably for much of her audience, reading the Qur'an in English.[77]

Additionally, in her khutbah, Lekovic affirmed her individual right to deliver a khutbah as a non-scholar. She stated in her introductory remarks, "I thank you sisters and brothers who are involved in the board for entrusting me with this privilege and for recognizing that someone other than a scholar can give a khutbah, which happens in other mosques all the time."[78] Here, she reads her invitation to be a khateebah as the WMA board's acknowledgement that non-scholars are capable of delivering khutbahs. She also attested to the regularity with which non-scholars serve as khateebs (male preachers) in other congregations, emphasizing the WMA's continuity with other Muslim communities. Claiming continuity with the tradition is congruous with the WMA's official narrative that women's spaces have existed throughout Islamic history.[79] At the same time, Lekovic's khutbah works to shift traditional understandings of religious authority. By highlighting her lack of formal Islamic credentials, she expands the parameters of Islamic authority to include lay Muslims, particularly Muslim women. Lekovic confers individual interpretive authority upon the WMA congregants, encouraging them to read and interpret the Qur'an for themselves, in order to connect with it on a personal level.

While Lekovic's assertion about the frequency of non-scholars as religious leaders in Muslim congregations is a way for her to claim historical continuity with the Islamic tradition, it is also reminiscent of practices in other American religious traditions with regard to popular female preaching. More specifically, Lekovic's self-positioning as a non-scholar resonates with the renowned twentieth-century Black Protestant preacher Lucy Smith. Smith rose to prominence during the Migration era as the founding pastor of Chicago's All Nations Pentecostal Church, as well as satellite institutions including other churches and a community center.[80] Originally from the rural South, Smith came from an impoverished background and never received a proper education.[81] She was often described as having an "easy informality" along with a vernacular preaching style, in contrast to other pastors who appeared as "stuck up and lived separated from the people."[82] Smith foregrounded her humble Southern roots and lack of educational credentials when preaching the Gospel, and Lekovic likewise cultivates an authoritative persona in which the authority arises from her lack of scholarly credentials, not in spite of it.

Lekovic's support for non-scholars to give khutbahs is congruent with themes in feminist exegeses of the Qur'an, specifically in Asma Barlas's work. Barlas claims that Qur'anic exegesis should extend beyond Arabic speakers or scholars, and she critiques the tendencies in American Muslim communities to venerate select Arab male scholars and privilege their often patriarchal interpretations that marginalize women.[83] She argues that scholars do not have a privileged relationship to the Qur'an:

> [The Qur'an] does not tie interpretive rights to race, sex, class, or even literacy. Literacy and scholarship have never been the hallmark of prophets or sages, or for that matter, of most believers who have always been unlettered. To assume that these people cannot understand the Qur'an because they lack scholarly knowledge is to disregard significant aspects of the Qur'an's religiosity and universality and to confuse knowledge of God's words with their "inner meanings," a distinction the Qur'an itself makes.[84]

Citing the lack of literacy among God's Prophets, Barlas argues that scholarship is not a prerequisite for religiosity. She extends the Qur'an's "interpretive rights" to include lay Muslims, and envisions women's inclusion in the interpretive enterprise, making space for a project like the WMA.

Barlas's scholarship also justifies the use of the Qur'an in translation. She argues that if Muslims accept the universality and divinity of the Qur'an, then the Qur'an is "equally real in all languages."[85] She further contends, "If the word of God is no longer real when it is not in Arabic, then it must also mean that the Qur'an is not a text for all humanity since humanity is not all Arab or Arabic-speaking or even literate."[86] To Barlas, the medium of language should be considered secondary to the content of the Qur'an, which is divine and therefore transcends language. Barlas, like Lekovic in her khutbah, promotes the idea that individual believers have a moral imperative to read and interpret the Qur'an. Barlas challenges the idea that Arabic proficiency confers accuracy on Qur'anic interpretations, highlighting that even the Prophet's Companions had differences of opinion in their understanding of the same verses. Stating that the Qur'an contains multiple layers of meaning, she emphasizes that its exegeses depend upon hermeneutical models and interpreters' specific values rather than linguistic expertise.[87]

Similarly, Lekovic critiques Arab male interpretive authority and asserts that non-scholars have the right to interpret scripture. In fact, she shared with me that Barlas's monograph *Believing Women in Islam* inspired her own spiritual journey, stating that it equipped her with vocabulary to articulate the importance of women's engagements with scripture.[88] For Lekovic, Qur'anic literacy is not tied to Arabic. She states in her khutbah that she rarely memorizes Qur'anic verses in Arabic because it is a "challenge," and then promptly follows another Arabic recitation with its English translation.[89] Lekovic admitting her difficulty with Arabic memorization creates rhetorical distance between the Arabic language and her engagements with the Qur'an. By privileging the translated Qur'an in her own life, Lekovic disassociates Arabic from Islamic authority and authenticity.

Lekovic also associates textual engagement with legitimacy in Muslim communities: "The textual stuff to me is important because I deal with mainstream Muslim communities a lot and I know the legitimacy piece is often going to come back to the text. And I want the Women's Mosque of America to be taken seriously as both a place that nurtures and a place that teaches and empowers through text."[90] Lekovic sees Qur'anic literacy as important for the WMA because of its capacity to empower individuals and as a tool for wider communal legitimacy. In other words, she wants the WMA to gain the approval of other US mosques where male authority is the norm. Yet she simultaneously critiques the male norms in these other mosques, citing the need for lay Muslim women's voices in mosques. These seemingly contradictory attitudes toward continuity with the Islamic tradition on the one hand and new interpretations and praxis on the other are perhaps, as Howe suggests, a feature of US Muslim communities making sense of their particular contexts.[91]

Lekovic affirms that reflecting on the "meaning and the relevance of the Qur'an" is the key to spiritual fulfillment, and attests to the importance of cultivating a personal relationship with God through the Qur'an.[92] Here, English translations play a central role since they provide her, a non-native Arabic speaker, and much of the WMA congregation, access to the Qur'an's meaning. She therefore offers an implicit critique of Arab male interpretive authority. The value of the Qur'an in English for Lekovic is the unmediated connection to God that it provides. The accessibility of the text in turn facilitates the process of applying particular verses to the daily lives of believers, which is something that Lekovic practices in her own life. She recounts in her khutbah that at MPAC she and her colleagues "read a few verses each week and collectively reflect on their meaning and relevance to us in our daily lives."[93]

Moreover, for Lekovic, the experience of having a direct relationship with the Qur'an, and thus with God, was entirely absent from the Islam that she "inherited" from her parents.[94] Inherent within this admission is a serious objection to an Islam that is associated with authoritative teachings passed down by local religious leaders and devoid of personal engagement with religious teachings. Here again, it is worth reflecting on the omnipresence of amina wadud, even when she is not directly invoked; wadud makes a similar critique that Arab immigrant men presume authority over African American Muslims through the entitlement they feel from a cultural heritage rather than spiritual criteria of devotion or knowledge.[95] wadud highlights how those who are dismissive of feminist voices perpetuate centuries of male privilege and patriarchal readings of the Qur'an.[96] She would therefore likely support Lekovic's exercising of non-scholarly interpretive authority, irrespective of whether the subsequent interpretations were fully polished, as the process itself is progress toward female inclusion. To this end Lekovic, like wadud, also privileges the criteria of devotion and knowledge. She laments that, as non–Arabic speakers, her parents were required to rely on outside sources for religious knowledge. For her, reliance on authority figures was both a result of a lack of religious education, and the reason for lay Muslims' lack of direct access to the Qur'an. In Lekovic's view, the inherited Islam of her parents' generation constitutes spiritual passivity, which fails to elicit spiritual nourishment.

Another early WMA khutbah touches on many of the same themes as Lekovic's inaugural khutbah about the importance of engaging the Qur'an on an individual level. Dr. Laila Al-Marayati's khutbah from June 2015, during the WMA's first Ramadan, is ostensibly about the struggles of fasting. But at its core, it addresses the importance of striking a personal, meaningful relationship with the Qur'an and with ritual practices. Al-Marayati talks about the difficulties that Ramadan poses in terms of fasting while also keeping up with one's various professional and family commitments, particularly in the summer months when the daylight hours are long. She shares how she has long personally struggled with achieving the spiritual high that other Muslims around her describe experiencing during Ramadan. Al-Marayati states that, by contrast, her Ramadan experiences have always been both a physical and spiritual challenge for her. She struggled with fasting while trying to balance exams in college and medical school, and then through the long hours of her medical residency. Yet she always prioritized fasting despite experiencing these hardships because she understood it as critically important, regardless of the impact on her health.[97]

In reflecting on the physical hardships of her past Ramadan experiences, Al-Marayati emphasizes how people should not place themselves in a position where their health is at risk. She supports this by referring to the Qur'anic concept of God wanting "ease and not hardship for us"[98] and citing a hadith tradition from Bukhari, which in her view demonstrates the importance of understanding the "spirit of the law."[99] This hadith, which she summarizes for the congregation, narrates a scenario about a group of the Companions of Muhammad, only half of whom were fasting while undertaking a journey during Ramadan. Al-Marayati explains that those among the group who observed fasting were unable to participate in pitching the tents for the night, and the burden fell disproportionately on those who did not fast. The hadith goes on to assert that those who did not fast were the ones who received the spiritual reward that day. To her, this hadith corresponds to the Qur'anic verse that states, "Do not fast if you are ill or on a journey," and demonstrates the importance of keeping perspective while observing religious rituals. In referencing this hadith, Al-Marayati emphasizes the importance of being connected to the internal dimensions of a ritual practice, rather than simply observing the external motions.

By emphasizing reading the Qur'an for oneself, both Al-Marayati and Lekovic implicitly draw on American Protestant values of individualism, rationality, and a critique of mediated religious learning. More accurately, these are also the values of American secularism, which is rooted in "Protestant-inflected models of 'religion.'"[100] Here, the analytical frame of the "Protestant secular" helps us to understand how the principles of secularism in the US dictate what forms of religion—including Islam—are palatable. The WMA's display of these Protestant secular attributes, then, reflects a broader trend in which American Muslim communities have negotiated their marginalized positions and adopted religious values that privilege the individual religious believer and unmediated religious experiences. These values appear throughout different WMA khutbahs and are made explicit in Al-Marayati's and Lekovic's respective reflections on fasting and daily prayer. For them, individual experience and the independent act of reading a sacred text for its meaning is valued over its recitation in ritual practice. Where Lekovic describes falling out of love with prayer because of a broader disconnect to the meaning of her Arabic recitations, Al-Marayati similarly describes feeling unmoved by Ramadan because of her focus on observing the external ritual of fasting despite the physical hardship it posed due to her demanding work schedule. Elaborating on this sentiment, Al-Marayati states in her khutbah:

> I would always do my best to pray Tarawih but since I don't always understand the Arabic, the Qur'an being recited at the mosque, I had a hard time experiencing the intense spiritual awakening felt by so many others. I kind of felt like I was just going through the motions and that my Ramadan experience was not as it should be. But what made all the difference for me was my attempt to read the Qur'an, first in English and later in English and Arabic. Year after year I managed to complete the text during Ramadan, which ended up shaping my identity as a Muslim, creating a relationship with Allah (swt) through his message.[101]

Al-Marayati, like Lekovic, credits reading the Qur'an in English as a personally transformative experience that helps to resolve the tension between carrying out a ritual and feeling moved by it. Al-Marayati emphasizes how she failed to experience an intense spiritual awakening while praying Tarawih, the supererogatory nightly prayers during Ramadan often observed in congregation, because she did not understand the Arabic recited at the mosque. Al-Marayati addresses this lack of spiritual awakening by returning to the Qur'an in order to cultivate a personal "relationship with Allah" through the text.

The assumptions undergirding Al-Marayati's self-reflections on her expectations of what Ramadan "should be" are worth considering here. Al-Marayati treats an "intense spiritual awakening" as a necessity for religious observance during Ramadan. In her reflections on past Ramadans, rather than feeling as if she fulfilled her religious duties by observing her fasts, Al-Marayati instead laments that there is something missing from her experience. Here she prioritizes individual religious experiences over communal practices. The observance of practices such as fasting and praying Tarawih during Ramadan to Al-Marayati somehow lack in value when not accompanied by an individual sense of spiritual fulfillment and a connection to God through the Qur'an. This is very similar to Lekovic's admission that she "fell out of love with prayer" and was struggling to engage in what had become, for her, an empty ritual devoid of personal meaning. Both Al-Marayati and Lekovic characterize their ritual practices as lacking in meaning when performed without an individual connection to the Qur'an.

Additionally, in her khutbah, Al-Marayati goes beyond describing her personal transformative experience that resulted from reading the Qur'an on her own to encourage the WMA congregation to do the same. She asserts the necessity for women in particular to develop a relationship with the text to feel connected to its meaning:

> I know this may seem obvious, yes of course we all read the Qur'an in Ramadan, that's what we do. But somehow I feel our connection to the actual content of the Qur'an itself, the meaning of the words, if you will, has gotten lost amongst all of the chatter about Islam. Restoring our relationship with the text *in a language we can understand, especially as women* will bring us back to the essence of Islam as a message of hope with justice as the cornerstone. . . . Unfortunately this is a concept that we must constantly be reminded of, especially when the letter of the law is applied so assiduously, while neglecting its spirit.[102]

Here Al-Marayati again makes a distinction between ritual observance and personal engagement. In this case, she identifies two distinct but related ways of approaching the Qur'an. One is the act of reading and recitation, as is customary for many Muslims around the globe during Ramadan, and the other is engaging it on an intellectual level for content. She encourages the WMA congregation to include the latter approach as they read, developing a relationship with the text in their respective native languages. Al-Marayati does not overtly disqualify the importance of carrying out external rituals of fasting or reciting the Qur'an, but she does place a greater value on individual engagement in these rituals in gendered terms. She thus encourages the WMA congregation to connect with the meaning of the text to arrive at the "spirit" of Islam, which she understands as defined by hope and justice. In Al-Marayati's view, Muslims' commitment to practicing particular rituals fails to reflect the spirit of Islam, and this is due to the disconnect between the Qur'an as approached in Arabic as ritual, as opposed to in one's own language for content.

As this section has shown, one way the WMA helps women cultivate interpretive authority is by emphasizing the centrality of the English language and privileging the meaning of the Qur'an over its liturgical practices in American Muslim communities. As we noted earlier, the value of understanding the Qur'an in English already prevails among the African American congregants at the WMA. For many African American Muslims, knowledge of the Qur'an and its meaning is integral to their ideas of Islamic authority, and to their own Muslim identities. Zahara and Kenyatta, like Lekovic and Al-Marayati, essentially suggest that the Qur'an in Arabic cannot be meaningful without a personal connection to its content in English. Their emphasis on the meaning of the Qur'an derives from the legacy of the Nation of Islam and the leadership of W. D. Mohammed, whose "community's language was based on the Qur'an."[103] Mohammed's khutbahs served as cultural translations of the Qur'an into the US context, and they corresponded with the contemporary concerns of his communities.[104] The fact that the WMA's most regular congregants are older African American women with ties to W. D. Mohammed's communities suggests that their preexisting attitudes toward the Qur'an and its English translations help to authorize the WMA's interpretive project. Other congregants are also receptive to the WMA's new criteria for interpretive authority; in particular, they value lay Muslim women's khutbahs above those from men with formal Islamic credentials.

WMA board members and khateebahs actively seek to include English alongside Arabic as a sacred and centrally important language of the Qur'an for US Muslims. It is, however, worth noting here the WMA's usage of the Arabic terms "khateebah" and "khutbah" over "preacher" and "sermon." As the WMA otherwise promotes English language translations of the Qur'an as a means toward accessibility of the text, its insistence on using Arabic terms to connote ritual positions of authority stands out as a part of a broader bid for Islamic authenticity.

Hearing Women's Khutbahs: Creating Community

WMA congregants are diverse in age, race, socioeconomic class, and ethnicity. The women in this study reflect this diversity, and also include born Muslims and converts from their early twenties to late sixties, each with different relationships with religious community. While all of the women had distinct reflections on what the WMA meant to them, they recognized it as a platform for women's interpretive authority. Moreover, congregants honored khateebahs' engagements with scripture as valuable contributions to Islamic knowledge, and in so doing, conferred interpretive authority on them. Congregants' receptive attitudes toward WMA leaders and khateebahs demonstrate the triangulation of power and authority between them. Power and authority flow between congregants, khateebahs, and board members, and together legitimize the WMA as an authentic expression of Islamic practice.

Crucially, WMA congregants are not only open to WMA's brand of interpretive authority based on lay Muslim women's khutbahs, but they also consider it to be more credible than authority based on formal Islamic credentials. In particular, many of the women featured in this book felt strongly that lay Muslim women's khutbahs at the WMA filled a gap in Islamic authority that men's khutbahs at other US mosques could not adequately address. They were particularly drawn to ideas about forging personal and intimate connections with the Qur'an, revealing that as a community of congregants, khateebahs, and board members, the WMA is bound together by their investment in scriptural meaning.

To illustrate congregant attitudes toward lay Muslim women's interpretive authority at the WMA, we first turn to Seher, whom we met earlier. South Asian and in her mid-thirties, Seher was drawn to the khutbahs at the WMA because they were different from khutbahs at other mosques, and she saw that as a welcome departure. For her, the lack of formal Islamic credentials among most WMA khateebahs was an asset rather than a barrier to Islamic legitimacy, and she appreciated how women at the WMA had a preaching style distinct from that of the male preachers she was accustomed to hearing in other mosques. Specifically, Seher thought that a lack of formal religious credentials rendered an "everyday" woman in contrast to a *hafidh* (a man who has memorized the Qur'an) more relatable as a khateebah, because she would be more

Figure 2.1. An overview of the congregants at the Women's Mosque of America during the Friday sermon (August 2015). Source: Faezeh Fathizadeh, the Pluralism Project at Harvard University

likely to foreground her experiences rather than simply quote from the Qur'an.[105] She states, "Because it's everyday women giving khutbahs, everyday women aren't necessarily in their mind instantly going to the Qur'an when they think about motherhood or something . . . their connection is more like their actual lives."[106] To Seher, hearing about "their actual lives" makes WMA khutbahs more engaging, indicating how women's experiences can serve as authoritative.

Notably, Seher describes WMA khutbahs as less focused on the Qur'an than those at other mosques.[107] This contrasts with the WMA's own claim to being Qur'an-centric. While it is useful to analyze points of tension between the WMA's official rhetoric and congregants' particular experiences, I interpret Seher's distinction between the WMA and other mosques as a broader observation on *how* the Qur'an is deployed in these different settings. For example, in her comments contrasting men and women's respective preaching styles, she highlights their different approaches to the Qur'an:

I noticed that men versus women are always yelling from the pulpit even if they don't need to . . . that's just the style of a man giving a khutbah—they're like [raises voice] "AND WE'RE TALKING ABOUT SURAH AS-SHAMS" and everything is just like yelled as though they don't have a microphone. And they're saying awesome things, but . . . the khutbahs are very judgy, like "you guys need to be doing this, and this and this," and drawing verses from Hadith and Qur'an about that, versus the khutbahs I hear at the Women's Mosque that reference the Qur'an in a much more nurturing way, [a] maternal way. It's all about the nurturing sense and not the fiery pulpit sense.[108]

Contrasting the "fiery pulpit" tone of khutbahs at other US mosques, Seher felt that WMA khateebahs approached the Qur'an in a more caring and motherly way. This illuminates her earlier comment about how everyday women are less likely to "instantly" refer to the Qur'an. To Seher, WMA khateebahs speak from their experiences first, and then relate their lives back to the text in an uplifting way. By contrast, she characterizes khateebs as didactic, drawing from Islamic scriptures to support a litany of moral demands.

Moreover, to Seher, the nurturing tone of WMA khutbahs reflected a sense of personal authenticity, creating the sense that khateebahs were not simply "performing" for the congregation:

It's conversational, people are telling a story [at the WMA] more than "AHHHHH!" [mocks yelling and chuckles]. . . . I don't know if people [male preachers] get it from other mosques outside of America or just kind of the Christian model of speaking from a pulpit, but I think for women, since there is no model, they just act like themselves. It's just how they speak; it's very different . . . rather than putting on this showy, fiery performance.[109]

Here Seher does not reject the value of khutbahs at other US mosques, highlighting that "they're saying awesome things" that enrich her religious learning. Yet she ultimately characterizes them as more performative than WMA khateebahs, whom she perceives as "just act[ing] like themselves." Importantly, her teasing tone as she imitates how men "yell" from the minbar (pulpit) demonstrates an implicit critique of male models of preaching in mosques. Her reflections indicate that the general value placed on traditional credentials in a given community does not neatly align with even that same community's sensibilities of what warrants their respect as religious practitioners. Seher values the knowledge shared in the didactic khutbahs that readily reference Qur'an and Hadith, but the fiery performative elements of male preachers elicit for her a sense of ridicule rather than reverence. By contrast, even as she recognizes that WMA khateebahs are less equipped as "everyday women" to make abundant references to scripture, she indicates a level of respect for their natural oratory style and is drawn to their ability to relate religious themes to their daily experiences.

Seher simultaneously critiques male styles of preaching, affirms the value of Qur'anic expertise, and advocates for everyday women without this expertise to have a religious platform. Moreover, her views were not uncommon among the other congregants with whom I spoke. The layered and intersecting values in her reflections make relevant discussions of the polyvalent nature of Islamic authority and how living communities respond to various credentials. The layered relationship to religious authority among the WMA congregation brings to mind Jennifer Thompson's ethnographic study of women with positions of Jewish leadership in their families.[110] Thompson shows that while Jewish laity may officially defer to traditional forms of male authority, on the level of lived religious experiences, they defer to the authority of their wives and mothers. These women shape their family's Jewish practices rather than institutional Jewish leaders. Therefore, on the level of community, embracing alternative forms of authority does not necessarily presume a forthright rejection of its traditional forms. Rather, as is the case at the WMA, community members may recognize traditional conventions of authority based on formal credentials, but may also find an alternative approach, such as one based on lay Muslim women's experiences, more compelling.

The WMA is not the first community in LA to embrace lay Muslim women's authority. Carolyn Rouse's ethnography of African American Muslim women in LA establishes a local precedent for understanding women's interpretive communities. Rouse shows that in women-only gatherings in their LA mosque, African American Muslims promote their "feminist" values through oral exegeses, elements of which sometimes figured into their male imam's Friday khutbah.[111] In this way, women partook in generating new moral spaces alongside men. Likewise, at the WMA, lay Muslim women, many of whom are African American like Rouse's interlocutors, are also participating in their own interpretive space. However, since the WMA is a multiracial congregation, there is less thematic coherence in their interpretive engagements in comparison to those of Rouse's African American interlocutors, whose shared racial identity informs their particular views on the family structure and gendered roles within it. While African American women's experiences in LA mosques are not homogeneous, their social realities of economic and racial oppression underpin their embodied exegeses and their acts of resistance in communal Muslim life.[112] Moreover, as a women-only congregation, the dynamics of authority at the WMA are distinct from that in other US mosques, even those also in LA. Namely, since women themselves deliver the Friday khutbahs at the WMA, their exegetical ideas are not beholden to the approval of male leaders; they are the sole arbiters of what constitutes valid exegesis.

Furthermore, some WMA congregants not only accept lay Muslim women's interpretive engagements as valid exegesis, but also identify khateebahs' lack of formal religious training as a key part of their appeal and legitimacy. For example, Sufiya, a South Asian American in her thirties, states that she likes the fact that women who are not leaders of a religious community are the ones delivering the khutbahs:

> I can tell that there is a difference in the khutbahs themselves, between khutbahs in regular mosques. It might be a woman thing, but I think it's also because it's not necessarily like leaders of the Muslim community or imams . . . they are just different women coming from different experiences and walks of life. It gives a different type of credibility. So I love the fact that we can learn from each other. There is no hierarchy in Islam anyways and it feels like that value is cultivated [at the WMA].[113]

Sufiya, like Seher, attests to the differences between khutbahs at the WMA and at other mosques. She further explains that, for her, having khateebahs who are "just different women" rather than imams or religious leaders grants the WMA a unique credibility and flattens the usual hierarchy in an appealing way. Sufiya further asserts her belief that there is no hierarchy in Islam, referencing that imams are meant to simply lead prayer rather than have moral authority over lay Muslims. She believes that the WMA honors this principle and allows women to learn from each other. Her reflections on the WMA depict an intimate image of religious community in which members are learning and cultivating religious faith together. This is in contrast to a relationship between a religious leader and a congregation, where the former assumes the role of teacher to a group of students. Sufiya's sentiments here cohere with how Seher characterized khateebs at other mosques as didactic, as they tell their congregants "you guys need to be doing this, and this and this" based on their readings of Qur'an and hadith, in contrast to the nurturing tone at the WMA.[114]

Leila, who is Arab American and in her thirties, was also specifically drawn to the WMA's khutbahs because of how they differed from those she had heard in other mosques. Like Seher, she felt that WMA khateebahs encouraged congregants how to better themselves rather than just identifying a set of issues that need addressing. She recalled one particular WMA khutbah that stuck out to her as memorable because it emphasized activism and offered specific, practical steps for congregants to follow. She said, "If I remember correctly, the sermon was about putting pain into action. I liked that emphasis. It was like, 'here's what we can do,' not just like, 'here's all the things that are wrong.'"[115] Leila was particularly appreciative of how WMA khateebahs encouraged congregants to take action, and she attributed this emphasis to the fact that it was run by women of color.[116] She, as well as many other women with whom I spoke, attested to how powerful and moving it was to have women preachers at the minbar speaking on religious matters from a personal perspective because it made the content more relatable and compelled them to take it more seriously. Leila, like Seher and Sufiya, emphasized the differences between khutbahs at the WMA and at other mosques. All three women were either current regular members of other mosques, or had been extensively involved in other mosque communities in the past. They had thus heard countless khutbahs by men, and were drawn to how the WMA was different—a space where khateebahs and congregants approached religious texts and moral issues together as a community.

WMA khutbahs enabled congregants to envision a particular type of religious community for themselves—one that nurtured, encouraged, and empowered them through knowledge of the Qur'an. Yasmin, for example, was drawn to the khutbahs that gave her insight into the Qur'an, stating, "I want keep hearing the stories [from the Qur'an], I want to keep learning because I know so many surahs by heart but it doesn't mean shit if I don't know what I'm reciting or what it means. So having that kind of explanation I really like."[117] Yasmin was eager to associate meaning with the Qur'anic chapters that she grew up memorizing. As we saw earlier, Yasmin entered the WMA community in early 2017, after not having set foot in a mosque since she was thirteen years old. She was therefore not present for Lekovic's and Al-Marayati's 2015 khutbahs that touched on identical sentiments about the importance of the Qur'an's meaning. That Yasmin's personal goals so closely cohere with the two khutbahs discussed in this chapter demonstrates how the WMA appeals to congregants who share their overall ethos of Qur'anic literacy. Additionally, to the extent that WMA members like Yasmin appear less concerned with aspects of the Qur'an that other Muslims around the world take for granted, such as the blessings associated with its Arabic recitation, they can be situated within a rationalistic cosmology that intellectualizes the Qur'an.[118]

Furthermore, as the khutbahs changed in tone over the course of 2017 to focus less on the Qur'an itself, some of my interlocutors expressed dissatisfaction at this shift. They preferred khutbahs that engaged more substantially with scripture, including Qur'an, Hadith, and traditional biographies, to those that focused on the broader themes of spirituality and self-care. Yasmin admitted, "The last one [khutbah], I was not very drawn into it. I don't know, it just wasn't really telling me a story that I needed to hear, and I didn't feel like it was telling me anything from the Qur'an. But I feel like we [at the WMA] *should* talk more about the Qur'an."[119] Yasmin felt unmoved by khutbahs that did not advance her goal to achieve Qur'anic literacy. But she was still very invested in the community at the WMA; she wanted to explore the Qur'an in more depth *with* the WMA community, not outside of it as an individual. She even expressed how she wished that the WMA held Jummah more than once a month, or that members got together informally as a group or on Skype to continue their reflections from the khutbahs.[120]

Other congregants shared variations of Yasmin's critique of some khutbahs, including Ana and Sarah. Ana, a Latina congregant in her forties, similarly expressed that she would like for khateebahs at the WMA to engage more directly with the Qur'an and the Islamic legal tradition. She stated:

> I like the fact that all the women there have different perspectives and backgrounds, women can learn from each other . . . but if it's going to be a learning environment, I think that it would be important to have people who are very well trained and educated and know Islam. . . . I didn't see anyone there leading [the discussion circle] like, "well actually in the Qur'an it says this, or the hadith say this, or this school of thought, the Maliki school says this and Hanbali," you know what I mean? . . . That's fine if they have different backgrounds, and different schools of thought, because that's what's great about it, that there can be a mixture of different practices . . . but it's important to know why they think that, like where did you learn that from? What school of thought?[121]

At the time of our interview, Ana had been to only a couple of WMA khutbahs since she did not live in LA full-time, but she was interested in becoming a more regular congregant. In her remarks above, she expressed appreciation for how the WMA opens up space for women to share their unique views in khutbahs, but she also wanted women with extensive knowledge of Islamic texts to facilitate the discussion circles after the prayer so that they could answer questions that people might have. Ana was interested in khateebahs explaining their opinions through the lens of the legal tradition, or based on particular texts from the Qur'an or Hadith. She firmly stated that she considers different schools of thought to be equally valid, but that she would like for the khateebahs to make clear which textual sources they use as a basis for their khutbahs. She had worries based on her experiences with other Muslim communities that, without this transparency, personal opinions might masquerade as religious facts.

Somewhat similarly, Sarah, white and in her twenties, felt that the WMA did not engage with the Qur'an as much as she would prefer. She stated, "I personally feel like a lot of the khutbahs at the Women's Mosque don't really use enough Qur'an, they kind of just go off of one verse, or like they'll have a topic and they'll kind of pick a Qur'an verse that fits in with it."[122] To Sarah, many WMA khutbahs did not focus deeply on the Qur'an, though she conceded that khutbahs at other mosques also did not always focus on scripture—"then again not all mainstream masjids do either." As a regular attendee at other LA mosques, Sarah ultimately preferred what she called the "traditional method of preaching" at her home mosque. Nevertheless, Sarah appreciated the different styles of khutbahs at the WMA and enjoyed hearing the personal perspectives of women, even when there was less of a direct emphasis on the Qur'an. Sarah preferred khutbahs that were more rooted in scripture, but perhaps because she was also a part of another mosque community, she did not necessarily look to the WMA to fulfill this preference in the same way as Yasmin; nor did she share Ana's concern for more explicit references to the Islamic legal tradition. Ultimately, regardless of their specific reflections on the WMA, Yasmin, Ana, and Sarah were all clearly invested in Qur'anic literacy, and each valued engagement with the meanings, histories, and logic behind specific verses. Their reflections here, coupled with board members' "return to the Qur'an" outlook, indicate how the WMA as a community and an institution is bound together with a focus on scripture—regardless of the manner in which every individual khutbah addresses the Qur'an.

Some congregants like Amal, whom we met earlier, were more explicit in describing their investment in cultivating a personal relationship with the Qur'an:

> I consider myself a Qur'anic Muslim. I'm not very invested in Hadith, to be honest—I am enriched by it, but I go back to the Qur'an. And then also, taking ownership of the Qur'an not as a document as the words of God to be interpreted by imams and scholars exclusively, but fundamentally to be interpreted by us and supported by scholars—like you use the specialist opinion as you need. And that's what kept me Muslim. I felt like I went from being a renter to an owner when I made that step and went to Qur'an classes.[123]

Here, Amal asserts the importance of the Qur'an in her personal engagement with Islam as a source of empowerment and authenticity. Significantly, she understands the Qur'an as a text that is first and foremost meant to be interpreted by everyday believers rather than specialists, a characterization that shifts the power dynamic between

Muslim scholars and lay people. Amal's attitude toward the Qur'an as a text "fundamentally to be interpreted by us and supported by scholars" not only opens up space for non-scholars to engage directly with scripture, but also privileges their individual engagements with the Qur'an over that of scholars. In other words, for some congregants, WMA khutbahs were relatable and therefore authoritative *because* they were coming from lay Muslim women and not scholars. For these congregants, the fact that most khateebahs had no formal Islamic credentials bolstered the WMA's credibility. It was precisely khateebahs' conversational storytelling style of preaching that appealed to congregants.

The congregant reflections highlighted above all gesture toward the ways that individual engagement with the Qur'an is integral to the broader ethos of the WMA. WMA culture—among congregants, khateebahs, and board members alike—encourages cultivating personal intimacy with the text. Referring back to Al-Marayati's and Lekovic's khutbahs, both attribute their own commitment to Islam to their individual engagement with the Qur'an. Lekovic affirms that she would have likely cast aside her faith in search of something more meaningful as she reached adulthood had she not read the Qur'an for herself. In the beginning of her khutbah, she states, "What changed in my life that changed me to the core was when I actually read the Qur'an on my own, when I engaged the text and read it from cover to cover and allowed God to speak to me directly."[124] WMA leaders echo these precise sentiments in media interviews about the WMA. Maznavi states that in the days after 9/11, when she heard verses of the Qur'an being taken out of context, she decided to read the Qur'an in English from cover to cover for the first time, which "proved to be the single most empowering act of my entire life as a Muslim woman."[125] Muttalib, the former co-president of the WMA, similarly attested to being spiritually moved based on her reconnection with the Qur'an during law school, which subsequently motivated her desire to "help the real Islam be lived in society."[126]

While I take seriously board members' and khateebahs' claims to continuity with the Islamic tradition, the WMA is also continuous with trends in other American religious communities of women. This is especially true in terms of how WMA members like Lekovic, Al-Marayati, and Maznavi describe their relationships with the Qur'an as deeply personal and intimate. Most notably, their invocations of spiritual intimacy with the Qur'an resemble how the Evangelical women featured in scholar of American religion R. Marie Griffith's study of the Pentecostal Women's Aglow Fellowship describe reading the Bible. While the Pentecostal Women's Aglow Fellowship is an Evangelical group based on charismatic healing through the Holy Spirit, several key figures from the WMA display striking similarities in their attitudes toward scripture. Griffith's informants "speak of the Bible as a 'personal love letter from God to His children,' the key to understanding his loving wisdom in difficult situations and to feeling his presence and direction in one's life at all times."[127] WMA leaders speak of the Qur'an in such personalized terms as well, and attest to being individually moved by its words. WMA leaders also each insist on their status as free independent thinkers who consciously turned to the Qur'an and Islam on the basis of rational, individually informed decisions. This language is again quintessentially Protestant, with its emphasis on Enlightenment values of individualism and rationality and its critique of mediated religious learning. The WMA's Protestant inflections are likely not premeditated on the part of its individual khateebahs or leaders as a bid to assimilate to US secular culture. Yet their values are formed by the discourse of the secular nation-state, which necessarily shapes our assumptions about what constitutes good religion or freedom.[128] In other words, the resonances between the WMA and different Protestant groups are not random, but an inevitable outcome of being a religious community in the secular US state.

Also, Lekovic's and Maznavi's rhetoric of choice and rationality supports Grewal's observation that American Muslim women leaders "are deeply invested in demonstrating that their religious lives emerge from free choice; they want to redeem Islam's image in the West as an excessively patriarchal tradition but also to resolve the crisis of Islam by reestablishing space for women religious authorities."[129] Grewal demonstrates the contentious nature of constructing authoritative spaces for Muslim women; they simultaneously feel compelled to defend their religious choices and also actively seek reform from within the tradition. To this end, WMA founders and the khateebahs referenced here all refer to the Qur'an as the ultimate source from which to claim Islamic authenticity and implement women's inclusion in interpretive activity. Therefore, the WMA actively expands and renegotiates the criteria for religious authority to privilege the unique credentials that each khateebah brings to her engagement with scripture. Moreover, in their engagements with scripture, members of the WMA community emphasize the importance of the meaning of the Qur'an in English over its Arabic recitation in ritual practice.

The WMA is a community based on scriptural meaning, and its members collectively promote the English translations as a powerful way to engage and connect with the Qur'an on an individual level. English translations facilitate access to the text and imbue meaning onto ritual activities such as prayer or fasting. Board members and khateebahs conceptualize the WMA as continuous with the Islamic historical tradition and understand themselves as reviving the legacy of Muslim women in positions of authority. By promoting a Qur'an-centric worldview that values content and meaning over disembodied recitation and ritual, the WMA unlocks opportunities for lay Muslims, particularly women who are excluded from formal Islamic training, to assert religious authority and interpret scripture without the requirement of mastering the Arabic language.

Moreover, congregants are receptive to the WMA's turn to lay Muslim women's authority; and in fact, some of them actually identify khateebahs' lack of formal religious training as a key part of the WMA's appeal. Congregants' receptive attitudes toward khateebahs may appear unremarkable given that their attendance at the WMA at a minimum indicates that they deem the space worthy of their time. However, it is not inevitable that congregants also accept the WMA's Islamic authority; some of them would often hear from family members or folks in their other mosque communities that the WMA sounded great in principle but should not be considered a mosque but a women's center, where women get together and deliver talks, not khutbahs. It is worth noting, then, that even the congregants we met earlier, who were unsure about the legal validity of woman-led Jummah, all took for granted that the women leading Jummah in any given month were indeed khateebahs delivering khutbahs at a mosque, rather than female speakers giving talks at a women's center. The concept of a khutbah by a woman did not require reframing on their parts, and they took seriously khateebahs' interpretive authority. Most importantly, they welcomed "everyday" women's interpretive engagements with the Qur'an. Furthermore, for many congregants, khutbahs at the WMA filled a gap in Islamic knowledge precisely because they came from the perspectives of lay Muslim women. By embracing lay Muslims as khateebahs, the WMA provides a powerful platform for them to cultivate authority grounded in their embodied experiences as women. In the next chapter, we explore how khateebahs engage sacred texts on the basis of their lived, gendered experiences to offer insights on subjects—like motherhood or gender violence—that congregants consider women to be more authoritative on than their male counterparts.

3

Embodied Authority

Women's Experiences as Exegesis

I feel like the East Coast buries their emotions under blankets of snow. There is a kind of looking down on experiential things, and always having to justify things statistically. You can't be anecdotal . . . whereas the West Coast is a lot more like, "Experiences matter." I feel this because the entertainment industry is out here, and it's like story-story-story. There is an emotional health that is here. . . . Even if the [Islamic] tradition says this, this, and that, because THIS experience has this much weight, I am just going to do something about it. Whereas [on the East Coast] I think you would have to debate about it forever: debate, then justify and engage with tradition . . . and there is value to that too, there's a rigor to that, but in terms of getting something done, if you believe in something, there's more fire to get things done here [in LA].
—-Sabrina, South Asian American, in her thirties

Sabrina, a South Asian New Englander who works in the television industry, credits West Coast culture for the development of women-led mosques like the WMA and the Qal'bu Maryam Mosque in Berkeley. She believes that, through the entertainment industry, Los Angeles culture promotes personal narratives and experiential learning over statistics and impersonal data. To her, LA's storytelling culture and the emergence of the WMA were inherently connected: the West Coast gives Muslims energy to take action without getting caught up in debates over knowledge for its own sake. Sabrina's privileging of experiences over "justify[ing] and engag[ing] with tradition" does not perfectly align with the WMA's institutional emphasis on scripture, as discussed earlier. Yet

Sabrina's attitude is indeed representative of that of other congregants who like her also explicitly value women's experiences *over* scripture.

On her own relationship to scripture, Sabrina's attitude toward the Qur'an has changed over time. While she still believes that the Qur'an is the word of God, she sees the text as having "literal and nonliteral" aspects. Elaborating, she explains how she takes the patriarchal frameworks set up in the Qur'an "with a grain of salt."[1] Chuckling as she relays how the Qur'an positions men as the "protectors of women," she says that while women may have been socially and economically vulnerable in the context of seventh-century Arabia, this is no longer the case, certainly not for her. Explaining that women like her in the US today have governmental and judicial protections, she states: "I don't need a man to protect me. I understand the text and the context in which it was revealed . . . I get it. Whereas a man who is more traditional would just take it for what it is and not consider the context of how things are different now."[2] In her words, Sabrina is able to reconcile aspects of the Qur'an that support patriarchal structures by understanding the context of revelation. Her assertion that "things are different now" and her ability to accept the Qur'an as the word of God despite disagreeing about its purported literal relevance follows modernist exegetical trends that many feminist Muslim interpreters, as discussed earlier, adopt in their readings of scripture. With respect to the Qur'anic verse (4:34) to which Sabrina refers (though does not directly reference), feminist exegetes such as Omaima Abou Bakr, a women's activist and a professor of English and comparative literature in Cairo, have problematized dominant interpretations that assert men's authority over women by interrogating alternative meanings for the verse.[3]

Sabrina's willingness to grapple with parts of the Qur'an that, in her view, do not cohere with her self-described progressive values is noteworthy. By contrast, the WMA's institutional position on the Qur'an affirms that it is a gender-egalitarian text. And at the time of my conversation with Sabrina, none of the WMA khateebahs had explicitly drawn attention to verses like Qur'an 4:34 that might challenge this description or otherwise suggest that the Qur'an might pose limitations to their professed commitments to gender equality. WMA khateebahs' avoidance, whether deliberate or inadvertent, of addressing potentially contentious discussions of patriarchal verses in the Qur'an began to change by December 2020, during the COVID-19 pandemic. The format of a fully online Jummah made it possible for Omaima Abou-Bakr, the feminist exegete, scholar, and activist referenced above, to deliver a WMA khutbah over Zoom from Cairo, Egypt, on the ethics of gender justice based on her activism and scholarship. In her khutbah, Abou-Bakr addresses patriarchal interpretations of particular Qur'anic verses and explicates different exegetical moves that could render gender-egalitarian readings of the text. These moves include viewing the Qur'an as a whole that should be interpreted according to its overall themes—aimed at deriving its ethical message—rather than broken down into fragments and decontextualized verses.[4] Then in July 2021, as WMA Jummahs continued to be held virtually due to the ongoing pandemic, Abla Hasan, a scholar of Arabic language and culture at the University of Nebraska–Lincoln, delivered a khutbah over Zoom titled "The Truth about 4:34—the Qur'an's Most Controversial and Misunderstood Verse." Later in this chapter, we return to a discussion of Qur'an 4:34, which is controversially referred to as the "wife-beating verse," but Hasan's khutbah, like Abou-Bakr's, similarly addressed alternative interpretations that challenged patriarchal readings of scripture. Yet even before Abou-Bakr and Hasan delivered khutbahs that directly challenged patriarchal interpretations of the Qur'an, Sabrina had viewed the WMA as broadly compatible with her relationship to the Qur'an. This indicates how WMA congregants bring with them their own fully formed positions on particular subjects, such as how to approach patriarchal elements of sacred scriptures. Congregants receive official WMA narratives through their own lenses, and at times, project their own values on institutional moves and on specific khutbahs. For example, when Sabrina reads the Qur'an, she decides which verses are and are not relevant to her life. Likewise, she also reads her own values of emphasizing personal experiences over strict deference to the plain meaning of the Qur'an or the Islamic legal tradition into the WMA's institutional positions. Congregants' individual and collective contexts inform their engagements with WMA khutbahs and wider policies.

There is a triangular flow of power in which WMA congregants, khateebahs, and board members negotiate norms and criteria for religious authority in real time. The boundaries between WMA members are distinct but porous, and continually negotiated. Khateebahs wield considerable influence as they promote women's experiences as authoritative through khutbahs on sexual violence, marriage, or motherhood. Yet board members—Maznavi and her rotating team—also shape the form of khutbahs by encouraging khateebahs to reference some textual sources over others and to employ particular rhetorical strategies. Furthermore, the discussion circles held after the prayer service provide a platform for congregants to respond to khutbahs and suggest future topics. Therefore, congregants also wield power, as khateebahs and board members must answer to their concerns or risk diminishing the WMA's relevance, which may result in the loss of congregation members.

While they occupy different roles within the WMA, congregants, khateebahs, and board members all emphasize women's lived experiences as an important criterion for Islamic authority. Specifically, they view women's experiences as a valuable basis through which to interpret scripture and authoritatively comment on issues affecting American Muslim communities. In the process, they recognize new forms of religious authority that are specific to the embodied experiences of women.[5] In fact, WMA members not only privilege women's experiences in interpretations of the Qur'an, but also posit that men lack insight to speak on certain subjects with nuance. To wit: Sabrina's speculation that a man reading the Qur'anic verses that designate men as protectors of women would be more likely than a woman to take them at face value without considering their original social context. Notably, then, many of the women with whom I spoke viewed women's exegetical insights on particular subjects as necessarily more authoritative and nuanced than those of men. Additionally, since many khateebahs are from Southern California, they are often regular WMA congregants as well, and not just passing members of the community who occasionally lead prayer and preach. Likewise, over the course of the WMA's tenure, board members and congregants have also served as khateebahs (in fact, Maznavi encourages them to do so), so there is fluidity and overlap among these three categories themselves.

As a collective, the WMA promotes female embodied experiences as a valid source of religious authority, creating space not only to address Islamic scriptures from a distinctly feminine perspective but also to approach subjects such as sexual violence, marriage, and motherhood as a community of women. This chapter argues that various WMA actors—

board members, khateebahs, and even some congregants—deploy embodied authority, rooted in what they deem as the "feminine" principles of vulnerability and nurture, as a means to contest patriarchal readings of text and also build community resilience through female solidarity.

The first part of the chapter explores how the WMA has developed a new genre of khutbahs based on women's experiences, and I suggest that khateebahs do not reproduce existing male forms of leadership. Rather, I frame their intervention as filling a critical gap in which specifically feminine forms of Islamic authority, predicated on vulnerability, have been missing. Within this feminine form of authority, women's bodies serve as important sites of knowledge through which to approach Qur'anic exegesis, and the second part of this chapter spotlights two khutbahs that address gender violence through this lens of female embodiment. One of these khutbahs, delivered by a sexual assault survivor, generated a "Me Too" moment at the WMA in 2015, which notably was before the 2006 movement launched by Black activist Tarana Burke entered into the American mainstream in 2017. This section also explores how khateebahs' openness in discussing sensitive subjects creates a nurturing atmosphere in which congregants also feel comfortable sharing their own vulnerabilities. In the final section, I analyze five khutbahs related to marriage, motherhood, and grief, reflecting on how they emphasize women's roles as nurturers, further distinguishing Islamic authority at the WMA from male forms.

Toward a Feminine Model of Religious Authority

I think the [WMA khutbah] topics are in a way directed to not only women but [they have] sort of a woman's approach. . . . It is personal but also includes the Qur'an . . . so it could be more meaningful for women to attend these khutbahs.[6]
—Isabella, Latina, in her fifties

In September 2017, news about the sexual misconduct of Nouman Ali Khan, a popular American Muslim preacher and the founder of a Muslim educational institution in Texas, polarized Muslim communities across the US. Long-standing rumors about Khan's predatory behavior toward his female students through sexual pursuit, harassment, and payments for victims' silence were confirmed by an independent investigation led by prominent American Muslim leaders and victims' testimonies.[7] Many American Muslims experienced anger and crises of faith as a result of these revelations, while others defended Khan and denied he did anything immoral. American Muslims were also divided in 2015 when multiple women came forward with their experiences of sexual assault and child sexual abuse at the hands of Mohammad Abdullah Saleem, a widely respected Chicago imam and Islamic educator.[8] We will return to a discussion of Muslim women's layered vulnerability and participation in the "Me Too" movement in the next section, but it suffices here to note that, for many American Muslims, the prevalence of exploitative Muslim male leaders only further underscores the need for women's religious leadership.

Anthropologist Shabana Mir argues as much in a guest post for Patheos, a media website dedicated to global conversations on faith, spirituality, and religion:

> There has been a public Muslim American discussion on the need to foster women religious leaders. . . . Usually, however, this gender inclusivity comes across as charity, as if the only people who benefit from gender inclusivity are these women leaders. . . . The truth is, the entire community benefits from women religious leaders. . . . There is an *urgent need* for Muslim women religious leaders, speakers, preachers, mentors and organizational decision makers. . . . With knowledgeable and experienced women mentors, young women can be *safer* from a life of guilt, secrecy and lost faith.[9]

Mir states that American Muslims should not consider including women in positions of Muslim leadership for the sake of being politically correct or as an act of "charity." Instead, they should pursue gender inclusivity for the benefits it confers on communities as a whole. She highlights the need for more women in positions of Islamic authority as scholars and preachers who can act as spiritual mentors for young Muslim women and safeguard their interests. Mir cites a tweet from Ingrid Mattson, who was one of the scholars who took part in the investigation that confirmed Khan's predatory behavior, that reads: "Sisters: discouraged?

Don't be anti-religion, be auntie-religion. They may be nosy, but they'll never advise you to have a secret marriage."[10] Mattson and Mir are both referring to the spiritual trauma and religious disillusionment that many young Muslim women experience when they are lured into inappropriate relationships with celebrity preachers who then become their fallen idols. Mir and Mattson suggest that if Muslim women have other Muslim women to turn to for spiritual guidance and support, they can protect their own interests and safety. Mir connects the overall well-being of American Muslim communities to the presence of women in positions of religious leadership.

Mir's reflections on the need for Muslim women leaders provide a useful framework to think about the WMA's institutional goals of "strengthening the Ummah by increasing women's access to Islamic knowledge, encouraging female participation in mosques, and fostering female leaders and scholars for the benefit of the entire Ummah."[11] As we saw earlier, the WMA promotes the notion that any woman, regardless of her scholarly credentials or lack thereof, is fit to serve as khateebah. Not requiring formal credentials for women to serve as khateebahs opens up opportunities for women like Edina Lekovic and Laila Al-Marayati, who are not Islamic scholars, to take up authority. Yet the WMA's democratization of Islamic authority through its inclusion of "everyday" women as khateebahs should not be understood as doing away with the notion of credentials altogether. Rather, when WMA leaders promote the voices of everyday women, they posit a new template for authority that caters to their prevailing ideas about womanhood. This approach by default excludes men because it is predicated on the embodied experiences of women. I read the WMA's woman-centered conception of authority as a corrective to women's exclusion from forms of formal training associated with Islamic authority in mainstream American Muslim communities. However, rather than viewing women's Islamic authority as a replacement for (male) forms of authority predicated on formal credentials, WMA leaders portray female Islamic authorities as filling a specific gap and representing a different model altogether.

Given that those who contest women's Islamic authority frequently claim that Muslim women lack adequate credentials to engage in authoritative interpretations of religious texts,[12] it is worth noting that WMA leaders do not respond to these claims on their critics' terms.

Rather than inhabiting a defensive posture, the WMA as an institution intervenes in the debate by asserting that traditional credentials are not a prerequisite for religious authority. In so doing, khateebahs at the WMA serve as one of many examples of Muslim women around the world who have cultivated different types of Islamic authority. Many studies have investigated Muslim women's authority in different geographical and denominational settings while attending to how these various leadership roles relate to Islamic knowledge. These include studies of women's mosques and woman *ahong* (religious leaders) in China,[13] the *murshidah* (woman preacher/spiritual guides) in Morocco,[14] state-sponsored women preachers in Turkish mosques,[15] the *Qubaysiyyat* (female ulama of a Sunni revivalist movement) in Syria,[16] and Islamist women's active involvement and public roles in movements like the Jamaat-e-Islami in Pakistan.[17] In each of these cases, women derive their authority through different means, and they also have distinct roles within their respective communities.

Yet with respect to promoting particular forms of feminine authority, there are parallels between WMA khateebahs and Muslim women authorities in the global context. For example, Saba Mahmood's groundbreaking study of women's piety movements in Cairo documents how *da'iyat* (female preachers/teachers) in different mosques, who for the most part are well versed in the canonical traditions of Islam, conduct religious lessons for Egyptian women. She includes an example of how one *da'iya* also challenges a prominent male shaykh's legal opinion on woman-led congregational prayer, indicating her command of the Islamic legal tradition and confidence to assert the authenticity of her claims even as they go against customary practices in Egypt.[18] Ellen McLarney also speaks to the Egyptian context and analyzes the contributions of women public intellectuals with various credentials, who she argues had a profound influence on Islamic revivalism. These public intellectuals include Bint al-Shati' and Heba Raouf Ezzat, whose respective writings made religious knowledge accessible to the middle class and centered women as key figures of religious authority. I highlight Mahmood's and McLarney's works in particular because both refer to the ways that the Egyptian women revivalists in their studies emphasize feminine forms of knowledge and authority. For example, Mahmood discusses how *da'iyat* encourage mosque participants to cultivate modesty and shyness as essential feminine virtues,[19] while McLarney highlights how Bint al-Shati' perceived women as "particularly equipped for the 'discursive arts' by virtue of their 'authentic instinctual preparation' and their affective nature."[20] McLarney further argues that, despite this essentializing view of women, Bint al-Shati' "discursively [situates] women's voices as authentic expressions of an Islamic worldview, destabilizing the idea of a male monopoly on religious knowledge and authority."[21] In a similar way, the WMA promotes a distinct type of feminine Islamic authority based on leaders' and members' assumptions about women as nurturing and emotionally sophisticated.

The WMA's *Khateebah Guidebook*, a sixteen-page document delineating requirements and suggestions for khutbah practices, provides a solid basis for understanding their model of a feminine Islamic authority. Maznavi wrote the *Khateebah Guidebook* in early 2017, approximately two years into the WMA's tenure, based on an iterative process of dialoging with board members and respective khateebahs, reflecting on past khutbahs and practices they felt were most effective. The *Khateebah Guidebook*, which emphasizes vulnerability and nurturance as particularly feminine traits, contains the official WMA policies for future and potential khateebahs. It has eight sections with information ranging from basic requirements and scheduling logistics to guidelines for structuring a khutbah and leading prayer. There is also specific information about which *du'as* (supplications) khateebahs should recite and when.[22] Additionally, there are rules of engagement for the khutbah and the question-and-answer discussion circle after the prayer. All of these rules and guidelines relate to being respectful of all congregation members since, as the opening remarks of the document state, some of them are "unmosqued," meaning without a religious community, and should be protected from further alienation.[23] Lastly, the guidebook also lists previous khutbah topics along with several suggestions for topics identified by congregants as subjects of interest. The *Khateebah Guidebook* provides insight into the WMA's developing ideology on the criteria for religious authority and its conception of religious community.

With the procedural focus of the *Khateebah Guidebook*, Maznavi and her team institutionalize khateebahs' authority while they simultaneously render Islamic authority accessible to lay women. By providing guidelines on the format of the khutbah—that it should comprise two distinct parts and require three particular du'as before and after the first part, and then after the second part—WMA leaders assume no prior knowledge on how to deliver a khutbah. This extends the role of khateebah not only to women who lack formal Islamic credentials, but also to those who may not attend Jummah regularly enough to be familiar with the proper format of a khutbah. Presumably, men with formal credentials or men and women who are regular mosque-goers would not need these guidelines made explicit. WMA leaders thus provide support and reassurance to prospective khateebahs by acknowledging their lack of experience and promising to guide them into the role. By encouraging otherwise inexperienced women to step into the authoritative role of khateebah, WMA leaders create new possibilities for women's authority. At the same time, by formalizing these khutbah practices through a guidebook, the WMA negotiates its authenticity and authority by strictly adhering to the mainstream Sunni[24] Muslim format of a khutbah.

The guidebook also illustrates the triangular flow of power and authority between WMA leaders, khateebahs, and congregants. Maznavi and her fellow board members wield power by dictating the parameters for khutbah practices and guiding khateebahs as they prepare. While the guidebook does not restrict khateebahs to specific subjects, it dictates clear expectations for them and requires that they submit a written version of their khutbahs at least two weeks in advance to be approved by the board.[25] While my interviewees tended to describe Maznavi's editorial role as minimal, her involvement is nevertheless significant in showing how WMA leaders formalize particular conventions of authority. The khateebahs I interviewed explained that Maznavi and other board members typically gave feedback on revising particular language that might come across as marginalizing to some congregants, but did not change or make suggestions on content. As was the case with the WMA's rule about menstruation and prayer leadership, a couple of women told me that they took issue with the idea of sending their khutbahs in advance for approval, however lightly edited they might be in the end, because the rule itself posed an uncomfortable level of control for them. These women declined to serve as khateebahs. Beyond this anecdotal knowledge, it is hard to speculate on the number of women who might take issue with having to send their khutbahs in advance since this book focuses on those within the WMA community, who at a minimum accept its rules. However, taking note of how some women are put off by Maznavi and her board's exertion of authority over khateebahs helps us to more fully understand the broader power dynamics among different actors at the WMA. For their part, the khateebahs I interviewed did not characterize their khutbah-writing processes as unduly regulated and did not give any indication that they felt censored by the WMA's conventions. One khateebah did share that she would have ideally preferred to deliver remarks in an improvised fashion and that she found it challenging to write out her khutbah in advance, but described it as a new learning process for her. Some expressed appreciation for Maznavi's hands-on approach and involvement, particularly if they were nervous at the prospect of giving their first khutbahs. In this sense, as opposed to a narrative about control, another way to understand the power dynamic between the WMA board and its khateebahs is one of mentorship and guidance, in which Maznavi and her team take it upon themselves to prepare and train women how to give a khutbah. After all, the stated purpose of the *Khateebah Guidebook* is to offer direction and support for women as they step into a new, unfamiliar religious role that has not previously been available to them. However, it also clear that the length that Maznavi and her team go to in order to ensure quality control of WMA khutbahs does not appeal to everyone.

Yet this flow of power is not one-sided. Since women's khutbahs draw on their individual personal experiences, the WMA board cannot dictate what subjects or perspectives khateebahs should engage. Khateebahs exercise autonomy in the construction of their khutbahs with respect to content and wield authority through their platform of speaking before a congregation and interpreting sacred texts through their own personal lens. They also often confer authority on congregants by encouraging them to interpret sacred texts on their own terms and through their own experiences. Additionally, congregants wield power and influence over both WMA leaders and khateebahs by sharing their expectations on which topics they would like to see addressed, which Maznavi then incorporates into the *Khateebah Guidebook*.

The *Khateebah Guidebook* demonstrates that the WMA takes seriously the role of khateebah and considers it an esteemed position with responsibilities toward the community. In the first section of the guidebook, Maznavi states that khateebahs are held to a different standard from congregation members because of the responsibility that comes with leading a congregation. For example, any potential khateebah must self-identify as a Muslim and as a woman, and display excellence in character, particularly in interactions with congregants. The guidebook also stipulates that to lead congregational Jummah prayer a khateebah should believe in the validity of woman-led prayer and plan not to partake in the optional four-unit dhuhr prayer afterward. A woman who feels uncertain about the validity of woman-led Jummah should not deliver a khutbah or lead prayer "so that the intention of the imam matches the intention of the congregation."[26] Additionally, she must have completed reading the entire Qur'an in her native language and choose a khutbah date when she will not be menstruating. As discussed earlier, the guidebook notes that while some Muslim women may choose to pray while menstruating, out of respect for congregation members who may disagree, a khateebah should avoid leading prayer during this time. The subjects of belief in the validity of female-led Jummah and praying while menstruating are two examples of how WMA khateebahs are held to a different set of standards than congregation members, as congregants can proceed as they choose regardless of their status or position on these subjects.

While those who are unsure about the validity of woman-led Jummah or those who are menstruating on the day of the WMA Jummah are not invited to lead prayer, as we saw earlier, they have the opportunity to deliver a pre-khutbah bayan. A bayan is a short lecture given before the Friday khutbah and, as the WMA website states, originates in Hanafi fiqh (jurisprudence), one of the four major Sunni schools of law.[27] As one of the WMA board members explained to me, pre-khutbah bayans were also an option for women who do not feel comfortable taking on the title of khateebah for whatever reason. The bayan and the khutbah at the WMA are usually similar in length. Based on my conversations with WMA congregants, bayans and khutbahs were viewed similarly in that one type of orator was not considered more or less authoritative than the other. In fact, many WMA members did not distinguish between bayans and khutbahs when referring to examples of khutbahs that they found meaningful; they saw the presence of a bayan as a "bonus" and described it as meaning there were two khateebahs that day.

Underpinning the guidelines throughout the document is the WMA's inclusive mission statement and Maznavi's desire to preserve and maintain a middle-ground environment. The ground rules for engagement stipulate that khateebahs must be respectful of the WMA's "come as you are" dress code and they are therefore prohibited from policing others' clothing. Other rules include avoiding gender stereotypes and the use of identity labels, and exhibiting sensitivity to the various life experiences of those in the WMA congregation. To this end, the guidebook states that if a khateebah wants to talk about motherhood and her own experiences with it, then she should "be sensitive that you don't say anything that might hurt the feelings of women who have chosen another path in life."[28] While the WMA does not identify as feminist, the language of this particular point is indicative of their adherence to a feminism of choice, as it ends with the statement: "We celebrate each woman's ability to make her own life choices, and at the same time, we want to empower each woman in the role she has chosen for her life."[29] This phrasing exhibits leaders' embeddedness in the US context of liberal feminism even as they avoid the feminist label; it also indicates the ways that the WMA as an institution is distinctly American.

The guidebook also elevates the role of the Qur'an over Hadith at the WMA, which as we saw above resonates with the broader trends among Muslim feminist exegetes. Just as Qur'anic exegesis is central to the Muslim feminist project in the United States, so too does the WMA identify Qur'anic literacy as the single greatest source of empowerment for Muslim women.[30] The *Khateebah Guidebook* stipulates that khutbahs need to reference at least one Qur'anic verse. Such verses, as well as any other Arabic terms or phrases used, must be translated into English out of respect for the WMA's several non-Muslim congregants and Muslims who are not familiar with Arabic. Here Maznavi includes four online resources for English translations of the Qur'an.[31] The guidebook further states that citing verses from Qur'an is preferable to references to hadith, but that any hadith cited should be *sahih* (sound) traditions. "Since many problematic/misogynistic issues within Islamic practice stem from weak and fabricated hadiths that are harmful toward women, it is important that any hadiths used are sound, strong, and fact-checked," the guidebook explains.[32] "Weak" hadith are those without a reliable chain of transmission that can be traced back to the Prophet Muhammad and therefore not considered authentic. The WMA's attribution of misogyny in the Islamic tradition to weak or fabricated hadith is in keeping with Muslim feminist

scholars who hold similar attitudes toward the Hadith and the jurisprudential tradition and also emphasize the Qur'an as a source of divinely
sanctioned gender egalitarianism. This demonstrates how American
Muslim feminist scholarship influences the shape of emerging institutions like the WMA in debates over female interpretive authority.

In addition to its emphasis on the Qur'an, the *Khateebah Guidebook*
also evinces an explicit commitment to foregrounding female experience. Khateebahs are instructed to make their khutbahs as personal as
possible to keep the subject matter interesting and relevant. Under the
section for best khutbah practices, the guidebook includes the following:

b) Please keep in mind that one of the things that makes our mosque
unique is the ability to hear from the first-hand female experience,
so we encourage you to make your khutbah as personal as possible.
The more stories and words of wisdom you can share from your own
personal spiritual experience and growth, the better!

c) Don't be afraid to be vulnerable. Your vulnerability helps the congregation open up and connect with you; it inspires them to know that their
leaders also struggle just like they do. By humbling yourself and exposing your own struggles/fears/doubts, women in the audience will
be able to see themselves in a leadership position like yours one day,
because they will no longer believe they need to be perfect in order to
lead others towards good.[33]

These instructions highlight how the idea of khateebahs deriving religious authority through their experiences is not coincidental, but
intentional. Khateebahs are specifically instructed to incorporate a personal story and to show vulnerability by recounting a spiritual struggle.
These imperatives are relevant to consider in light of my interlocutors'
observations about how WMA khutbahs are different both in their
delivery and content from those at mainstream mosques. The guidebook
demonstrates that this departure is by design rather than by chance.
Rather than attempt to emulate the (male) style and content of khutbahs
at other mosques, WMA leaders attempt to cultivate a very different
form of authority, finding strength in the admission of weakness.

In other words, this distinctly feminine authority at the WMA, cultivated through women's khutbahs, is marked by its difference from other

conventions of preaching that focus on specific Qur'anic verses or hadith and then explicate them systematically. This is not to say that some of the WMA khutbahs cannot or have not taken this form, as each khateebah has her own preferences and style. In fact, one of the khutbahs that I attended in person was a close reading and analysis of Surah Fatiha, the first chapter of the Qur'an. However, on the whole, a personalized narrative is the preferred khutbah format of WMA leadership. This indicates that the WMA does not extend its platform to those without scholarly backgrounds in order to be more inclusive, but to champion, as the guidebook dictates, "first-hand female experience" as something meaningful in and of itself. The WMA thus provides opportunities for women to take up religious leadership on the basis of their lived experiences as women, not merely as an alternative in the absence of formal Islamic credentials, but as a discursive statement about valuable forms of Islamic knowledge and authority.

In their expectation for women to display "vulnerability," the WMA solicits a particularly gendered performance of emotion from their khateebahs. While it is also the case that lay Muslim men routinely deliver khutbahs at mosques all over the US, they typically do not share personal experiences from the minbar. Rather, they usually adhere to a format of speaking about a few Qur'anic verses or hadith traditions or relaying a Qur'anic narrative, for example. The WMA thus departs from other mosques not only in that women rather than men preach, but also through the content and design of the khutbahs themselves. By providing guidelines that encourage khateebahs to share their personal stories and struggles, the WMA promotes embodied knowledge through experiences and emotion as valuable.

The WMA's institutional expectation for khateebahs' vulnerability reveals gendered assumptions about women's roles as gentle, emotional, and nurturing. Many attendees as well as WMA khateebahs share these assumptions about womanhood and they frequently differentiated between feminine- versus masculine-led spaces. One example of this is Mariyah's description of the WMA and women's forums in general as different from mixed-gender settings:

It's more gentle energy and there is a different level of openness and intimacy when it is just women together in a space that somehow changes when men enter it. Not necessarily in a negative way, but it definitely changes. . . . At the WMA, there is an attention to detail and making things look and feel good that is often times missing when you are in mixed-gendered spaces or men are in charge. You know they don't necessarily think about making things look and feel pretty.[34]

Mariyah's experiences of women-led and women-only groups included emotional intimacy and support as well as a pleasing aesthetic usually involving "decorations and flowers."[35] Along similar lines, we saw earlier how Seher set up contrasting images of the typical male khateeb "shouting" judgments from the minbar versus WMA khateebahs speaking in level tones, tenderly sharing information with the congregation. In their observations of the differences between male and female leadership, congregants like Mariyah and Seher offer their thoughts on the criteria that they consider authoritative in their religious leaders. Many WMA members, particularly those in their thirties and younger, extolled the nurturing environment of the WMA community.

A number of congregants across all ages were also drawn to the storytelling aspects of the WMA khutbahs. They felt that khateebahs' sharing of personal stories made them more relatable than other religious leaders. This is another illustration of the triangular flow of power at the WMA: when participants describe hearing personal narratives from the minbar as powerful, they validate the experiential knowledge of the khateebahs. Congregants wield influence by conferring authority on khateebahs who conform to their ideas about the value of feminine forms of preaching. As such, these gendered distinctions between male- and female-led mosques allow the WMA, in the eyes of its congregants, to create an entirely different framework for authority that does not compete with even laymen's models of religious leadership, since male khateebs do not claim to draw their authority from personal experiences, even in the absence of formal credentials. Indeed, for many congregants, WMA khutbahs, because they were rooted in women's embodied experiences, filled a gap in Islamic knowledge that was not being addressed in other mosques. They also felt that the WMA provided a unique, nurturing space in which to meaningfully engage khutbah topics like gender violence that, in their view, could be safely addressed only in a community of supportive women. The next section explores two such khutbahs.

Beyond Vulnerable Bodies: Addressing Gender Violence

It wasn't until I started sharing my own story that I also came to know just how many survivors there were within our Muslim community, amongst our Muslim leaders [and] community members. And I also came to know, to have the certainty when walking into a room like this, that there have already been people in this room who have whispered in their hearts and their chests the words, "Me too." I know this because it happens every single time I share my story. And the survivors I speak of within our community include women who were assaulted despite the hijabs they wore, despite the jilbabs they wore, or even the niqabs. Women who are sexually abused by the very *mahram*, the family protectors who are meant to protect them from harm. These are also boys, young men who are raped by their Qur'an teachers or molested by an uncle, or even a neighbor. What this means is that we are not doing our job to protect one another.[36]
—Sumaya Abubaker, from her April 2015 khutbah, "Sexual Violence and the Necessity of Compassion and Justice"

When Sumaya Abubaker addressed the subject of sexual violence in her WMA khutbah, she spoke to the congregation as a survivor. She had been assaulted as a teenager in her own home by a family friend, and again in young adulthood, at a mosque by an imam. By sharing her personal experiences of abuse, Abubaker made a lasting impression on the congregation, even in the years that followed. In the summer of 2017, when reflecting on khutbahs that were most memorable to them, many of my interlocutors mentioned Abubaker's. While some of these women were present at the WMA in April 2015, others, like me, had listened to the khutbah online. Each of these congregants noted that, before Abubaker, they had never heard anyone address the subject of sexual violence in a mosque, making her khutbah even more arresting for them. One congregant who was there that day explained that she was moved to share her own experiences of rape from two decades earlier during the discussion circle. Previously, she had discussed this trauma with very few people.[37] Hearing Abubaker open up about experiencing sexual violence in a mosque by a religious leader made her feel that Muslim communities need to do more to actively protect their girls and boys and ensure that their mosques are safe.[38] Other women who were present that day also described listening to Abubaker's khutbah as a powerful, difficult, and intimate experience.

The WMA creates opportunities for women to challenge existing Islamic frameworks on sexual violence that leave them vulnerable to bodily harm by promoting lived experiences as one of the primary criteria for Qur'an interpretation. Here scholar-activists Sa'diyya Shaikh, amina wadud, and Debra Majeed, introduced earlier, all provide models for thinking about women's experiences in textual exegesis as a way to destabilize male privilege and bring women's voices from the margins to the center.[39] For example, in her study of marital violence among Muslims in South Africa, Shaikh advocates for a *tafsir* (exegesis) of praxis, a hermeneutical tool that includes believers' lived experiences in interpretations of sacred texts.[40] Like wadud and Majeed, Shaikh scrutinizes the absence of women's voices in canonical texts and the dominance of male subjectivity. Their observations provide us with a way to frame both WMA khateebahs' gendered approach to the Qur'an and congregants' expectations that women read texts differently because they read through the lens of their experiences. For example, congregants welcome the notion that khateebahs read and interpret Qur'anic verses as women, and even assert that they necessarily derive different theological norms from those produced through male subjectivities.

This brings us back to Sabrina, the South Asian congregant in her thirties from the opening of this chapter, who engages sacred texts based on her own circumstances and experiences. She reflects on the Qur'anic concept of men as "protectors" of women through the lens of the social context of seventh-century Arabia in which the Qur'an was revealed, arguing that it does not ring true in her own life. Her interpretive methods here again demonstrate the influence of feminist scholar-activists like wadud, Shaikh, and Abou-Bakr, despite the fact that she does not name any of them. For instance, wadud observes that Islamic legal understandings of the family are embedded in norms that do not reflect women's social realities, and calls for Islamic legal reforms that recognize women's experiences and promote gender-egalitarian concepts of family.[41] Such reforms would be based on social realities, not abstract textual ideals. wadud states that the Islamic expectations of mothers as nurturing caregivers and husbands as financial supporters do not account for dissolved marriages in the American Muslim context, where child custody is often the domain of the mother. Single mothers are not only the financial providers for their children; they are also in charge of their moral upbringing even in the absence of societal structures of support. wadud's observations resonate with Sabrina's previously described reflections on men as protectors of women, where she argues that the social context of the Qur'an does not align with her own, in which she is socially and economically capable of protecting herself. Sabrina's experiences play a key role in her understanding of this particular Qur'anic tenet. Moreover, if we think about how Abubaker's khutbah reveals the frequency of sexual violence within Muslim communities, we can start to imagine the power of communal recognition that the gender roles set forth in dominant interpretations of the Qur'an—of men as protectors—do not align with many women's social realities. This is especially the case in instances when women need to be protected *from* men rather than by them. Khutbahs grounded in women's experiences, like Abubaker's, facilitate this type of communal recognition that, in her view, will ultimately contribute to increased safety for vulnerable members of Muslim communities.

In the eyes of the congregation, Abubaker's experiences as a survivor qualify her to speak with authority on sexual violence and right Muslim practice while also lending credence to her interpretations of the Qur'an. Here, Majeed's Muslim womanist approach is helpful to frame how Abubaker claims authority through her experiences. Muslim womanism, Majeed argues, is "an epistemology, or way of knowing, that positions the experiences and wisdom of women at the forefront of any consideration of Muslim family life."[42] Majeed's philosophy of Muslim womanism derives from and builds on Christian womanist ethics, which "involves black women's commitments to understand and change oppressive, systemic structures and alienating experiences."[43] Likewise a Muslim womanist approach focuses on African American Muslim women's experiences as they relate to racist and patriarchal US culture, with an emphasis on their efforts to seek Islamic legitimacy.[44] In her ethnography of polygynous marriages in African American Muslim communities, Majeed promotes the authority of experience as a Qur'an-sanctioned method of interpretation that centers women's voices.[45] She argues that women's experiences of polygyny in African American Muslim communities constitute a valid source of Islamic knowledge about its practice. She shows that African American Muslim women whose husbands have multiple wives are positioned to authoritatively interpret Islamic sources on polygyny because their interpretations would reflect the day-to-day realities more accurately than a disengaged exegesis of the same Qur'anic verses. While Abubaker does not refer to particular verses of the Qur'an that she asserts are specifically about the issue of sexual violence, she, like Majeed's interlocutors, advocates for particular readings of the Qur'an based on her own lived experiences.

While Abubaker preaches as a survivor, she also draws on her professional experiences in the nonprofit organization that she co-founded that facilitates support for victims of sexual violence in American communities. She represents alternative ways whereby women can claim interpretive authority based on their experiences rather than formal religious credentials. By preaching as a survivor, Abubaker models how reading texts through one's own experience produces particular Qur'anic interpretations. Underpinning her khutbah is the Qur'anic concept of *rahma*, or compassion. In her experience, Muslims do not always convey compassion when dealing with victims of sexual violence, instead silencing, blaming, and shaming them. She recounts that when she was sexually assaulted as a teenager, others blamed her for it and she struggled with depression, guilt, and self-loathing throughout her early adulthood. To Abubaker, this lack of compassion and unwillingness to stand up for victims of sexual abuse perpetuates the conditions that allow such violence to continue.

Abubaker further argues that a culture of silencing has created the illusion of safety in Muslim communities, and she characterizes that silence as the complete absence of *rahma*. Her khutbah is meant to help heal victims and also encourage Muslim communities in their entirety—encompassing victims, perpetrators, and witnesses—to collectively address sexual abuse. Noting that *rahma* is one of the most mentioned concepts in the Qur'an, and the most mentioned attribute of God, Abubaker argues for a Qur'anic moral imperative that human beings embody compassion in all of their interactions. This is a very intentional interpretive strategy; she does not highlight a particular verse and then analyze it, but rather draws on broader themes of the Qur'an that exist across the text as a whole. These themes are then made applicable to specific circumstances. She uses this method to derive a different form of authority. By foregrounding general themes of the Qur'an, Abubaker gives the appearance that the text is speaking for itself.

To Abubaker, compassion without justice is ultimately inadequate. Here she does specifically invoke a Qur'anic verse from Surah an-Nisa:

> You who believe, uphold justice and bear witness to God, even if it is against yourselves, your parents, or your close relatives. Whether the person is rich or poor, God can best take care of both. Refrain from following your own desire, so that you can act justly—if you distort or neglect justice, God is fully aware of what you do.[46]

She interprets this verse as stating that no topics should ever be considered taboo regardless of the discomfort they might cause in the community. As such, she argues that this verse provides an imperative to stand up against sexual violence and to work toward justice, despite the difficulties of navigating particular social norms or of perhaps having to disclose that a relative, friend, or superior is a perpetrator of sexual abuse. In Abubaker's engagement with this Qur'anic verse, she envisions Muslims as a single moral community in which individuals have certain rights and responsibilities toward each other. Rather than place herself as a "detached" observer speaking from the periphery of her subject matter, she foregrounds her status as a survivor, which stands in contrast to a traditional (male) style of preaching that might decenter the khateeb's personal context and focus solely on the text.

In calling for a Qur'anic imperative to stand up against sexual violence, Abubaker demonstrates an alternative model for producing religious knowledge through experience, rather than through traditional or secular religious education. In this regard, we can use Patricia Hill Collins's Black feminist epistemology, which upholds the value of knowledge derived from emotions and experiences, rather than only rational "facts," to analyze Abubaker's khutbah. Hill Collins argues that for "most African-American women those individuals who have lived through the experiences about which they claim to be experts are more believable and credible than those who have merely read or thought about such experiences. Thus lived experience as a criterion for credibility frequently is invoked by U.S. Black women when making knowledge claims."[47] Rather than separate information from ethics, Black feminist thought instead distinguishes knowledge from wisdom, which is conferred through experience. Within Hill Collins's Black feminist epistemology, lived experiences, emotion, empathy, and personal character are all valid forms of arriving at and assessing truth claims.[48]

Not all WMA congregants are African American women, but Hill Collins's comments help to explain why they are receptive to khutbahs like Abubaker's that are rooted in women's experience. Congregants believe that khateebahs who are everyday women have more credibility than preachers who deliver sermons professionally as regular imams.[49] Furthermore, Hill Collins addresses how the "actual contours of intersecting oppressions can vary dramatically and yet generate some uniformity in the epistemologies used by subordinate groups."[50] Black feminist thought, then, can account for the experiences of WMA congregants as a subordinate group of Muslim women of color in the US; it provides a framework to understand how marginalized groups produce alternative modes of knowledge to empower themselves.[51] Here I situate WMA members' interpretive attitudes about the role of experiences in exegesis within the larger bodies of scholarship that have tended to women's experiences. As Shaikh and others have advocated, rather than take them at face value, I understand experiences at the WMA as "always imbricated in complex and intersectional configurations of power that require multi-dimensional analyses."[52] Grounding Islamic authority in women's lived experiences at the WMA is not the same as universalizing individuals' experiences and using them as "evidence" to promote specific sets of knowledge as applicable across communities at all times. Rather, as we unpack how and to what end the WMA emphasizes women's experiences as authoritative, we can begin to understand one of the ways that religious knowledge and authority are produced in the American Muslim context. To the extent that the WMA constructs authority and produces Islamic knowledge based on women's experiences, it can show us how models of embodied authority can be deployed to build communal resilience and resistance in the face of gender discrimination in religious communities. Moreover, the WMA shows us how embodied authority can also be utilized to contest and resist patriarchal readings of text.

For instance, the WMA's production of Islamic knowledge based on women's experiences as it pertains to gender violence provides an alternative to classical Islamic legal frameworks that privilege male power over female bodies. Classical Muslim jurists, for example, stipulate that a husband is permitted to physically discipline a "disobedient" wife and limit his wife's movements to ensure his sexual access to her at any given time. Kecia Ali highlights that while gender was not the only factor that jurists considered in establishing power hierarchies within marital and sexual relationships—since categories of enslavement, virginity, age, and religion also figured into determinations of power—rights within marriage were always decidedly gendered.[53] While a free Muslim man had the right to take his female slave as his concubine, a free Muslim woman could not take a male concubine and have sexual ownership over him.[54] Even within a marriage between a free man and woman, the wife was subjected to her husband's sexual control since an Islamic marriage contract granted him sexual access to her in exchange for financial maintenance. As such, the concept of rape within marriage was not formally recognized by classical jurists as a sexual violation, though as Hina Azam notes, physical injuries, such as vaginal tearing, incurred as a result of coercive sex constituted criminal behavior and could warrant monetary compensation from husbands to wives.[55] Broadly speaking, however, premodern jurists facilitated the male exertion of power over female bodies.

Nevertheless, there were ethical guidelines delineating how premodern jurists facilitated this dominance and defined the parameters of domestic violence. Islamic studies scholar Ayesha Chaudhry explains how in engagements with Qur'an 4:34,[56] the "wife-beating verse," premodern jurists meticulously regulated the extent to which physical discipline was permissible against wives.[57] These jurists differed on the particularities of striking that were permitted and debated what types of behavior constituted wifely *nushuz*, or disobedience.[58] It was not the case that they sanctioned unbridled violence against women, but they did—like many contemporary Muslim scholars still do—uphold a husband's right to discipline a wife. Moreover, in lived practice, the jurisprudential regulation of sexual violence has not protected Muslim women from harm. As Azam shows, the institutionalization of male authority over female bodies has facilitated further harm against Muslim women with respect to rape laws in several Muslim-majority countries, which routinely punish victims of rape for fornication or adultery.[59] Despite jurists' nuanced engagements with men and women's respective rights within marriage and their attention to the ethics of wife beating, the Islamic legal tradition has not consistently upheld a woman's right to bodily integrity and safety. Contemporary Muslims with gender-egalitarian sensibilities, like those in the WMA community, have therefore often found premodern frameworks around marital violence insufficient to meet their moral needs. These Muslims find existing rulings on sexual violence contradictory to their understandings of human dignity in the Islamic tradition.

Najeeba Syeed's October 2015 khutbah, which addresses domestic abuse, highlights these contradictions. A professor of interfaith studies and a social justice activist, Syeed contrasts her understanding of the values promoted by the Qur'an that uphold human dignity with legal frameworks that regulate spousal violence. She makes a case for moving beyond the Islamic jurisprudential frameworks that facilitate male power over female bodies. She calls for moving past a framework that assumes women's bodily vulnerability and takes for granted the premise that a wife's safety is secondary to a husband's control within a marriage. Like Abubaker, Syeed makes a case for women's bodies as an important site of knowledge. She calls for a new exegetical discourse rooted in the norms of gender justice by emphasizing God's infinite mercy and believers' right to bodily integrity. Syeed advocates for going beyond limiting the extent of violence permissible toward wives by husbands.

Syeed's khutbah demands setting aside classical legal frameworks defined by male power for a gender-egalitarian worldview that upholds the human body as sacred. Underpinning Syeed's remarks on domestic abuse is the Qur'anic concept of *ahsan at-taqweem*, of human beings as created in the best of stature. She states:

> The body is love itself. Your body, my body is the manifestation of the Creator's love. . . . We need to move beyond: what is our right to harm a woman's body? How far can we go? What is allowed? What may a man do to his wife that is permissible? And return to the source of looking at *ahsan at-taqweem* [best of stature]. . . . If these bodies are the *ahsan at-taqweem*, we need to elevate the discourse and see the manifestation of restorative love, see a version where there is no harm done to these bod-

ies. . . . It is not a question of my right and how far I should go. It is not a question of how much I can hurt someone. It is a question of how do I restore and how do I view my body and your body as sacred? How do I live in a world where I practice a principle of no harm of such bodies? How do we work towards a society where women's bodies are not an interruption, where women's bodies are not policed, where women's bodies in their homes [should] be safest when we know the most unsafe place for a woman's body is often in her own home?[60]

Syeed calls for Muslim communities to affirm the Qur'anic characterization of human beings as the best of creation, by embodying *ahsan at-taqweem* in their practices. In her emphasis on bodily dignity, she calls for a new framework based in social justice and restorative love, rather than one based on power and control of women's bodies. For Syeed, it is insufficient to leave the physical safety of a wife to her husband's discretion, because that would violate the sacred nature of the human body and go against the Qur'anic characterization of humans as the best of creation. While Syeed does not explicitly cite Qur'an 4:34 or make overt reference to Islamic legal rulings on wife beating, there is an implicit invocation of both of these sources when she speaks of moving beyond the metric of how much violence against women is permissible and toward a more holistic foundation of viewing the body as holy. These reflections reveal that she is acutely aware of the Islamic legal discussions that preserve men's rights to harm their wives through physical discipline. Moreover, she grounds her critique of Qur'an 4:34 and its interpretations in the Qur'an itself, upholding the concept of *ahsan at-taqweem*. Like Abubaker, Syeed draws on general themes of the Qur'an to argue for the importance of gender justice.

This again demonstrates the influence of Muslim feminist thinkers like wadud, who calls for incorporating external sources of knowledge outside of Islamic texts in her discussion of Islam and sexuality. wadud examines Qur'an 4:34 in regard to monogamous wives' contracting HIV from their husbands as a way to rethink the concept of a wife's obligation to be sexually available. Here wadud argues that Islamic texts sometimes serve only as inspiration for, rather than the foundation of, practical religious knowledge.[61] Specifically reflecting that a wife's unconditional sexual availability to an HIV-positive husband renders her and her future children vulnerable to disease and death, wadud upholds the centrality of experiences. Specifically, her suggestion that Islamic texts serve to inspire rather than provide a set of solutions to any given issue helps us understand Syeed's promotion of *ahsan at-taqweem* as a guiding principle for thinking about domestic abuse and moving beyond juristic limitations on the extent to which a husband may physically abuse his wife.

Additionally, in upholding the sacred nature of creation, Syeed draws a parallel between physical violations of the body in the context of domestic abuse and broader systems of injustice in the US whereby bodies are controlled and violated by the state. Here Syeed speaks to systems of oppression in the US in which police brutality and the criminal justice system systematically violate and discard bodies, particularly Black and brown ones. She challenges existing Islamic legal frameworks on domestic abuse by positing a new discourse based on social justice, sustained by the Qur'anic concept of human beings as the best of creation. She also connects Qur'anic imperatives to strive toward justice to social problems that are plaguing the country, arguing that Muslims have a moral imperative to resist state systems of injustice that violate the sacred nature of the human body. Ultimately, Syeed argues against taking for granted women's bodily vulnerability and their susceptibility to violence within their own households and communities. In place of this, she posits a model of marriage, family, and community that is rooted in a strength that is not defined by exerting force over others, but based in restorative love, the principle of non-harm, and bodily integrity.

Syeed's khutbah was not the only time the WMA addressed domestic violence. Six years later in 2021, as we saw earlier, khateebah Abla Hasan used her khutbah to address Qur'an 4:34. The WMA's monthly newsletter promoting Hasan's khutbah described Qur'an 4:34 as causing "considerable harm to female members of our community," further asserting that "many young Muslims who haven't been able to reconcile their doubts about existing male-led scholarly explanations on this verse have lost their faith." Billing Hasan's khutbah as "possibly . . . the single most important khutbah you will have ever heard in our mosque to date," the newsletter promises that congregants "will walk away from this jumma'a with a newfound clarity, empowered confidence, and an understanding of Verse 4:34 . . . your faith will be strengthened and renewed in the absolute perfection of our beautiful religion."[62] Hasan, like Syeed, advocates for using the egalitarian and moral thematic frameworks of the Qur'an to argue against the assertion that the text makes permissible violence toward wives. Additionally, the WMA newsletter, emailed to its subscribers, gives us insight into how the institution frames such khutbahs—as a defense of the Qur'an itself against any charges of gender injustice.

Both Abubaker and Syeed show how WMA khateebahs can use sacred texts to produce new norms around sexual violence that emphasize the Qur'anic themes of justice and compassion. Their respective khutbahs push the discourse on sexual violence forward to more accurately reflect gender-egalitarian values. Both khateebahs insist that compromising the bodily integrity of Muslim women, whether through physical abuse or a culture of silencing sexual assault survivors, reflects poorly on the moral integrity of a Muslim community as a whole. Their khutbahs set aside classical legal frameworks defined by male power and instead posit a gender-egalitarian approach to scripture that treats the human body as sacred. Their methods illustrate Abou El Fadl's concept of taking a "conscientious pause" when confronted with interpretations of texts that promote harm, for example in the face of violence committed by Muslims in the name of Islam, suggesting that Muslims assess the prevailing assumptions that could have contributed to those harms.[63] Both Abubaker and Syeed take a conscientious pause to reflect on American Muslim attitudes toward victims of sexual violence and evaluate them as insufficient to, in Abou El Fadl's words, "uphold the integrity" of Islam.[64] They both use Qur'anic concepts to promote a new way to think about the culture of gender violence.

Abubaker and Syeed carefully navigate the patriarchal gazes of both the American Muslim and non-Muslim publics. They occupy a precarious position in which their internal critiques of problematic trends within Muslim communities are susceptible to being co-opted by Islamophobic narratives. Muslim women, while seen as oppressed victims of their religion and its men, nevertheless remain key targets of anti-Muslim violence in the US. Abubaker and Syeed are thus adamant in addressing gender violence within Muslim communities. In her ethnography of American Muslim anti–domestic violence work, Hammer observes that the majority of imams in the US do not address domestic violence in their communities, unless to briefly declare that it goes against Islamic teachings before avoiding any further engagement.[65] The WMA stands apart from this trend, and these two khutbahs and the positive receptions to them make it clear that its members are not willing to remain silent in the so-called service of protecting Muslims from Islamophobia.

Nevertheless, Islamophobia is indeed a major concern for Muslim women when they consider whether to disclose their experiences of sexual violence to others within and outside of their communities. There is added pressure on Muslim women to stay silent about their experiences of sexual violence because of the shame that people in their communities would inflict on them on the one hand and the broader Islamophobia that their narratives would fuel on the other. This burden placed upon Muslim women came to the fore in public discussions in which many Muslims criticized and attempted to discredit the victims who spoke out against the predatory behaviors of prominent Muslim male leaders like Nouman Ali Khan, mentioned earlier, and Tariq Ramadan, the Swiss Muslim public intellectual. Mona Eltahawy describes Muslim women's position as being caught between a rock and a hard place, or in other words between "Islamophobes and 'our men.'" She explains:

> The rock is an Islamophobic right wing in other cultures that is all too eager to demonize Muslim men. Exhibit A is President Trump, who has himself been accused of sexually harassing women and was caught on tape bragging about it. Nevertheless, he has used so-called honor crimes and misogyny (which he ascribes to Muslim men) to justify his efforts to ban travel to the United States from several Muslim-majority countries. . . . The hard place is a community within our own faith that is all too eager to defend Muslim men against all accusations. . . . Too often, when Muslim women speak out, some in our "community" accuse us of "making our men look bad" and of giving ammunition to right-wing Islamophobes.[66]

Eltahawy describes how Muslim women are demonized by their own communities and accused of promoting Islamophobia if they choose to speak up about the abuse they suffered. Those who do speak out are either not believed or advised that they should suffer in silence to protect their communities from external critique. This dilemma rings true for Black women outside of Muslim communities as well. When Black women level accusations against "their own" men, there is uproar within their communities about how they are fueling anti-Black racism. These dilemmas expose hierarchies of whose vulnerability matters, demonstrating not only the gendered nature of sexual harassment violence[67] but its racialized dimensions as well.[68]

Anti-Muslim and anti-Black racism pose additional obstacles for American Muslim women to come forward with their experiences of sexual violence because of the antagonism they experience from their own communities. This broader climate of hostility makes Abubaker's khutbah and the "Me Too" moment it generated among WMA congregants in 2015 all the more notable. This was before activist and community organizer Tarana Burke's 2006 "Me Too" movement that raises awareness of survivors' experiences of abuse went viral on social media in September 2017, initiated by sexual assault allegations leveled against Hollywood producer Harvey Weinstein by nearly eighty different women. The subject of sexual violence in 2015 was not openly discussed in mainstream American culture in the way that is more common today. This timeline helps situate Abubaker's khutbah in a different cultural moment than what followed it, and highlights how women of color like Burke, a Black woman, have been leading national conversations and participating in grassroots activism about sexual violence long before key actors in mainstream white American culture began to support, and many times co-opt, their labors. It is relevant, then, that Abubaker, who as a Yemeni American is also a woman of color, co-founded an organization that supports victims of sexual violence in American Muslim communities. It is not a coincidence that the WMA, which is led by women of color, hosted difficult conversations about sexual violence in American Muslim communities in 2015, demonstrating the importance it places on women's lived experiences as a source of knowledge. By cultivating a community of women who share their vulnerabilities and support and nurture each other, the WMA models resilience to gender discrimination within US Muslim communities. Additionally, through its emphasis on women as nurturers, the WMA's model of embodied authority is distinctly gendered and does not compete with male forms of authority.

Gendered Authority: Women as Nurturers

I just think it's so important that there's a place where women
can talk about whatever they want to talk about, especially
when it comes to women's issues. . . . When you go to regular
Jummah at regular mosques . . . it's just very general, you
know?[69]
—Ana, Latina, in her forties

WMA congregants routinely identified khutbahs on subjects like sexual
violence, marriage, and motherhood as particularly valuable because
they came from a woman's perspective. Many characterized these topics as "women's issues" and commented on how the WMA provided a
nurturing environment in which to discuss them. In their khutbahs and
discussion circle conversations, WMA members collectively construct
gendered ideas about the strengths of women-led communities, specifically upholding nurture as a core characteristic. This section examines
five sources that exemplify how the WMA addresses "women's issues,"
including Muslema Purmul's Mother's Day lecture, khutbahs by Shabnam Dewji and Sarah Nadeem, and bayans by Sabina Khan-Ibarra and
Eman Hassaballa Aly. Each provides insight into how WMA actors conceptualize womanhood and further demonstrates how women can be
considered religious authorities on the basis of their embodied experiences. While this type of embodied authority does not directly compete
with traditional male forms of authority, it nevertheless undermines it
by highlighting the value of a distinctly gendered authority.

In a special Mother's Day lecture at the WMA in 2016, Purmul, like
the *Khateebah Guidebook*, promotes the nurturing of younger women as
an ideal component of female Islamic authority. Specifically, her lecture
discusses the relationships between mother and daughter "types," and
also includes her reflections on sacred women in Islamic history such
as Maryam, mother of Jesus; Khadijah and Aisha, two of Muhammad's
wives; Fatima, Muhammad and Khadijah's daughter; and Asiya, wife of
Pharaoh. To recap from chapter 1, Purmul is an Azhari-trained scholar
in Southern California who publicly opined that woman-led Jummah
was invalid on the eve of the WMA's inauguration in 2015. Some therefore interpreted her participation in the Mother's Day event as her ap-

proval of the WMA, despite her opposing legal stance. This is despite the fact that Purmul's lecture was neither a khutbah nor a bayan, and not at all associated with a Friday prayer service. Rather, it was a part of a special "Mother-Daughter High Tea" event held on a Sunday.

While Purmul's lecture briefly touches on relationships between biological mothers and daughters, it mostly focuses on female mentors and mentees. In particular, she discloses her own struggle to find the perfect female mentor. During her religious training in Egypt, she had been in constant pursuit of a mentor that she could regard as a mother figure, and was always disappointed because her female religious teachers were never nurturing toward her. Purmul readily admits to her audience that she held her female teachers to a different standard than her male teachers, whom she did not expect to become mentors. Nevertheless, she conveys a broad criticism of female religious teachers in the Middle East as gratuitously strict and "difficult," thereby making it a challenge to cultivate personal relationships with them.

Significantly, Purmul attributes the strictness of her female teachers in Egypt to the fact that they were emulating their male counterparts in order to gain an equivalent level of respect and authority. By contrast, in her account of sacred women in Islamic history, figures like Khadijah, Aisha, and Fatima always acted like their "true selves" and played to their own unique strengths.[70] Purmul's female teachers did not allow themselves "just to be females, to wear flowers," exposing their true selves. She compares them to women in corporate America, who in her view are required to dress in "gray and black suits" as if these colors should be considered more professional than more feminine clothing patterns and designs.[71]

Purmul's critique of her female teachers is rooted in her expectations of the ideal qualities of mothers and daughters. For her, these ideal characteristics are based on two hadith from Bukhari and Abu Dawud, which are two canonical Hadith collections. The first hadith narrates a woman coming to Aisha with her two daughters seeking charity. When Aisha has only a single date to offer, the mother splits the date in half and distributes the two portions to her daughters, taking nothing for herself. Aisha is very moved by this, and when she later recounts the event to Muhammad, he states that this woman's two daughters will serve as protection for her on the Day of Judgment. Purmul interprets this hadith as demonstrating that the natural disposition of a mother should be someone who prefers her daughter to herself, and does not hesitate to sacrifice for her.

The second hadith describes Purmul's view of the ideal disposition for a daughter. This hadith narrates the story of a woman who vowed to fast for a month if she was able to successfully complete a voyage. This woman had a successful voyage but passed away before she could fulfill her vow. A younger woman (whom Purmul describes as a daughter-figure; the hadith does not make clear if she is a daughter or a younger sister) asks Muhammad what to do, and he replies that she should fast on the deceased mother-figure's behalf. In Purmul's commentary on this hadith, she states that Muhammad, when approached by believers with particular questions, would give them the answer that they were already predisposed to. In this case, Purmul reads the daughter-figure in the hadith as wanting to carry her mother's burden in appreciation of her own experience. She further explicates that this daughter-figure's knowledge about the oath her mother had made reveals the intimacy of their relationship.

Purmul uses the above hadith to assert that the ideal daughter fulfills the role of a best friend and supporter, somebody a mother can lean on to help carry her burdens. Purmul's reflections on the ideal characteristics of mothers and daughters, and her critiques of her female teachers, show us how particular assumptions about women's "ideal" nature influence conceptions about female religious authority. To Purmul, women should ideally embody compassion, nurturance, and a willingness to sacrifice for others. However, rather than provide an example of a woman sacrificing for a male figure in her life, a husband or a son, Purmul upholds her view that women should nurture other women.

Purmul's reflection on motherhood and ideal female characteristics is one of many articulations of womanhood at the WMA that emphasize nurture. Shabnam Dewji, speaking from a Shi'i perspective, raised similar points about sacred female figures in Islamic history in her khutbah on Fatima from November 2015, but to a different end. Dewji, like Purmul, highlights the importance of Khadijah and Fatima as role models for Muslim women because of their strength, independence, and ability to meet hardships with resilience. She also emphasizes their nurturing qualities, explaining that Khadijah was Muhammad's primary source of emotional and financial support. After Khadijah died, Fatima then took on this role for her father, to the extent that Muhammad had affectionately referred to her as "the mother of her father."[72] However, in a departure from the themes in Purmul's lecture, Dewji highlights Fatima's nurturing relationship as a means to support women's independence and assertiveness.

Dewji uses Fatima's example to argue against gender segregation in Muslim communities as well. She states that Fatima supported Muhammad by accompanying him in public wherever he went, and therefore had a front seat to witness his political and religious activities. Dewji further states that segregation is considered an Islamic ideal only as a precautionary measure, but as Muslims in American society where all aspects of life are gender-integrated, it is essential that daughters are confident and understand their worth. She emphasizes that raising confident girls requires teaching them how to act appropriately with the opposite gender and advocates for raising sons and daughters in the same way, affording them the same privileges.

Nurturance is also a theme in Dewji's khutbah, and she emphasizes the importance for women to surround themselves with those who nurture them, as a reminder to take care of themselves. In speaking about marriage, she instructs the congregation that "if you choose to have a spouse, then choose one who will be right there with you to support you." Dewji's approach to womanhood and nurture differs subtly from Purmul's, in that she urges women to both give and receive nurture. There is a significant amount of overlap between their talks, though Dewji's reflections on Fatima explicitly champion an image of women who are independent and strong-willed, whereas Purmul emphasizes sacrifice and care. Both, however, center the importance of nurture and care for women, whether toward others or themselves.

What is striking about how both of these women emphasize nurturance and care as desirable feminine qualities is that they understand these feminine qualities as assets for women as they step into leadership roles in the public sphere. This is in contrast to how gendered understandings of women as soft, emotional beings suited to care for others might be deployed by critics of feminism, both Islamic and Western, to argue for limiting women's roles to the domestic sphere. For instance, we saw earlier that American Muslim public figure Yasmin Mogahed criticizes women who desire to lead prayer or pursue work outside of the home. She characterizes such women as engaging in a "crusade to follow men" rather than valuing the "selfless compassion" that they were divinely endowed with through responsibilities like motherhood.[73] Mogahed, like Purmul and Dewji, recognizes sensitivity and compassion as feminine qualities, but to her, the natural conclusion of such attributes are the pursuit of homemaking and motherhood, as well as the disavowal of "worldly leadership," which she situates squarely within a masculine domain. Purmul and Dewji frame their understandings of "feminine" qualities of nurture and care as sensibilities that women should lean into in all of their pursuits—in their professional and personal lives. For instance, Purmul criticizes her female religious teachers as insufficiently "feminine" to be good, compassionate mentors, but she is not criticizing their public roles as religious authority figures. Views like Mogahed's that explicitly criticize women for pursuing careers or wanting to lead men in prayer would likely be unwelcome at the WMA based on the *Khateebah Guidebook*'s instruction to avoid passing judgment on women's various life choices. By contrast, the differences between Dewji's and Purmul's reflections on womanhood more accurately exemplify the kind of diversity of views the WMA aspires to by showcasing different perspectives on similar topics.

Another example of the WMA's diversity of views occurred in April 2016, when the pre-khutbah bayan and khutbah at the WMA addressed the subjects of grief, loss, and divorce from two different perspectives. Sabina Khan-Ibarra, who gave the bayan that day, is a freelance writer who runs her own platform, Muslimah Montage, specifically designed for Muslim women to share their personal stories. She also regularly contributes to online publications such as altMuslimah and MuslimARC. Sarah Nadeem, who gave the khutbah, is a practicing attorney originally from London who has been involved in different types of advocacy work, including fundraising for orphans with the Islamic Circle of North America (ICNA).[74]

Khan-Ibarra's bayan refers to several subjects, including divorce and interracial marriage, but is most powerful in her discussions of grief and loss. She delivers her bayan as a personal narrative of her life, beginning with her experiences growing up in a devout Pashtun Muslim family in the US and then moving to England at age eighteen after having an arranged marriage. This marriage ended in divorce seven years later due to abuse. She describes how her parents were unique within their extended family and within the Pashtun community for supporting her divorce. Despite their support, Khan-Ibarra felt ostracized by other relatives who used her divorce to exclude her from family events and wedding traditions based on their belief that she would bring bad luck. She shares with the congregation how she used this period in her life to focus on her education and career, while becoming closer to God through daily prayer and direct conversations that made her feel understood.[75]

Khan-Ibarra later remarried at age thirty to a non-Pashtun man who had converted to Islam nearly twenty years earlier and was accepted by her family. She describes feeling content at this period in her life, imagining that this moment, after finally overcoming the trauma of her previous marriage and subsequent ostracization, marked the start of her "happily ever after."[76] She states, "For some reason, maybe it was the stories that I had read, the movies that I've watched, unless a story was ridiculously miserable, the protagonist had one major sad plot that once overcome ended in happily ever after."[77] As a listener, I was unnerved to learn that her early descriptions of her abusive first husband and in-laws were ultimately among the lighter themes of her bayan, as she went on to recount the heart-wrenching tragedy of losing her infant son to a rare genetic heart condition just days after his birth. Her bayan portrays the raw emotional experiences of the aftermath of the tragedy in the period following her loss as she shares with the WMA congregation her internal torment and anguish, and the lack of support from among her Pashtun extended family, some of whom suggested that she simply move on. One woman suggested that her son's death may have been the result of her being divorced and marrying a non-Pashtun, and not "following the right path."[78]

At this stage in her life, she began to reflect deeply on mortality and on God's will, and ponder questions such as "Was I a sinner for being divorced? Did my marrying a non-Pashtun make me less Muslim? Was I the only mother to lose a child?" She answers these questions one by one, first referring to the Qur'anic verse 49:13,[79] which describes how God has created human beings into different peoples and tribes so that they may know one another. Khan-Ibarra interprets that passage as suggesting that marrying outside of one's culture is indeed one of God's commands. Then she refers to the biography of Muhammad and high-lights the tragic losses he experienced throughout his entire life, from being orphaned and living with his grandmother to losing his grand-mother and going to live with his uncle, then having the uncle die in the same year that he lost his first wife, Khadijah. She also mentions how Muhammad outlived six of his seven children, including his infant son Ibrahim. Citing a hadith from Bukhari, per the WMA guidelines to cite only *sahih* (sound) traditions, she recalls how Muhammad wept openly for Ibrahim. She also refers to the Qur'anic narrative that the Prophet Yaqub's (Jacob) eyes turned white from his tears, effectively blinding him, when he thought he had lost his son Yusuf (Joseph). Citing other hadith that document times when Muhammad shed tears, she affirms that she was not wrong to express her grief. She explains that the overall aim of her bayan was to destigmatize conversations about abuse, grief, divorce, and mental health. Like Abubaker in her khutbah from exactly one year prior, Khan-Ibarra calls for cultivating safe and empathetic en-vironments where Muslims listen to each other's stories.

The khutbah that followed Khan-Ibarra's powerful bayan dealt with the same theme of loss, but highlighted miscarriage and the passing of elderly relatives. Delivered by Sarah Nadeem, a returning khateebah from the previous month, this khutbah was the second installment of a two-part segment titled "Grief, Loss, and Divorce." She begins with general reflections on mortality, highlighting that all things that are in the world, including people, belong to God alone. She then relates the experience of losing her grandmother when she was twenty years old and a recent bride. Shortly thereafter, she experienced her second en-counter with death, this time "within my own body," stating: "Miscar-riage is another form of death. . . . I treasured every moment of those three months of my first pregnancy but that was all I was meant to have from the life that was growing within me, just three months."[80] Nadeem asserts that everything, including one's self—body and soul—belongs to God. She states that it is only when individuals fully grasp that concept that they can come to terms with loss.[81] She repeats the Qur'anic verse "We belong to God, and to Him we will return" throughout her khutbah. Nadeem's miscarriage is one of the four losses she mentions in her khut-bah, but it stands out as an example of why many women feel that the WMA is a safe venue for them to open up about issues they would not feel comfortable discussing in a mixed-gender forum. Between Khan-Ibarra's loss of her infant son and Nadeem's miscarriage, the WMA has served as a platform to share a range of women's experiences around motherhood and loss.

Representing another aspect of women's experiences with motherhood, Eman Hassaballa Aly, a Chicago-based digital strategist with a background in social work, spoke from the perspective of a daughter in her May 2015 bayan, titled "The Power and Responsibility of Motherhood." Like most of the other khateebahs and speakers at the WMA, Aly spoke from her personal experiences as a daughter, and also from her professional experiences with counseling children, which has taught her about parenting. In her bayan, Aly first describes how the effects of parenting linger on children, and how being a parent is not an obligation in the Islamic tradition, but rather a trust from God. As such, she argues that parents should be sure that they are able to provide children with all of their spiritual and emotional needs. Her ideals about motherhood are similar to Purmul's and Dewji's as she states that mothers are "supposed to be nurturing."[82]

Her bayan further coheres with Dewji's advice on mothering sons and daughters equally as she reports that she was raised very differently from her brother. She and her sisters, unlike their brother, were restricted from sports and instead channeled into religious education. As Aly grew up, her mom increasingly declared things haram (forbidden) for girls on the basis of the Qur'anic verse "The male is not like the female."[83] This included mundane restrictions like not being allowed to drink coffee to more substantial limitations on traveling or higher education. Aly also met resistance when she pursued her bachelor's and master's degrees. Although her mother was ultimately proud of her, she did not understand why her daughter would need a higher degree to become a wife and mother. While Aly was able to heal her relationship with her mother as an adult, crediting both God's help and professional therapy, she states that many people are not that fortunate. Some people's relationships with their mothers are too deeply rooted in trauma and different forms of abuse to recover.

Like Purmul and Dewji, Aly discusses the elevated position of mothers in the Islamic tradition, citing examples of exceptional mothers in the Qur'an. One key difference in Aly's approach is her assertion that mothers have to earn this status. To her, having a child is a trust and a test from God, and mothers must hold themselves responsible. In her bayan, Aly encourages congregants to reflect on the relationships they have with their mothers and recognize the effects on their upbringings. She advises that those who still experience harm should honestly assess the level of damage and take measures to minimize that harm, even if that means reducing interactions with their mothers. She further advocates pursuing therapy or confiding in a friend or spiritual guide. Ultimately, Aly states that while everyone should attempt to have a fulfilling relationship with her mother, sometimes this will not be possible. In these cases, the loss should be acknowledged and grieved.

Aly's bayan has a different narrative arc than either Purmul's lecture or Dewji's khutbah. While the latter highlight the ideal qualities of mothers to encourage women to embody them, Aly addresses how to approach situations when women do not live up to those ideals. She emphasizes the responsibilities of motherhood alongside its elevated status, and speaks honestly about difficult mother-daughter relationships that involve too much trauma to safely salvage. Aly's personal reflections on motherhood engage both the Qur'an and Hadith, and elevate women's experiences as a basis for Islamic knowledge and authority. Aly's bayan came up a handful of times in conversations with WMA members when I asked them to reflect on Jummahs that were memorable to them. They appreciated Aly's humor and raw honesty in how she spoke of her strained relationship with her mother while she was growing up. It is worth mentioning that Aly delivered her bayan at the WMA a year prior to joining the controversial Muslim Leadership Initiative (MLI), an interfaith program that invites North American Muslim leaders to visit Israel and engage with Jewish leaders.[84] MLI is problematic to many American Muslims for a number of reasons, not least because it lends credence to the assumption that the root cause of the Israel-Palestinian conflict is religious intolerance that can be resolved by Muslim-Jewish dialogue without attending to Palestinian grievances, a process known as faith-washing. While Aly does not have a significant public platform among US Muslims, her association with MLI would have likely been a point of contention for some in the WMA community. However, possibly because her bayan was from 2015 (and her khateebah biography on the WMA site had not been updated since) and she did not join MLI until 2016,[85] it did not appear that any of the congregants I spoke with were aware of her background. After all, Aly had traveled to the

WMA from Chicago and was not a local Muslim leader in Southern California who would have been familiar to many in the congregation, nor was her bayan related at all to interfaith dialogue. In fact, those who referenced Aly's bayan in conversations with me were not even able to identify her by name, but rather mentioned specifics from the bayan itself, explaining how its content about a strained relationship with one's mother resonated with them. To congregants, Aly's authority to speak on mother-daughter relationships derived from her own experiences as a daughter and as a professional counselor, and from her willingness to speak frankly about these experiences.

Broadly speaking, WMA congregants were receptive to each of the khutbahs and bayans described in this section in which women's experiences functioned as the primary criterion for religious authority. They valued women's everyday experiences and often made claims about the unique nature of the WMA, stating that other mosques did not make similar attempts to deal with pressing and difficult subjects like sexual violence. It is not possible to assess whether the WMA is indeed the first Muslim space to discuss subjects like sexual violence or the nuances of motherhood and loss, but it is still important that WMA congregants frequently mention that it was the "first" or "only" mosque in their experience to prioritize topics like sexual violence, or Black Lives Matter and social justice. To these congregants, the WMA offers a uniquely cathartic forum for Muslim women to engage timely and sensitive subjects.

More than any individual khutbah topic, however, the discussion circle held after each monthly Jummah provide the most compelling evidence for the WMA's commitment to female nurturance and feminine models of authority. Most, if not all, of the congregants I spoke with identified this part of the Jummah program as uniquely enriching, especially in comparison to their other mosques and religious communities. During the months that I attended WMA Jummahs, it was typically Maznavi or Hannah Kim, one of the board members at the time, who would start ushering congregants to sit in a large circle on the floor; though as most congregants were regular attendees by then, they would typically begin this process themselves. This would be after the few, usually five to seven, congregants who opted to pray the optional dhuhr finished their prayer. The khateebah would sit on the floor in the front

Figure 3.1. WMA congregants reflecting together after the Jummah khutbah. Source: Faezeh Fathizadeh, the Pluralism Project at Harvard University

of the room, facing all of the congregants with her back to the minbar that she had just preached from. A handful of the older congregants for whom sitting on the floor was not physically comfortable or tenable would sit in chairs dispersed throughout the circle, though typically situated on either side of the room or at the back.

Standing just outside the perimeter of the circle, Maznavi would then make a few announcements using a microphone, explaining that this was an opportunity for attendees to engage in a Q&A session with the khateebah and share their reflections and comments. She routinely made it a point to encourage new attendees and those who had never spoken in prior discussion circles to speak up, assuring congregants that this was a safe space and adding that for those who were shy or anxious about public speaking that this was a good opportunity to practice being more at ease. Maznavi would also announce each time that these discussion circles were being recorded for online posting at a later date to be accessible to a wider community. Congregants could opt out of being recorded by not using the microphone and notifying one of the board members in advance so the videographer knew not to film them. After these announcements, Maznavi would join the circle and facilitate the session from the floor, rising up intermittently to pass the microphone.

The discussion circle sessions all began in a similar fashion—the first few congregants to speak up would begin their comments by thanking the khateebah for her efforts and complimenting specific aspects of the khutbah. These compliments differed from month to month, sometimes focusing on speaking style and delivery, and other times on how important the topic was. Following their compliments, congregants would ask specific questions about scriptural sources, usually framed by an interest in wanting to research a particular subject further, rather than challenging facts, the authenticity of particular claims, or the speakers' authority to make those claims. Khateebahs for their part were required by WMA leaders to come to the Q&A discussion circle with full citations and references from their khutbahs in hand.[86]

The subject of discussion often moved away from the topic of the khutbah by the end into other subjects on congregants' minds. This was an intimate space, and congregants, even if meeting each other for the first time, appeared to feel comfortable and safe with each other. Rather than directing comments and questions solely to the khateebah, congregants would also address their reflections to one another and, in turn, respond and offer advice or resources for further study. At the Q&A discussion circle on June 30, 2017, one congregant, a South Asian American in her mid-thirties and the mother of a toddler girl who was also in attendance, shared her pain, frustration, and sadness at the brutal murder of Nabra Hassanen, a Nubian-Egyptian American teen who was visibly both Black and Muslim. This tragic event, which had occurred just weeks prior in the DC area, affected many American Muslims, for whom the racial and gendered dimensions of Hassanen's assault and murder were obvious. As this congregant shared her thoughts, she became openly emotional and then began to cry. Those sitting nearest to her in the circle were quick to offer comfort through a hug or supportive touch.

Shortly thereafter, one of the older African American congregants said that in the current political climate—referring to the context of a Trump presidency and increased incidents of anti-Muslim hate—it was especially important for Muslim women to learn to defend themselves. She elaborated that Muslims, especially women, should learn self-defense so that they could be more aware of their surroundings and

Figure 3.2. A toddler sitting in the middle of a WMA discussion circle. Source: Alexa Pilato

fight back in life-threatening situations. Others in the circle agreed, and the conversation moved to whether women who wear the hijab should consider removing it for safety. More members began to speak up, with some of the older congregants offering sincere advice to younger congregants about prioritizing their safety over everything else.

I was also processing the trauma of Hassanen's murder along with many in the congregation. Though I generally did not contribute much to these discussion circles so I could focus on listening, I briefly shared my concerns that if we focused this conversation about a tragic murder on personal accountability, on the need for self-defense and changing our styles of dress, it would appear as though victims of violence were being held responsible for the hate directed at them. I felt that, in many situations, no act of self-defense or wearing different clothing would be sufficient to save one's life. After the circle dispersed, I continued discussing this topic with some congregants who felt similarly, and they expressed that American Muslims need to have a bigger conversation about how to process these tragedies. I did not have any alternatives to the suggestion of learning self-defense, nor did I necessarily disagree on its importance, but sharing my thoughts in the circle was a way to articulate my own grief. In the process, I experienced some of the catharsis that my interlocutors described in their reflections.

Also during this same discussion, another congregant suggested that the WMA address this tragedy directly. The July 2017 khutbah subsequently focused on honoring Nabra's life. This is an example of the way that WMA members collectively negotiate new norms and criteria for religious authority in real time; together, leaders and members create their own interpretive community, where they value their own and other women's experiences as a way to derive religious knowledge. Because congregants claim that men lack the insight to speak with authority on particular subjects like sexual violence, domestic abuse, and motherhood, they create new opportunities for a type of female religious authority that they perceive to be more relevant and nurturing than men's. As we have seen, this model of women's religious authority does not compete with male authority, but rather fills a distinct need in American Muslim communities, in which women's voices are missing. Yet at the same time, this embodied authority grounded in experiences undermines male forms of authority that are disengaged from everyday women's perspectives because it is elevated as more relatable and relevant to congregants' lives.

According to many in the WMA community, women in positions of Islamic authority are uniquely positioned to speak on subjects like gender violence, marriage, and motherhood. As an institution, through its *Khateebah Guidebook* and selected khutbahs and bayans, the WMA emphasizes women's leadership roles as nurturers and posits lived experiences as an authentic means to derive religious knowledge and cultivate authority. In so doing, it also promotes particular ideas about womanhood that assume women's roles as nurturers and suggests that female religious authorities should act as mentors who provide support to younger women. Such gendered expressions of authority, rooted in notions of women's capacity to nurture, mother, and mentor, can effectively operate to replace male authority that simply cannot account for women's embodied experiences. In the next chapter, I turn to the WMA's commitment to social justice activism as another aspect of its project to cultivate a distinct type of Islamic authority. In particular, we explore how, within its nurturing community of women, the WMA navigates anti-Black racism as an institution and attempts to build and sustain a multiracial congregation.

4

Authority through Activism

Islamophobia, Social Justice, and Black Lives Matter

In El Hajj Malik's [Malcolm X] letter from Hajj to his followers, he said in part, "There were tens of thousands of pilgrims from all over the world. They were of all colors from blue-eyed blondes to the Black-skinned Africans. But we were all participating in the same ritual, displaying a spirit of unity and brotherhood that my experiences in America had led me to believe never could exist between the white and the non-white." This still resonates. And for sisters that have felt in any way lesser than, at Hajj you will be rewarded to see that you are the same as any believer. You are worthy, dear sister to make this journey. And part of the journey, I think particularly for women, is to know your self-worth.
—Hajjah Krishna Nunnally Najieb, from her February 2020 khutbah, "The Transformative Power of Hajj"

In her khutbah on the Hajj and its powerful effect on her as a Black Muslim woman, Krishna Najieb invoked the legacy of Malcolm X, who had performed this rite in 1964, one year before his assassination. Hajj is the annual pilgrimage to Mecca that is incumbent upon all Muslims to complete once in their lifetime if it is physically and financially feasible. In his letters and autobiography, Malcolm X described how worshiping alongside Muslims of different races and ethnicities had transformed him, and made him amenable to working toward Black liberation alongside white allies and the mainstream civil rights movement in the US.[1] Najieb connected Malcolm's experiences to her own, stating that participating in this ritual was likewise transformative and made her feel equal to her fellow Muslim pilgrims. The Hajj strengthened Najieb's personal relationship with God and validated her self-worth as a Muslim woman.

When Najieb realized that her Hajj journey coincided with the fiftieth anniversary of Malcolm's own, she felt further validated, as if God had been sending her signs her whole life. She had converted to Islam in her fifties but had been familiar with Malcolm X's account of the Hajj since she was a teenager. "I didn't realize until midway through our pilgrimage that it was the fiftieth anniversary of the Hajj journey for El Hajj Malik," she stated. "Looking back I now feel like Allah was leaving signs for me to get on the path even at the age of seventeen."[2] Being able to connect Malcolm X's Hajj experience with her own imbued an increased significance to her identity as a Black Muslim woman. To Najieb, it was a sign from God that she, as a Black woman, was just as worthy as any other Muslim believer. Throughout her khutbah, she reflected on Hajj as a process through which Muslim women, particularly Black women, could understand and affirm their own worth in Islam.

Through such reflections on her racial-religious identity, Najieb and other Black khateebahs have introduced prominent Black Muslim figures like Malcolm X, W. D. Mohammed, and Elijah Muhammad into the WMA's lexicon. These famous figures' entry into the WMA's worldview plays a role in merging the history of Black Islam in the US with the larger story of Islam in America, especially for non-Black congregants who are unaware of this history. Beyond correcting the erasure of Black Muslims from narratives of American Islam through some of its khutbahs, the WMA also creates opportunities for congregants to cultivate a shared moral consciousness across racial identity by committing to social justice activism, countering Islamophobia, and confronting anti-Black racism within Muslim communities.

Islamophobia, or anti-Muslim racism, has been a central concern for the WMA since its inception, before the start of Donald Trump's explicitly Islamophobic and xenophobic presidency in 2017. A number of WMA khateebahs have utilized scripture to encourage Muslims to proactively address Islamophobia through community building, civic engagement, or by creating spaces to safeguard and cultivate an American Muslim identity. Moreover, many WMA khutbahs have showcased how the normalization of white supremacy in the US public profoundly shapes how American Muslims see themselves and their communities as racialized others. This chapter investigates the way that American Muslims' status as social and political outsiders to the white mainstream informs how they engage sacred Islamic sources through the lens of social justice. It also analyzes how the WMA enables congregants to draw connections between multiple forms of oppression that afflict Black and non-Black Muslims alike, setting the stage for them to build interracial solidarity with each other.

The WMA facilitates interracial solidarity among congregants on multiple levels. On a discursive level, some khateebahs have addressed the shared histories of Black and non-Black Muslims in America in their khutbahs on Islamophobia. Others have put Islamic scriptures in conversation with specific American social issues like anti-Black racism, demonstrating how they affect Muslims across racial and ethnic identities. On the level of community, the WMA treats the mosque as a venue to confront anti-Black racism through its programming. WMA leaders hosted a discussion series on the Black Lives Matter (BLM) movement in 2016 for congregants to participate in dialogue with each other, and in 2020, hosted a virtual conversation on the Hajj, women, and race. The results of such programming do not reflect a linear trajectory of success in solidarity building, based on the many challenges of racial justice work. Congregants ultimately have mixed feelings about the extent to which they experience interracial understanding and solidarity at the WMA. Nevertheless, to these same congregants, the WMA's engagement with social justice issues like structural racism, environmental degradation, and gender discrimination bolsters its religious authority because it renders Islamic scriptures relevant to current events and to their political values and concerns. By exploring how these issues motivate WMA khateebahs to put Islamic scriptures in conversation with social justice causes, we can see how they cultivate authority on the basis of their activism.

A Multiracial Congregation

I didn't have that problem [of marginalization] in my mosque. I didn't have anybody telling me what I could and could not do . . . [but] I kind of know of the trials and tribulations of my immigrant sisters. They've got it a little bit more rough than we [African American Muslim women] do. We are kind of in your face and loud. We are not taking that

stuff. You all [South Asian women] got to get there. The idea
of a mosque being started by a woman—I could understand
the reasoning. Whether I had issues at my mosque or not,
we had no choice but to support our sister [Maznavi]. . . . I'm
old. She is such a youngster, just the bravery, it took some
guts to do something like that. I will support her till the day I
die and I will fight for it [the WMA] till the day I die.[3]
—Tina, African American, in her sixties

As a multiracial community, the WMA serves as a space in which African American, immigrant (including Black), Latinx, and white Muslims
can cultivate camaraderie across their experiences and construct a
shared identity. As a racially diverse congregation, the WMA is a useful
site to explore the relationships between African American Muslims and
their "immigrant" and white counterparts. Here I use "immigrant," as
my subjects do, to broadly signify the ethnic backgrounds of first-, sec-
ond-, and subsequent-generation Americans. As Islamic studies scholars
like Jamillah Karim and Sherman Jackson show, African American and
immigrant Muslims have a mutually conflicting relationship with American whiteness.[4] Despite the shared historical consciousness of African
Americans and immigrant Muslims through their brutal experiences
of subjugation through American slavery and European colonization,
Jackson argues, immigrant Muslims are complicit in anti-Black racism.
He states that, in fact, many immigrant and Black Muslim communities do not identify with each other.[5] Indeed, as cultural anthropologist
Zain Abdullah demonstrates, even Black African immigrant Muslims
dissociate themselves from African American Muslims since they have
"internalized stereotypes depicting African Americans as criminals or
people caught in a cycle of destructive behavior."[6] In other words, even
as they face anti-Black racism, African Muslims along with South Asian
and other immigrant Muslims lean into the trope of the "model minority" in which they attribute their upward economic mobility in the US
to their hard work and family values, overlooking the role of structural
racism that prevents African Americans from making similar gains.

Karim also observes that African American Muslim women often
view immigrant Muslim women as unduly subjugated by their men,
a sentiment that Tina echoes above. Tina characterizes South Asian

women in general as not standing up for themselves against their men to the extent that African American women do. Her eagerness to embrace Maznavi and the WMA (and to be interviewed for this book) was grounded in her desire to support a younger generation of South Asian women who, in her view, were making important strides in asserting their voices as Muslim women—whether through creating a women's mosque or, in my case, writing about it. Tina's anecdotal observations about African American and immigrant women in mosques conform to the available data on gendered experiences in mosques. While Muslim women's experiences across US mosques are multiple and varied, according to a 2011 study, African American mosques—particularly W. D. Mohammed's communities that came out of the legacy of the NOI[7]— and Shi'i mosques tended to be more "woman-friendly" in comparison to immigrant Sunni mosques. These mosques had more adequate women's prayer spaces and did not use physical partitions to separate women and men.[8]

Consistent with the trends reported in that 2011 study, African American women at the WMA, like Tina, attested to inclusive experiences at their own mosques. In fact, many African American women at the WMA were involved in leadership roles at their home mosques.[9] For example, Ibtihal, an African American in her late thirties, explained that her mosque community in Pasadena operated as one big family. While men exclusively led ritual prayer at her mosque, women were on the executive board. Ibtihal further explained that, though it was "by no means perfect" in terms of gender equality, she felt that her mosque included women's voices in leadership decisions to a great extent, especially in comparison to other communities.[10]

Zahara and Celeste, both African American and in their sixties, similarly characterized their respective African American home mosques as having better conditions for women than those run by Arab and South Asian leaders. Zahara described an incident from over a decade ago, when a male member of her African American congregation erected a partition to separate the women and men's prayer spaces. Zahara removed the partition, stating that it was simply not a viable option for her. He did not make a second attempt.[11] Black Muslim women like Zahara, and Tina above, characterize themselves as assertive members of their congregations. These women attributed their assertiveness, in part, to their experiences of African American Muslim congregations being structured as families, which to them made it more likely that women's voices would be heard and respected.

For this reason, African American congregants like Celeste and Kenyatta were somewhat hesitant to get on board with the WMA in its earliest stages. They were skeptical about whether an all-women's mosque constituted progress or was worthwhile at all. They were accustomed to worshiping in the same community as their male kin and felt that, if they were to give a khutbah, they would want to be heard by the men in their communities. As such, they were not initially sure if the WMA as a woman-only mosque was the right fit for them. Ultimately, however, among current congregants, those who initially harbored certain reservations about the WMA as a woman-only space came to appreciate it for the unique community it had become, and they embraced their own roles as mentors and models for younger members.

The majority of the older African American women in this study shared Tina's sentiment of supporting the WMA in solidarity. Many of them operated from a protective impulse to nurture and guide younger American Muslims of immigrant heritage who were marginalized in their own home mosques, or those who were generally without a spiritual community. Women like Tina support the WMA despite the fact that they do not feel similarly marginalized in their own mosques. These elder African American Muslim women are not only willing to give their support to the WMA and their "immigrant sisters," as Tina put it, but are also committed to constructing a shared religious community with them. I use "Black" and "African American" interchangeably in referring to my interlocutors, as they used both terms to describe themselves. It is worth noting that all of the Black WMA members in this study are African American; the women with whom I spoke did not include Black Muslims from immigrant backgrounds.[12] This does not mean that there are *no* Black immigrant women in the community, but there are a number of reasons we might consider when thinking about why African Americans might be more likely to gravitate toward the WMA.

As mentioned earlier, the dynamic between Black immigrant and African American Muslims can be antagonistic. Aware of how racial hierarchies operate in the US, Black immigrants often do not want to be associated with African Americans or Blackness and prefer to identify with their national identities.[13] Likewise, African American Muslims, particularly groups influenced by reform movements in the Middle East, can also be unwelcoming toward African immigrant Muslims, criticizing their dress and religious customs as not properly Islamic.[14] Beyond the anti-Black sentiment behind both of these impulses, there may also be general anxiety among Black immigrant Muslims about discussing politics or race in the mosque, based on the precarity of their own status as Americans. Particularly if they are undocumented, Black immigrant Muslims may not feel safe in a mosque with activist commitments, and may not want to draw additional attention to themselves as political agitators, particularly when US mosques are known to be closely surveilled by law enforcement. In other cases, some African immigrant Muslim communities forge ties with federal agencies and cooperate in counterterror efforts by policing their communities for signs of radicalization.[15] Given the long history of tension between NOI mosques and the FBI,[16] African American mosques affiliated with the NOI or W. D. Mohammed's communities are generally less trusting of law enforcement, and oriented toward political organizing. Despite Mohammed's shift away from the NOI's Black separatism, he remained committed to developing mosques as centers for Black autonomy and community building—as opposed to tools for assimilation and acceptance into white mainstream American society. In this way, these African American mosques resemble how the institution of the Black church has served African American Protestant communities.[17]

Because of the fear of surveillance, non-Black immigrant Muslims, and mosques with immigrant Muslim leadership, may be similarly hesitant to address social justice concerns that might render them politically "threatening" to white America.[18] Conflicting relationships between different US Muslim communities and law enforcement also pose substantial barriers to interracial solidarity, especially when immigrant mosques cultivate partnerships with local police departments at the expense of solidarity with Black Muslims, who are victims of rampant police brutality.[19] These dynamics give us a sense of some of the broader challenges to Muslims' coming together and building community across racial and ethnic identity. It also helps us to understand the type of American Muslim who might be more likely to be attracted to the WMA's social justice activism: African Americans whose Islam already appeals to racial equality, and more broadly those Muslims who are eager to leverage their various privileges (racial, economic, citizenship status) to engage social issues that matter to them. For such Muslims, being a part of a multiracial congregation that utilizes the mosque as a site for social justice activism is particularly appealing. The next section explores how the WMA navigates the idea of a shared community across racial identity by spotlighting a khutbah that links the histories of African American and immigrant Muslims. This khutbah provides a basis to think about how American Muslims—both Black and non-Black—are racialized and politicized as the "other," and how their intersecting marginalization could serve as a framework for solidarity.

A Shared History: Racializing Muslims

I struggled [deciding] between talking about asserting our civil rights, pushing back against racial profiling and the national security framework, police killings of African American civilians, FBI targeting of Muslims. . . . I would argue that it [Islamophobia] is the root of many of our challenges today. They might not be able to drone-bomb Yemen or Somalia if we weren't dehumanized as a community. We might have more allies in public office if they weren't afraid to associate with our community. . . . Last year I, as a Muslim woman of color, chose to question Memorial Day and the way we celebrate war in this country and the holy grail that is the military industrial complex. And for more than a week, I was profiled by Fox News, I had hate mail sent to my work. . . . I could not pick up my phone for fear of death threats and silencing, so much so that it not only made me afraid, it made the people around me afraid. Every time I questioned war . . . I must consider: am I permitted to do this as a Muslim woman of color?[20]
—Zahra Billoo, from her July 2015 khutbah, "Combatting Islamophobia"

Addressing Islamophobia in mainstream American culture has figured prominently in the broader agenda of the WMA. As a nonprofit organization, the WMA does not endorse any particular politicians or propositions, though the *Khateebah Guidebook* encourages khateebahs to promote voting and civic engagement.[21] Accordingly, over the course of the WMA's tenure, khateebahs have urged congregants to engage in civic activities, build community, and participate in local governance, often framing these actions as a means to resist Islamophobia. In her khutbah, Billoo, a labor-rights advocacy lawyer who is the executive director of CAIR (the Council on American-Islamic Relations) in the Bay Area, defined Islamophobia as "close-minded prejudice or bigotry against Islam and Muslims." Islamophobia, she asserted, was responsible for the US bombings in Yemen and Somalia, a dearth of Muslim allies in US politics, and her own experiences of public censure as a Pakistani American Muslim woman following her critiques of the military industrial complex.

In her khutbah, Billoo portrayed Islamophobia as a multifaceted phenomenon of anti-Muslim racism promulgated by various individual and collective actors, including the US state apparatus. Her treatment here is consistent with Edward Curtis's argument that Islamophobia in the US "is not exclusively the reflection of certain cultural and political interests" but also "the product of the state's legal and extra-legal attempts to control, discipline, and punish Muslim American individuals and organizations."[22] Billoo's experience of targeted abuse aligns with both of Curtis's categories; not only was she subjected to threats of violence by individuals whose political and cultural interests differed from her own, but she was also targeted by corporate media, which enables state Islamophobia. Since mass media shapes public opinion by disseminating narratives that justify government policies like the War on Terror, it plays a key role in structural Islamophobia.[23] As a result of being on the receiving end of multipronged Islamophobia, Billoo questioned whether as a Muslim woman of color she would ever be permitted to critique her own government without being cast as a "terrorist sympathizer."[24]

Billoo's public censure as a Muslim woman of color has a long history in the US and can be traced back to the legacy of state repression of African Americans. The media and the government have long engaged in the systematic production of Islamophobia to control and repress American Muslims. Since the 1930s and throughout the civil rights era, African American Muslims (and non-Muslims) in particular were racialized by the state as political others who posed an inherent threat to national security.[25] Religious studies scholar Sylvester Johnson demonstrates that this process of racialization occurred through systematic FBI surveillance, harassment, and violence toward African American organizations. Organizations such as the Black Panther Party, the Nation of Islam (NOI), and unarmed Black student activist groups across college campuses were brutally repressed by the US state.[26]

Furthermore, the FBI disseminated anti-Muslim propaganda in the media to influence perceptions of the NOI as inherently dangerous to mainstream white American society. These propaganda campaigns advanced the idea that the NOI was not an authentic religious organization but a "hate-based political movement merely masquerading as a religion."[27] FBI training manuals, while implicitly maintaining the superiority and moral innocence of white Americans, portrayed Black Muslims as primitive, violent, and irrational as opposed to the adherents of "real Islam," which they deemed "a thoroughly spiritual religion of peace and brotherhood."[28] Despite these FBI manuals' distinction between African American Islam and "real" Islam from the Middle East, Johnson demonstrates that by the 1960s immigrant Muslims had also been recast as enemies of the state.

American Muslims' political marginalization was further intensified in the post-9/11 era.[29] Johnson shows that the same rhetoric the FBI had deployed against Black Muslims and immigrant Muslims in the 1960s, depicting them as fanatics prone to violence, was again applied to Muslims of immigrant background as they were "vilified as enemies of the West" immediately following 9/11.[30] The similarities between the racialization processes to which Black and non-Black American Muslims have been subjected indicates the continuity of the US national security paradigm across decades and how it renders Islam as intrinsically other than American.[31] Curtis argues that the US state's treatment of immigrant brown Muslims in the post-9/11 context and its treatment of Black African American Muslims pre-9/11 both reveal the systematic suppression of any Muslims who critique the US state.[32] Immigrant American Muslim women like Billoo have lived that experience and acknowledge the continuities of the national security paradigm in the US. For example, Billoo listed civil rights, racial profiling, national security, police killings of African American civilians, and FBI targeting of Muslims as elements that all relate to the pervasive structures of Islamophobia. In this way, her khutbah merged the narratives of Black and non-Black American Muslims rather than treating them as separate groups without a shared history.

Billoo's implicit linkage of early twentieth-century African American Muslims in the Nation of Islam with post-1965 immigrant Muslim narratives is noteworthy because many American Muslim communities do not consider Black and brown American Muslim histories as continuous. This is both because of "immigrant" Muslim perceptions (and, as Curtis and Johnson both note, academic, mainstream media, and FBI perceptions) of the NOI as a "heterodox" and inauthentic manifestation of Islam, and because of the anti-Black racist attitudes that pervade US Muslim communities. Despite these perceptions, anti-Muslim hate in the US, whether against Black or immigrant Muslims, is indeed linked. As American studies scholar Sylvia Chan-Malik argues, Islam in America is a "racial-religious form," and racial stereotypes have been attached to Muslim identity based on various political, social, and economic circumstances. Chan-Malik suggests that anti-Muslim hate in the US be understood through the lenses of not only "orientalism and xenophobia but also through the historical legacies of and contemporary expressions of anti-blackness, misogyny, sexual violence, and the acknowledgment of the United States as an imperial settler colonial nation."[33] WMA khateebahs like Billoo frame their understandings of Islamophobia in precisely these historically layered ways. Billoo accounted for the xenophobic underpinnings of her own experiences of anti-Muslim harassment as she recounted multiple incidents of white Americans telling her to "go back to her own country."[34] At the same time, she also included the issue of police brutality against African Americans under the umbrella of Islamophobia, the central subject of her khutbah. Billoo also identified how her gendered identity as a visibly Muslim woman made her susceptible to particular forms of harassment and accusations that she was not authentically American, with xenophobia, anti-Black racism, and misogyny all coming into play. Linking these phenomena together in her khutbah, she signaled how the racialization of Islam by the US state produces an Islamophobia that affects both Black and non-Black American Muslims.

In her khutbah, Billoo drew on specific examples of anti-Muslim discrimination that she deals with through her work with CAIR. She described Muslims not being able to maintain stable employment because of their religious identities, or being too fearful to reach out for support when they did face bigotry.[35] Here Billoo drew a comparison between the discrimination that American Muslims face in their lives with the hardships that the Prophet Muhammad and his Companions faced for being Muslim in seventh-century Arabia. To this end, she stated, "we have a rich tradition of responding to oppression with dignity and stead-fastness. Our tradition isn't one that simply reminds us of the sadness—instead it gives us hope and tools necessary to respond to make our best effort."[36] Like other WMA khateebahs, Billoo upheld the importance of the Islamic tradition in her khutbah, arguing that it contains within it tools to address American Muslims' contemporary and contextually specific concerns about Islamophobia. This relates back to the themes discussed earlier, in which we saw that WMA leaders and khateebahs tend to emphasize continuities with the Islamic tradition, even while congregants appear to have more flexible commitments to it.

Billoo also cited the Qur'an as a source that provides both hope and the tools to respond to Islamophobia, demonstrating how khateebahs put sacred texts in conversation with social issues, approaching it through an activist lens. From Qur'an 39:53, she quoted "Do not despair of the mercy of Allah" to argue that there are explicit Qur'anic instructions to perse-vere and stay positive.[37] She paraphrased other verses of the Qur'an[38] to emphasize reliance on God to get through hardships. Her advice to the WMA congregation about how to combat Islamophobia was two-pronged. Through a religious lens, she encouraged participants to read more Qur'an and draw strength from prayer, community, and charitable giving. In the second half of her khutbah, Billoo provided actionable ad-vice, encouraging Muslims to be on the front lines of civic engagement, working toward causes like environmental and social justice.

Notably, Billoo expressed appreciation for how WMA leaders remind khateebahs to select timely subjects and provide a system of quality con-trol with regard to guidelines for khutbahs. She lamented that khateebs (male preachers) at other mosques do not preach on timely subjects, im-plying that their messages are not always relevant to the social context of their congregants. As we saw earlier, many women similarly use binary descriptions to compare khutbahs at the WMA to those at other mosques through claims of relevance versus irrelevance, relatability versus abstrac-tion, or nurture versus judgment. Billoo's commentary indicates that making Islamic teachings, sacred texts, and Prophetic examples relevant to the contemporary lives of American Muslims is central to the aims and overall narrative of the WMA. Putting sacred Islamic sources in conversation with American social movements, as Billoo and other WMA khateebahs do, represents their commitment to social justice.

Billoo concluded her khutbah with an English supplication that in part reads: "[Oh Allah!] Empower us to turn our weapons used against our community to bring smiles to tired and hungry faces. Shower them with justice. . . . Our hearts and souls bleed, but we trust in Your mercy. Forgive all those who have been unjustly killed by racist police officers.[39] Grant those who have lost their lives paradise . . . fill our souls with humility. Ameen."[40] Her supplication, seeking God's mercy and forgiveness for those who have lost their lives as victims of anti-Muslim bigotry and police brutality, underscores the multifaceted manifestations of Islamophobia. Between her criticism about the typical irrelevance of khutbahs at other mosques and her closing supplication that addresses the varied faces of anti-Muslim racism, Billoo is arguing that the American mosque should be a site to address current issues of injustice. Moreover, she points out how anti-Muslim racism in the US affects Black and non-Black Muslims in related ways. She also incorporates her professional expertise from the realm of Muslim civil rights activism to cultivate her authority as a WMA khateebah, using scriptures to encourage congregants to be more civically engaged with social justice causes.

Toward Community Building and Civic Engagement

I can only hope that one day when Ramsey [my son] faces hate in this world . . . that he remembers that people love him and embrace him, that he is filled with enough compassion to respond with compassion, because eventually he will have to face it by himself.
—Aziza Hasan, from her May 2015 khutbah, "Empowering Youth to Respond to Hate with Compassion"

Khateebahs Aziza Hasan and Farrah Khan represent two additional models of activist authority with their messages to build community ties and become politically active. In her khutbah from May 2015, titled

"Empowering Youth to Respond to Hate with Compassion," Hasan, founder and director of the interfaith organization NewGround: A Muslim Jewish Partnership for Change, addressed the importance of teaching youth how to respond to religious hatred. Specifically, she spoke on the value of fostering relationships within the Muslim community and outside of it as a long-term tool to cope with anti-Muslim hate. Her khutbah focused on her personal experience of taking part in a Muslim-Jewish public prayer event that NewGround organized outside of Los Angeles City Hall. During this prayer event, Omar, the man who was designated as the leader for the Muslim prayer, faced a personal crisis when news broke that there was an active shooting in his hometown of Garland, Texas, where an anti-Muslim group had organized a "Draw Muhammad" contest. Rather than dropping out of the event, Omar instead decided to carry on as planned and relied on the support of the Muslim and Jewish communities who had gathered.

Hasan described being moved by this experience, especially since her four-year-old son, also in attendance, was able to witness the love and affection between supportive community members from two different faith traditions in the face of fear. Her message to the congregation was to find and keep compassion in the presence of hatred and to rely on each other for support. Hasan quoted Qur'anic verse 2:286 as inspiration to continue to do good works despite the existence of hatred:

> On no soul doth Allah Place a burden greater than it can bear. It gets every good that it earns, and it suffers every ill that it earns. Our Lord! Condemn us not if we forget or fall into error. Our Lord! Lay not on us a burden like that which Thou didst lay on those before us; Our Lord! Lay not on us a burden greater than we have strength to bear. Blot out our sins, and grant us forgiveness. Have mercy on us. Thou art our Protector; help us against those who stand against faith.[41]

Using this Qur'anic verse to ask for God's protection against anti-Muslim bigotry, Hasan explained that by remembering the compassion of God, Muslims could respond to rejection with compassion. As such, she extolled the virtues of creating new models of community, such as the interfaith alliances cultivated through NewGround. To her, building community is not only a virtue, but also a pragmatic tool to diffuse religious bigotry.

Whereas Hasan advocated for community building, Farrah Khan's khutbah from November 18, 2016—just ten days after the presidential election during which Donald Trump ran and won on an openly anti-Muslim, xenophobic platform—promoted Muslims' participation in local governance as a means to resist Islamophobia. Khan used verses from the Qur'an and specific hadith to urge the WMA congregants to become civically engaged and run for public office. She specifically cited Qur'an 13:11, which she translated as "Verily God does not change the people's condition unless they change their inner selves," as a basis for her claim. Khan framed her call for WMA congregants' increased involvement in local governance with personal reflections on losing a local election. Khan had run for city council in Irvine, California, that same month.

She recounted with pride that although she lost the election due to a last-minute smear campaign against her by an opposing candidate with greater financial resources, she had been successful in garnering the necessary endorsement from the Democratic Party and raising the requisite funds. To come to terms with her unsuccessful campaign, Khan cited this hadith: "If you ask, ask God. If you need help, seek it from God. Know that if the whole world were to gather together in order to help you, they would not be able to help you except if God had written it so. And if the whole world were to gather together in order to harm you, they would not harm you except if God had written it so. The pens have been lifted and the pages are dry." Khan used this hadith to assert the inevitability of God's will, seamlessly connecting sacred texts with the events in her own life. This mirrors the way that she and other khateebahs put scriptures in conversation with current social and political issues to promote activist causes—in this case her own foray into local politics and coping with her loss in the election.

Running for office helped Khan find peace and hope with the national election results after initially going through a cycle of denial, despair, and anger.[42] People from her Muslim networks who had not supported her campaign suddenly began to contact her in the days after the election, asking for advice on how to become trained in the US political system. Khan felt empowered seeing others participate in political protests since, in her view, the majority of American Muslims had been complacent for too long. Here she again invoked Qur'an 2:216 to bolster her argument about the necessity of civic engagement and fighting for social justice: "It may be that you dislike a thing while it is good for you and it may be that you love a thing while it is evil for you, and God knows what you do not."[43] Her primary focus was to encourage congregants to run for office, then secondarily to encourage those who did not want to run for public office to become involved in politics at the local level by participating in others' campaigns. As a third option, Khan said that those who were not inclined to participate in political campaigns should get involved with local policy makers who work on issues that they are passionate about, such as the environment, education, or safety.

Gendered Islamophobia

It's a question I pose to Muslim women in our society today: what will break first, our spirit or our body? Islamophobia is a spiritual jihad of our generation, meeting our struggle. And it's a collective struggle. . . . Some of us, like millennial Muslims, were born into it [an era of hatred]. Our formative years happened here. The development of who we are took place under a complete assault on our identities, especially for Muslim girls.[44]
—Amani Al-Khatahtbeh, from her January 2016 khutbah,
"A Message for Muslim Youth"

Amani Al-Khatahtbeh's khutbah, delivered on the one-year anniversary of the WMA's inception, addressed how Islamophobia has shaped millennial American Muslim identity. Al-Khatahtbeh, the founder and editor-in-chief of Muslim Girl, an online magazine for American Muslim women, reflected on how Muslim youth might navigate the post-9/11 Islamophobia that has shaped their generation. Al-Khatahtbeh spent much of her youth feeling uncomfortable being Muslim, and as a young girl, self-consciousness prompted her to deny her identity to peers. For millennial Muslims like herself, she states, Islamophobia is the "spiritual jihad of our generation."[45] Their formative years were defined by hatred: "The development of who we are took place under a complete assault on our identities, especially for Muslim girls. Entire wars have been built on our backs, both physically and ideologically."[46] By singling out the experiences of Muslim girls, Al-Khatahtbeh's khutbah highlighted the gendered nature of Islamophobia and how women are especially vulnerable to anti-Muslim violence, particularly if they wear the hijab.

Al-Khatahtbeh's khutbah alludes to the contradictory roles that Muslim women play in Islamophobic discourses. On the one hand, their visibility as Muslims through modest forms of dress renders them as oppressed, and in this way, their bodies serve as political pawns to justify wars abroad based on Islamophobic rhetoric that they need to be liberated. On the other hand, this same visibility also renders them targets of anti-Muslim violence. Juliane Hammer summarizes the dissonant attitudes toward American Muslim women in her analysis of gendered Islamophobia:

> As objects of hate crimes and discrimination, Muslim women have Islamophobia mapped onto them directly and as representations of Muslims in American society; as objects of anti-Islamic discourse Muslim women are represented as victims of their religion, culture, and Muslim men, and thus in need of saving, liberation, and intervention.[47]

Hammer juxtaposes tropes of the oppressed Muslim woman that pervade mainstream American society, in both neoconservative and liberal circles alike, with the wholesale rejection of these same oppressed Muslim women as alien and un-American. Other scholars have analyzed in more detail the hypocrisy of white feminists who support US military interventions abroad in the name of saving Muslim women, despite the fact that these interventions further harm rather than liberate them.[48] Scholarship that addresses the intersections of white feminism, US military interests abroad, gendered violence, and debates over Muslim national belonging show how American Muslim women occupy a precarious position within broader discourses of Islamophobia. As we have seen, Muslim women, especially those who are visibly marked as other through hijab and/or modest clothing, bear the brunt of Islamophobic hate. They are also put under added pressure to remain silent about violence against them perpetrated by Muslim men based on the fact that they might further fuel Islamophobia. This fraught position partially informed Al-Khatahtbeh's motivation for starting Muslim Girl when she was seventeen. She wanted to create a space where Muslim girls could be allowed to "simply exist."

Muslim Girl achieved widespread success; it gained an impressive readership and has been featured across mainstream media outlets like *Teen Vogue* and the *Guardian*. Additionally, Al-Khatahtbeh was included in *Forbes*'s 30 Under 30 in Media in 2016 and named one of CNN's twenty-five most influential American Muslims of 2018. Muslim Girl ultimately served as an outlet for its readers to thrive and strengthen their identities as young Muslim women. Al-Khatahtbeh exposed how the prevailing context of anti-Muslim sentiment, particularly in its gendered form, has adversely affected young Muslim women.

While Al-Khatahtbeh has successfully built a brand based on elevating Muslim women's voices, some former staff members at Muslim Girl have reported a toxic and exploitative work culture, where their work was not always credited or fairly compensated.[49] Given how the broader US culture of anti-Muslim sentiment inspired Muslim Girl's inception, one possible way to read the allegations about its abusive work culture is an internalization of Islamophobia that facilitates devaluing Muslim women's work. Alternatively, one can view Muslim Girl as a thoroughly American brand that emerged in a corporate culture where the exploitation of female labor is the norm. Indeed, Muslim Girl is a part of a larger trend in the tech industry, where companies that brand themselves as feminist replicate the very same patterns of inequality and abuse that they aspire to correct.[50]

Nevertheless, Al-Khatahtbeh's khutbah, like Billoo's and Hasan's, sheds light on how Islamophobia informs American Muslims' conceptions of their own identities. It encourages WMA congregants to stand up for themselves against anti-Muslim discrimination and "reclaim their narratives" in the media. Focusing on how Muslim women in particular are targeted by Islamophobia, Al-Khatahtbeh states in her khutbah that they need to prioritize taking care of themselves physically, mentally, and spiritually to be able to counter the discrimination they face. Her khutbah, like the others discussed in this chapter, demonstrates how the broader context of American Muslims' marginalization as social and political others drives them toward social justice causes, countering their own and others' intersecting oppressions.

Reading Islam as Social Justice

We sit here today in the City of Angels in the historic Pico Union Project miles from South LA where the city burned years ago because of police brutality and institutional racism against our Black brothers and sisters, which still runs deep. This is the city where immigrants seek gainful work for a better life while finding themselves struggling every day, a city where housing is not affordable, where race tensions are high, where water is scarce, where environmental segregation negatively impacts poor communities of color the most . . . this is the reality in a city that gets known for Hollywood films, luxury, and sunshine. This is the other Los Angeles, and I'm here today to talk to you about the *amana*, or covenant God bestowed on human kind, and the choice we have to take it on.[51]
—Sarah Jawaid, from her March 2015 khutbah, "Being a Steward of God's People and Planet"

Many congregants routinely identified the WMA as the first or only mosque they had seen address social justice issues, which contributed to its appeal for them. Yet Muslim preachers across the globe have often used Islamic scriptures to promote social justice causes. The particulars of their message, however, are always context-specific. For example, in Egypt, khateebs might draw on Islamic sources to address alleviating poverty and concerns such as the rising cost of bread. Similarly, Sarah Jawaid's khutbah, redolent of Martin Luther King Jr.'s 1967 speech on poverty and inequality "The Other America," in its reference to "the other Los Angeles," highlighted local social justice concerns. These concerns included police brutality against African Americans, the economic hardships of working-class immigrant communities, affordable housing, drought, and environmental degradation. I read congregants' claims to the WMA's "first-ness" as testimony that they feel their interests and values as American Muslims are represented at the WMA as opposed to their other American mosques. Moreover, khateebahs' regular references to structural racism, police brutality, and mass incarceration, which disproportionately affect Black Americans, indicate that the WMA cultivates a contextually specific American Islam.

In constructing an American Islam, khateebahs integrate new concepts—for example, social and environmental justice and anti-Black racism—into the conceptual universe of the Qur'an and the Prophetic tradition. WMA khateebahs are not unique in this interpretive move. For example, Islamic studies scholar Omid Safi describes progressive Muslims as engaging with scriptures while working toward social justice, gender equality, and pluralism.[52] These values align with the broader agenda of Muslim feminist scholars. Safi suggests that the imperative for social justice has always been "at the heart of Islamic social ethics" through the textual tradition.[53] Jawaid's khutbah, which focuses on the concept of *khilafa* (stewardship), conforms to Safi's imperative to use scriptural teachings to deal with "the here and now" rather than the distant future.

In her introductory remarks, Jawaid urges Muslims to take on the responsibility of stewardship: "I'm going to talk about social and environmental justice, which is how I am framing being a steward of the earth. To me, being a steward means owning your story, owning your impact on the earth, owning your power as a trustee of God's covenant. There is no one else coming; we are it."[54] Jawaid grounds her claims in the Qur'an, citing surah 33, verse 72, which in its entirety reads: "We offered the Trust to the heavens, the earth, and the mountains, yet they refused to undertake it and were afraid of it: mankind undertook it—they have always been very inept and rash."[55] As Jawaid explains, the Trust represents a covenant with God for human beings to do good to each other and to the earth. Given that Jawaid is a community organizer at a faith-based nonprofit and was previously the director of Green Muslims, an organization that promotes environmentalist causes from an Islamic perspective, her authority at the WMA derives from her environmental-activist profile.[56] Furthermore, she incorporates her professional commitments to environmental and social justice into her interpretation of this Qur'anic verse, thereby exercising authority through her activism.

In keeping with the WMA's emphasis on textual authority, Jawaid grounds her arguments for environmental and racial justice in scripture. She states that, in the Qur'an, God commands believers to reflect on the signs of nature, and highlights that many chapters of the Qur'an make explicit the correlation between nature and scripture. For her, this means that Muslims should protect the environment and reduce waste by conserving water during *wudu* (ritual ablution) and avoid using Styrofoam in mosques. Furthermore, Jawaid invokes the Sunnah to argue that Muslims should oppose injustice and help the vulnerable by working to dismantle mass incarceration. She argues that, if the Prophet Muhammad were alive today, he would work with the disadvantaged to protect the vulnerable. Additionally, in calling for the end of rampant police brutality and institutional racism against Black Americans, she references the Qur'anic narrative of Moses asking God to enable him to overcome his speech impediment in approaching Pharaoh, using it to argue that all Muslims should stand up against injustice.[57]

By framing Islamic scriptures as a means to address modern injustices like institutional racism, police brutality, lack of affordable housing, and environmental degradation, Jawaid makes a case for the relevance of the Qur'an and Sunnah in the local American context. Specifically, she uses Islamic teachings to articulate a moral critique of US policy, and further argues that American Muslims are obligated to address injustice. She emphasizes injustices that affect Americans across racial and ethnic identities, and calls on Muslims to unite as they strive to overcome them.

Jawaid's move toward Muslim unity is continuous with a longer historical trend in which American Muslims began to look to their religion rather than ethnic background to define their identities. During the Cold War era, American Muslims were united across ethnic and racial difference by their shared distress over US foreign policy, for example with respect to US support for Israel and Saudi Arabia and interventions in Iran and Vietnam.[58] Curtis argues that shared concerns over US exertions of power abroad unified American Muslims across their diverse religious forms.[59] Likewise, stating that the Prophet Muhammad himself would be striving to end mass incarceration, Jawaid identified social injustices in LA and the US as issues that *all* American Muslims should be concerned about in solidarity with Black Americans and other marginalized groups.

Building Solidarity: Toward a Collective American Muslim Consciousness

The first step is asking ourselves how does racism exist within us? . . . Our Muslim communities incorporate the same racial hierarchy that the rest of America does. A common criticism of an immigrant Pakistani or South Asian mosque is that they're not in solidarity with their African American brothers and sisters in Islam. If we're supposed to be living examples of the Prophet's message then we have to address this question. How will we deal with the racial hierarchy that exists inside our own communities?

—Sarah Jawaid, more from her March 2015 khutbah, "Being a Steward of God's People and Planet"

Jawaid's khutbah attends to local social justice concerns, bringing to the fore the idea of a "shared Muslim American consciousness" of Black and immigrant Muslims in the US. The emergence of a shared "Muslim American consciousness," as Curtis describes it, after World War II stands in contrast with trends in the first half of the twentieth century in which American Muslims typically emphasized their ethnic identities to argue for their recognition as citizens. This approach stemmed from exclusionary immigration and citizenship laws that restricted emigration from non-European countries and limited citizenship to white immigrants. Scholar of Islam in America Kambiz GhaneaBassiri notes how both Muslim and non-Muslim immigrant groups in the US in the first half of the twentieth century had to contend with the hegemonic "matrix of whiteness, Christianity, and progress that had come to constitute America's national identity."[60] Since citizenship was tied to whiteness (and by extension, Christianity) during the early twentieth century, Muslim immigrants focused on their ethnic and racial rather than their religious identities to make a case for their naturalization before the courts. Immigrants' (Muslim or otherwise) appeal to legal whiteness demonstrates how the requirements of US citizenship have historically pitted American immigrant communities against African American communities and one another. While the 1965 Immigration and Nationality Act significantly diversified the American demographic, normative American identity continues to be bound up in notions of whiteness and Christianity, and necessarily excludes Black Americans.

The impact of white supremacy in part accounts for contemporary divides between the Black and immigrant American Muslim communities that Jamillah Karim analyzes in her 2009 study of Muslim women in Chicago and Atlanta. Karim shows how Black and immigrant American Muslims have mutually conflicting relationships with whiteness, and that immigrant Muslims actually benefit from anti-Black racism. Immigrant Muslim communities in the US are focused on cultivating transnational ties with Muslims abroad rather than forging meaningful connections with African American Muslims in their own communities. Karim finds that her South Asian Muslim informants did not identify the socioeconomic struggles of their African American Muslim neighbors as a "Muslim cause," tending instead to focus on social justice concerns overseas in places like Palestine or Kashmir.[61] In Jawaid's khutbah, she laments the lack of solidarity from immigrant Muslims. The immigrant Muslim focus on social justice causes abroad is not only born from anti-Black racism in the US, but is also rooted in questions about Islamic authenticity. Zareena Grewal describes how, throughout the last few decades of the twentieth century, immigrant Muslims' cultivation of a counter-citizenship culture that committed to the idea of a global ummah "became a dominant mode of Islamic authentication."[62] As Muslim immigrants continued to arrive in the US throughout the late twentieth century, there was an increase in "the nostalgic sense of attachment to immigrants' countries of origins and the exaggerated political importance of the Middle East."[63] As a result, US mosques shifted from focusing on local concerns to "global political events in the Muslim third world."[64] Grewal marks 9/11 as a turning point when immigrant Muslim leaders began to lay claim to their identities as Americans. Nevertheless, her observations about the importance of transnational connections for immigrant Muslims may in part account for WMA congregants' critiques of the "irrelevance" of khutbahs at mainstream US mosques.

Jawaid also calls for immigrant Muslim communities to hold themselves accountable for how they replicate the racial hierarchies that devalue Black Muslims within their own communities. These racial hierarchies within Muslim communities are apparent in how, as wadud shows, African American Muslims are excluded from religious leadership roles in the United States. wadud argues that the marginalization of Black Muslims in America is intertwined with matters of class and financial resources, as immigrant Muslims in general are more affluent than African American Muslims. She also argues that there is an interpersonal arrogance and condescension that plays out in relationships between Black and immigrant

Muslims who are part of the same communities, wherein the latter often assume the role of teachers.[65] These are the trends to which Jawaid alludes in her khutbah when she criticizes how many Muslim communities perpetuate immigrant hegemony, wherein Black Muslims and their religious practices are infantilized and devalued as South Asian and Arab cultures are elevated as more authentically Islamic.

The history of Islam in the US is a complex web of encountering, intermixing, and negotiating religious and racial differences.[66] The histories of Black and immigrant American Muslims have always been connected but are not parallel. During the late nineteenth century, Bengali shipmen from British India migrated to New Orleans and New York City and integrated into Black and Latino working-class communities through marriage.[67] Though many of their Black and Puerto Rican wives converted to Islam and retained and passed down their Islamic practices to their children, the Bengali shipmen were legally categorized as "Negro" by the US state, thereby muting their Muslim identities. In the twentieth century, the NOI appropriated Islam as a religion that would help America's Black citizens restore their racial integrity.[68] At the same time, in critiques of Western imperialism, Islamic revivalists like the Pakistani Abul A'la Mawdudi "found common cause with many Muslim Black nationalists."[69] By the last few decades of the twentieth century, Black and immigrant American Muslim interests were not always aligned or uniformly opposed but consistently bound up in questions of race, American identity, and Islamic authenticity. The next section turns to how WMA khateebahs engage the question of Islamic authenticity by emphasizing how their commitments to social justice stem from their readings of sacred scripture, as opposed to externally held values.

Racial and Gender Equality in the Qur'an

I am a peacemaker and I am an activist because of my tradition, not in spite of it. I didn't come to this place because I moved away from my tradition; I came to this place of love, of restorative love, because of my tradition, and the love of the Qur'an and the love of the Sunnah.[70]
—Najeeba Syeed, from her October 2015 khutbah, "Restorative Social Justice and Radical Love"

Just as Jawaid refers to the Prophetic Sunnah and particular Qur'anic verses to support social justice causes, Najeeba Syeed's khutbah, excerpted above, does the same. Like others, Syeed credits her Muslim faith for her commitment to social justice activism. Using Qur'anic verses while also referring to specific hadith and the Prophetic Sunnah, khateebahs frame contemporary American social issues such as racism, environmental justice, and the representation of Muslims in US governance. Syeed for example, contends that Muslims have a moral imperative to stand up for those in their own communities and those outside of it, grounding her argument in the Islamic tradition. She references both contemporary and historical Muslim scholars like William Chittick (b. 1943), Ibn Arabi (d. 1240), al-Ghazali (d. 1111), and al-Shatibi (d. 1388) to support her broader arguments about what Muslims can contribute to achieving social justice.[71] Like other khateebahs, Syeed also draws attention to anti-Black racism and uses scriptural references to argue for the importance of the Black Lives Matter movement.

Khateebahs' attention to racial injustice sets the WMA apart from other US mosques since, as wadud describes, issues of race and class seldom receive attention even in progressive feminist Muslim discourse.[72] Many WMA khutbahs go against this trend and demonstrate the WMA's heightened sensitivity to issues of racism toward African American Muslims within their religious communities and the broader American context. These values are based upon readings of Qur'anic verses that incorporate particular ideas about social justice. For example, in her khutbah, Jawaid calls upon WMA members to examine their own biases and reflect on how everyone internalizes racial and gender hierarchies. She invokes the example of Hagar to argue for the elevated status that God granted a woman of color, and notes the central importance of Hagar's experience for all Muslim pilgrims on the Hajj. As WMA khateebahs tackle the issue of intra-Muslim racism and acknowledge Muslim complicity with the larger structures of oppression and white supremacy in US culture, they take up wadud's challenge to work toward a more inclusive collective space for American Muslims.

As we have seen throughout this book, wadud's scholarship and activism resonates with a number of WMA's khutbahs, whether she is explicitly cited or not. Jawaid's khutbah is no exception to this broader trend in the way that she also deploys the Qur'an to argue for social and racial justice. On the subject of racial and ethnic difference, wadud argues that the Qur'an "supports and acknowledges difference between peoples but does not use those differences as a standard of judgment for human worth."[73] As evidence of this claim, she cites three verses from Qur'an 49:11–13:

> Oh you have attained to faith! No men shall deride (other men) . . . and no women [shall deride other] women: it may well be that those [whom they deride] are better than themselves. Be conscious of God. Oh human-kind! Behold, We have created you all from one male and one female, and have made you into nations and tribes, so that you might come to know one another. Verily the most noble of you in the sight of God is the one who is most deeply conscious of God.[74]

wadud's understanding of these verses reflects her conviction that the Qur'an here endorses "ethnic parity."[75] To her, these verses champion an egalitarian society whose merits are based on God-consciousness, or *taqwa*, rather than gender, class, or race.[76] In wadud's view, then, the Qur'an has an essentially egalitarian nature, and attitudes of racism and sexism are therefore antithetical to Islam. Notably, Jawaid uses this same Qur'anic verse, 49:13, to challenge her audience to engage with other Muslims across cultures, and in particular to cultivate solidarity with African American Muslims.

Scholars throughout Islamic history have interpreted this surah quite differently. The institution of slavery, which is antithetical to contemporary understandings of social justice and egalitarianism, was very much a social reality in the seventh-century Arabian context in which these verses were revealed. And as recently as the twentieth century, the Egyptian Shaykh Muhammad al-Ghazali (d. 1996) saw these verses as specifically referring not to racism or classism, but to the sins of slander and backbiting and the importance of sincere faith-based *taqwa*.[77] By reading her particular ideas of gender, racial, and social parity as morally exemplary values into the Qur'an, Jawaid exercises her religious authority by then introducing and legitimizing this scriptural reading at the WMA.[78]

Jawaid's engagements with the Qur'an are of course historically situated in her US context, and I do not read her as claiming to reveal essential truths about the "true" meaning of the Qur'an. Deep-seated concerns about racial inequalities, universal human rights, and environmental waste are the product of a contemporary US moment, rather than based on the Qur'an itself. Jawaid has framed her Qur'anic interpretations with her professional and personal values by, for example, acknowledging in her khutbah that her interpretations of specific Qur'anic verses are informed by her work as a community organizer and anti-racism activist. While she presented racial and economic equality as moral imperatives, she never explicitly categorizes them as the only valid interpretations of the text. In fact, throughout her khutbah, Jawaid qualified many of her Qur'anic interpretations with the phrase "to me," adding "this is the Sunnah as I understand it" after invoking the example of the Prophet to advocate for anti-racist legal initiatives.[79] Jawaid's alluding to the essential nature of egalitarianism in the Qur'an can be read as a rhetorical strategy. She appropriated verses of the Qur'an and applied them to the circumstances around her, demonstrating the fluidity of the text itself.[80]

Jawaid does not argue for the essential coherence of a Qur'anic worldview that adequately measures up against contemporary standards of gender and racial equity. Instead, her rhetoric emphasizes her particular relationship to the Qur'an. This interpretative strategy is similar to that of wadud, who claims that individuals can arrive at an authoritative reading based on their own circumstances, irrespective of communal consensus (*ijma*).[81] In this vein, Jawaid enjoined her audience to act as stewards of the earth per the Qur'anic injunction, on the basis of their own individual circumstances and motivations.[82] Jawaid's khutbah thus challenges patriarchal notions of interpretive authority by not only claiming authority for herself, but also by conferring it upon the members of the WMA congregation. By authorizing congregants to take on social justice work both as individuals and as a community, the WMA acts as a venue for collective anti-racist work. This stance was exemplified in the 2016 discussion series on Black Lives Matter.

Black Lives Matter: A WMA Discussion Series

I heard the Messenger of Allah say, "Whosoever of you sees an evil, let him change it with his hand; and if he is not able to do so, then [let him change it] with his tongue; and if he is

not able to do so, then with his heart—and that is the weak-
est of faith."[83]
—from al-Nawawi's 40 Hadith, cited at the WMA's 2016
BLM Discussion Session 1

In the months of July, August, and September 2016, the WMA hosted
a three-part discussion series on Black Lives Matter (BLM) during the
regularly scheduled reflection circles after Jummah.[84] The first two were
co-facilitated by two Black Muslim women—Kameelah Wilkerson, one
of the WMA's past khateebahs, and Desha Dauchan, a member of the
BLM movement—while the last was led by mosque founder Maznavi.
Wilkerson and Dauchan approached the sessions using the above hadith tradition about condemning evil with the hand, tongue, and heart.[85]
They began a discussion with WMA congregants about hating injustice
in one's heart, then moving forward to speaking out against injustice,
until lastly taking action to address it.[86] Using this hadith to promote
racial justice in the US is continuous with broader trends in African
American Muslim communities that have historically engaged Islamic
teachings to resist racism. Through these and other structured conversations, the WMA attempts to challenge the anti-Black racism of many
American Muslim communities. As we have seen, the intersections of
anti-Black and anti-Muslim racism enable WMA congregants to cultivate a shared American Muslim social consciousness among Black
and non-Black Muslims. However, these same intersections also pose
specific challenges to the WMA's institutional attempts to address anti-
Black racism, and congregants come away with varied experiences of
these engagements.

Participants expressed mixed feelings about the efficacy of these 2016
discussions, in part because they approached them with differing expectations. Race, age, and political commitments informed WMA attendees' reflections on the series. Some felt that the discussions did not have
the depth that they would have liked, while others expressed satisfaction
with the series. On the other end of the spectrum, one of my interlocutors (white and in her seventies) explicitly stated her disapproval of BLM
as a whole, despite agreeing with the motivations driving the movement.
It is worth highlighting that I did not prompt each of the women in
this study to reflect on these sessions, but rather only asked those who

brought up the BLM sessions organically during our conversations. Despite clear differences in personal reflections on the series, there was general agreement that the sessions were valuable, even among women whose individual expectations were not met.

My interlocutors generally fell into three categories: those who felt the BLM series was well intentioned but unproductive, those who were disappointed and underwhelmed, and those who were proud and mostly satisfied. These different reactions were not neatly divided across racial identity or age, and therefore provide a window into the nonlinear and sometimes inconsistent visions of interracial solidarity throughout the WMA. Women in the first category believed that the BLM discussion series was a good idea for the WMA, but that it was perhaps premature for the congregation. For example, Zahara, African American and in her sixties, felt that many of her fellow congregants lacked the knowledge of African American history required to understand the BLM movement, much less learn how to be allies. Reflecting on the BLM sessions, she stated:

> The truth of the matter is so many of the people who were there truly did not have a background in the history of African Americans in this country. So it's not even a matter of them not caring; you're just asking them to understand more than they can understand. . . . The bottom line [is] you got to bring information first. You can't say to somebody, "I need you to understand the framework of this problem. I need you to commit to helping with this," et cetera, et cetera. They don't even know what the problem is. . . . The young women [among WMA congregants] did not know that there had been a commissioned study to actually move all the Africans from this country. You can't have a discussion with somebody about something they don't know anything about.[87]

While Zahara believed the BLM movement was an important topic to discuss at the WMA and in mosques more generally, she felt that the series was likely lost on most congregants. She summed up the attitude of some in the congregation as, "Their thing was like, 'Why are these Black people complaining about this culture? They just aren't trying.' They simply don't know the history."[88] Zahara spoke in a matter-of-fact tone with no hints of frustration as she described how some of her fellow WMA congregants had no prior knowledge of institutional anti-Black racism in the US, despite most of them having been born and raised there. Her evenness and patience likely comes with the experience of being Black in America for over six decades and being a part of different kinds of Muslim communities with all sorts of attitudes toward racism in the US. Rather than faulting individual congregants for their ignorance of US history and African Americans' place within it, Zahara attributed these congregants' attitudes to the racism embedded within the structure of American society. Specifically, she explained that erasure of Black history is part and parcel of the US education system, which is designed to promote and circulate white supremacy.[89] Indeed, in the years since Zahara shared these reflections with me, the role of schools in upholding the status quo of white supremacy has become a subject of heated political debate in the US. By July 2021, twenty-six states had already introduced legislation that would ban (or limit) teachers from discussing critical race theory and racism.[90] As far as Zahara's reflection on the WMA's Black Lives Matter discussion series, she connected WMA congregants' lack of ability to fully engage with the issues presented to structural racism.

As one of its most regular congregants, Zahara was deeply enthusiastic about and invested in the WMA as an institution, and appreciated that Maznavi and her team worked actively toward creating a "truly multicultural" space.[91] Her remarks were not a personal criticism of the WMA or its individual members, but rather a reflection of the structural barriers to forging meaningful interracial understanding even within the confines of a well-intentioned community. For Zahara, young non-Black Muslims needed basic education in African American history, from slavery through the civil rights era to the contemporary realities of Black experiences in the US, including but not limited to barriers to acquiring housing, access to better neighborhoods, and employment. Such education had to happen before a meaningful dialogue about race, and the movement for Black lives, could occur at the WMA.

Rana, a South Asian American in her early thirties, also felt that many WMA congregants lacked a nuanced understanding of African American history, but expected the BLM series to fill in these gaps. She represents the second category of those who were disappointed by the series as a whole. Describing the series as a "super-rudimentary discussion about race," Rana felt underwhelmed:

I would have liked to have a slightly more well thought-out actual in-
structional lesson on race and just the history of Black people in America.
I think a lot of people just don't know a lot of those nuances of . . . the
history of racism in this country. I think a lot of people hold the view, "oh
there was slavery, and then there was the civil rights movement, and then
it was done." They don't know about redlining and the housing policies,
mass incarceration, all the other things that happened that were codified
into law that held Black people back. So I wish we had gotten into more of
that stuff, like structural racism, and we didn't. It was very rudimentary.
So maybe for other people, that was a good place for them but . . . I don't
think they connected to real action.[92]

Rana was particularly critical of the final BLM discussion, where congregants were broken up into affinity circles of small groups of people
who shared their racial and ethnic identities. In Rana's estimation, this
ensured that a more nuanced discussion of race, with tangible advice for
congregants to implement into action, would be impossible. At the same
time, however, Rana went on to praise the WMA's leaders for hosting the
series in the first place. "Just putting it into context—how many other
mosques are having a BLM discussion series after their service?" she
asked. "It's great that they even did that. So I think that's the caveat—it's
great they did it, but it wasn't perfect."[93]

Other members of the congregation, especially those in their twenties
and thirties from immigrant backgrounds, like Rana, highlighted how
the WMA had set itself apart from other mosques by hosting a series on
BLM. This demonstrates the symbolic importance to young immigrant
American Muslims of the WMA openly discussing anti-Black racism.
Such direct engagement with anti-Black racism bolstered the WMA's
authority in their eyes, giving them the sense that the mosque aligned
with their progressive values. For example, Leila, an Arab American
in her early thirties, was drawn to the WMA's "visceral engagement"
with diversity and its acknowledgement that systems of oppression affect Black people differently than immigrant Muslims.[94] Rana and Leila,
young second-generation immigrant Muslims, felt that the BLM series
was a step in the right direction, particularly in attempting to address
the intra-Muslim racism and immigrant hegemony that typically characterize South Asian– and Arab-led congregations.

These women's assessments contrast with that of Ibtihal, an African American in her late thirties, who spoke to me of the frustrating experience of navigating the WMA as a Black Muslim. On the BLM series, she reflected:

> I felt like it was lip service to the conversation of BLM, but it wasn't really a conversation around BLM. It was just cluelessness, quite honestly. I feel like it was a sincere attempt . . . I just felt they were kind of clueless about things, you know? I say that with all due respect, but that's [my] experience of people who attempt to be allies.[95]

Ibtihal's comments indicate that there is a lot more work to be done in creating a worship space that can foster meaningful dialogue about the intersections of race, religion, and gender. When I asked Ibtihal to speak generally on whether she saw the WMA as a place where people were conscious of racial injustice, she responded that it was not a matter of people being unconscious or conscious of race. She felt that some at the WMA believed that all people of color, whether Black, Arab, or South Asian, had their own equal racial burdens to bear. This attitude frustrated her because she felt it precluded non-Black congregants from understanding the distinct African American experience. To her, such acknowledgement was required for a more substantial discussion on BLM.[96] That some congregants, according to Ibtihal, failed to differentiate between the struggles that non-Black people of color and Black Americans face highlights the broader challenges of interracial solidarity building. This dynamic can work to mask anti-Blackness in non-Black communities of color, or otherwise sideline and erase Black voices. Even in spaces committed to cultivating interracial solidarity, overcoming anti-Black attitudes and learning how to be an ally poses challenges for even those individuals eager to be in solidarity.

On the other end of the spectrum, the third category of response to the BLM series included those who had no criticisms to share. Sabrina, a South Asian American in her mid-thirties, expressed only positive remarks when thinking about the sessions, focusing on how remarkable it was that the WMA hosted such an event.[97] And Kenyatta, a Black attendee in her mid-forties and an activist in her own right, recalls the

BLM sessions with fondness while describing her personal journey of becoming a recent member of the movement herself.[98]

Maznavi facilitated the final BLM session with the affinity circles, and her own assessment of the series reflected a combination of congregants' different attitudes. Like others, Maznavi attested to the rudimentary nature of the 2016 sessions, but characterized elementary conversations about race as particularly valuable for non-Black Muslims. One of her motivations for hosting a BLM discussion series at the WMA was to help non-Black congregants develop an increased awareness of their "blind spots" regarding racial prejudice, so that they could learn how to "step up" and support "their fellow Black Muslims."[99] Pursuant to this goal, her affinity circle exercise (that Rana above was critical of) was designed to put congregants at ease and encourage them to express themselves openly within their own racial and ethnic groups without fear of judgment from others.

Overall, Maznavi was pleased with the affinity circle exercise because it pushed white congregants to think of themselves as racialized and elicited some discomfort from them. She explained,

> I thought it was extremely successful because the white group—so many of them were like, "Oh, we have to do this?" They were so uncomfortable, and afterwards a couple of them were cringing and coming up to me and really like, "Oh, I really didn't like that. I felt so uncomfortable." One of them literally said, "It's the first time I've had to feel like I'm a different race." I was like, "Oh, so you had no idea you were a different race so you just thought you were the norm." . . . I'm so glad that we did that because it was the first time that they thought of themselves as separate in the way that the rest of us [people of color] have [seen ourselves].[100]

Maznavi's aim for the BLM series, much like her approach to the WMA's goals more broadly, was to "meet people where they are" and facilitate a basic conversation.[101] She describes feeling satisfied with how the affinity group exercise pushed white congregants out of their comfort zone to think about what it means to identify as a racial group, as opposed to assuming that only people of color have a racialized identity. I did not ask any of my white interlocutors about their responses to the affinity circle exercise, though I expect they may not have been as forthcoming with me about their discomfort as they were with Maznavi, whom they knew well. I also did not share their white identity nor did I have the shared experiences of being there with them for any of the BLM sessions. Likewise, it is conceivable that Black congregants like Zahara and Ibtihal may have tempered their critiques of the BLM series since it was most likely the case that women who shared my South Asian identity or were otherwise non-Black were the ones unaware of Black history and of the differences between how Black Americans and non-Black people of color experience racism. Still, congregants' comments and critiques provide us with a snapshot of the spectrum of congregant reactions to the series.

Congregants' opposing perspectives on the discussion series cohered into a single narrative that ultimately demonstrated similar characterizations of the WMA community as a whole. For example, while Rana was critical of the affinity circle exercise, she conceded that, as Maznavi suggested, for some people it might have provided a much-needed rudimentary discussion on race. Likewise, Zahara and Ibtihal were respectively neutral and frustrated about the series, but both suggested that the majority of the non-Black congregants at the WMA were ill-suited at the time to be proper allies to Black Muslims and Black Americans more broadly.

The differences in WMA members' reactions to the BLM series reflect their contrasting attitudes toward the objectives of the sessions. The wide range of reactions also reflects the spectrum of congregants' individual understandings of what it means to have a racialized religious identity. For some folks, acknowledging their own non-Black racial identities as also constructed and embedded within hierarchical patterns of power and privilege was an important step toward understanding the experiences of Black Muslims and non-Muslims in the US. For others who were ready to explore tangible measures they and others could take to combat racial injustice at the structural and personal levels, the WMA's BLM series left much to be desired. There were also those who may have desired for themselves a more nuanced and sophisticated conversation around BLM, but did not feel confident that the majority of the congregation had the tools to engage at that higher level.

Since the WMA is a multiracial congregation, addressing anti-Black racism and Islamophobia as anti-Muslim racism together as a community generates multiple narratives and experiences among congregants. Anti-Muslim racism, which affects all American Muslims in distinct ways, is built on the broader institutional culture of anti-Black racism in the US. The broader American context therefore also informs how American Muslims appropriate anti-Black racism into their own communities. Moreover, the WMA's effort to address anti-Black racism can be seen as a part of a deeper legacy of Islam as a religion of protest against racial oppression in the US. In the contemporary context of the BLM movement, anthropologist Donna Auston has shown that its Muslim women participants view their anti-racist activism as a part of their religious obligations.[102]

Congregants' reflections on the BLM discussion series at the WMA demonstrate how American Muslims, both Black and non-Black, contend with the linkages between anti-Muslim and anti-Black racism. As a multiracial space, the WMA provides a way for Black and immigrant Muslims to construct a shared American consciousness based on social justice. Drawing from their justice-oriented interpretations of the Qur'an, WMA members fit into a broader historical trend of Black and immigrant American Muslims turning to religion as a way to address moral injustice. While some aspects are challenging, such as creating meaningful dialogue about anti-Black racism across multiple racial and ethnic identities, the WMA seeks to cultivate a socially and politically conscious congregation in addition to providing prayer services. Participating in events like the BLM discussion series, in turn, further crystallizes these congregants' sense of their own authority in and outside of the mosque, since they are having discussions of social justice in the wider context of the US as Muslim women.

Cultivating Sociopolitical Values at the Mosque

The truth is that this country was built on the brutal land grab and near genocide of the Native Americans and on the vicious African slave system that made the United States the richest country in the world. The common reference to all of us as immigrants seeking the American dream or a better life in the United States is patently untrue. It ignores history, excludes and marginalizes the original people of this land,

and attempts to ignore four hundred years of chattel slavery
of Africans, followed by a vicious racist system that Americans must battle to this very day.[103]
—Hajjah Abrafi Sanyika, from her October 2019 khutbah, "Balancing Religion and Culture—from an African-
American Muslim"

The WMA's khutbahs on Islamophobia and social justice, and its 2016
BLM sessions, demonstrate how for its congregants it is more than an
alternative worship space where women gather for prayer. It is also a
discursive space where its members reflect together on contemporary
American social issues. The WMA provides an outlet for American
Muslim women to cultivate not just Islamic literacy through knowledge
of the Qur'an but also particular sociopolitical values through a variety
of means, including khutbahs like Sanyika's above that provide counterhegemonic narratives of history. These counterhegemonic narratives
engage with the reality of the US as a settler colonial state rather than
accepting at face value its euphemistic designation as a "nation of immigrants." Such views are absent not only from mainstream US mosque
culture but also the nation's public education system more broadly,
making Sanyika's khutbah and others like it at the WMA all the more
notable.

One way to understand how the social and political dimensions of
the WMA fit into American religious history is through the example of
the Black church and women's roles within it. Historian Evelyn Brooks
Higginbotham argues that, during the period between 1880 and 1920,
the Black church functioned as "a discursive, critical arena—a public
sphere in which values and issues were aired, debated, and disseminated
throughout the larger black community."[104] In her analysis of the National Baptist Convention, one of the largest Protestant denominations
of Black Americans, she contends that Black women were integral to the
discursive arena of the church; they actively contested racism and advocated for voting rights, desegregation, equal employment, and education
opportunities in the US.[105]

Higginbotham's example of the political activism of the Black church
in the late nineteenth century has a parallel in American Islam, albeit
a bit later. Curtis notes that, by the mid-twentieth century, American

mosques began to resemble churches and synagogues in their organizational structure but also in the fact that they became "more than a place for prayer," as the site of community and the discussion of politics.[106] The legacy of the Black church and its role in developing a national consciousness among Black Americans, alongside the evolution of American religious congregations as sociopolitical spaces of community, provides a template to think about the WMA project as a whole. It is a mosque that is committed to not only providing worship services for women but also fostering political and social activism. Khateebahs attempt to generate collective American Muslim interest in particular social justice concerns like anti-Black racism in American society, including within its Muslim communities.

Sanyika's 2019 khutbah educates congregants on the history of the US and the legacies of African slavery. It is particularly salient within the political context of 2020 and efforts by then President Trump and Senator Tom Cotton of Arkansas to ban schools from teaching the 1619 Project, a Pulitzer Prize–winning *New York Times* initiative by Nikole Hannah-Jones that sheds lights on the centrality of slavery and anti-Black racism in US history. In September 2020, Trump announced a commission to promote a "patriotic education" curriculum that would further downplay slavery and its enduring legacy, and designate critical race theory as "left-wing indoctrination" in an effort to instill "pro-American" attitudes in students.[107]

Yet Trump's preferred whitewashed version of US history had already been the norm prior to 2020. Sanyika's remarks excerpted above were part of her reflections on a khutbah she had heard at a local mosque where the imam, an immigrant from Turkey, had "encouraged the Muslim ummah, the community, to be loyal and grateful for our acceptance into the United States where he said we have come to pursue a better life." She recounted feeling "appalled" at this broad, generalized statement that applied only to immigrant Muslims: "It erases the experiences of many of us in the congregation. African Americans did not come here for a better life, nor did the Native Americans who were already here." Her sentiments are broadly reflective of the widespread erasure of African Americans and Natives in revisionist characterizations of all Americans as having immigrant origins, a narrative that works to conceal the nation's enduring systems of racial oppression. Moreover,

Sanyika's khutbah draws attention to the erasure of Black Muslims in US history, both the enslaved African Muslims forcibly brought to US soil through the transatlantic slave trade and early twentieth-century movements like the Moorish Science Temple and the NOI that were led by Black American Muslims.

Sanyika's khutbah offers a corrective to the inaccurate assumption that Islam in America is exclusively the domain of "immigrant" Islamic cultures. This idea is widely perpetuated by non-Black Muslims, whether inadvertently or as a part of a conscious effort to delegitimize expressions of Black Islam as inauthentic.[108] Black American Muslim scholars like wadud, Su'ad Abdul Khabeer, and Donna Auston refer to these tensions in their scholarship, addressing the deteriorating relationship dynamics between Black and immigrant American Muslims, and the "doubly liminal"[109] space that Black Muslims occupy in the US, where Black culture is valued over and at the expense of Black lives.[110]

Describing a very similar exchange to Sanyika's encounter with the Turkish American imam at a California mosque, wadud states that when she describes herself as "American by force," Muslim immigrants routinely reply, "'If you don't like it . . . then you should leave.'"[111] As wadud explains, "There is nothing in my statement that says what I like or dislike. . . . I will always be American because my options to be something else were taken away once my fore-mothers were raped by white owners and my blood line was further blended with other Black, native-American and white lines throughout my past."[112] The hostile reactions that wadud receives from immigrant Muslims reveal a fundamental misunderstanding about African Americans' place within US history. Sanyika's khutbah, with its explicit references to the enduring legacies of slavery and the roles of prominent Black Muslim leaders in US history from Noble Drew Ali of the Moorish Science Temple (MST) to Elijah and Clara Muhammad and the broader impact of the NOI on the trajectory of Islam in America, fills in some of these critical gaps of knowledge.

Moreover, Sanyika's khutbah addresses the tensions between immigrant and indigenous Black (and Latina and white) Muslims in the US while acknowledging the "false dichotomy" that these categories present, given that immigrant Muslims come from all over the world, including from Black African countries. She asserts that although American Mus-

AUTHORITY THROUGH ACTIVISM | 189

lim communities defy easy generalizations because of their diversity, it is critical that all Muslims understand the history of African Americans. Sanyika states plainly:

> I do not naively think that immigrant Muslims came here to involve themselves in the anti-racist struggles of African Americans. I'm sure most immigrants have their own struggles just trying to figure out their new culture or escaping religious or racial persecution in their own countries. However, coming to the United States to enjoy the incredible wealth created by African slavery while turning a blind eye to those very people who suffered to make this country so wealthy is insensitive at best and extremely hurtful to those who share that painful legacy.[113]

Further, Sanyika argues that regardless of whether someone was born in the states or immigrated, they must not only acknowledge the brutality of US history and combat anti-Black racism, but do so as Muslims. She states, "If you recognize anti-Black prejudices in your home, in your workplace, or anywhere within your culture or life please work hard to shed it within yourself and encourage others to do the same, because it is against the very spirit of Islam." This is another example of how WMA khateebahs not only put Islamic teachings in conversation with social justice activist causes but also actually understand Islam as rooted in anti-racism. Sankiya's khutbah demonstrates how WMA actors lean into activism as a basis for their Islamic authority because it is rooted in some of their very ideas of core Islamic teachings.

More specifically, Sanyika implores Muslims to get to know one another better, "as God tells us in the Qur'an," quoting from Qur'an 49:13.[114] Stating that Muslims are not a cultural monolith, she reaffirms that they should learn about each other and "admit to our personal prejudices and work to eliminate them. This is a mandate from our Creator and from our Prophet, peace and blessings be upon him."[115] Like other WMA khateebahs before her, Sanyika understands anti-Black racism and cross-cultural understandings as moral mandates from the Qur'an and the Prophetic example.[116]

Through khutbahs that address themes of social justice and Islamophobia, or anti-Black racism like Sanyika's, the WMA constructs itself as a platform for cultivating social and political values. In the years since the 2016 BLM series, some of the sources of dissatisfaction that congregants described then, such as observing that many non-Black congregants lacked adequate knowledge of American history, have been addressed in subsequent khutbahs. As power and authority flow between congregants, organizers, and khateebahs, there is a dialectical relationship among the various members of the WMA who collectively determine what issues and topics will be addressed in the monthly khut-bahs. In other words, since the WMA promotes lay Muslim women's authority, at any given time a congregant has the opportunity to suggest a khutbah topic or even serve as a khateebah and speak on a subject that she deems urgent. Within this model of Islamic authority, power shifts and flows among various actors, giving congregants who take issue with specific attitudes or trends recourse to correct and educate their community.

Beyond a khutbah like Sanyika's that directly calls on Muslims to ac-knowledge US history beyond revisionist narratives that erase the brutal legacy of slavery, other khutbahs educate the WMA community on race and Islamophobia. In the wake of the 2020 murder of Black American George Floyd in Minneapolis that set off protests against police brutality around the world, the WMA hosted a Facebook livestream Q&A ses-sion on Zoom that in part addressed how to support the movement for Black lives.[117] By enlisting khateebahs from different ethnic and racial backgrounds, the WMA exposes its congregation to a multiplicity of American Muslim experiences and authorizes all of them. By endowing lay Muslim women with authority and helping them together to cul-tivate particular religious, social, and political sensibilities, the WMA facilitates the larger ongoing process of creating a multiracial commu-nity based on knowledge and respect. This commitment to justice in turn helps the WMA: congregants generally felt that its attempt to en-gage structural racism through Islamic teachings bolstered its authority and relevance to US Muslim communities, even when it fell short of its stated goals. They also appreciated its interfaith outreach to Jewish and Christian women, a topic to which the next chapter turns.

5

The Politics of Community Building

Intrafaith Inclusivity and Interfaith Solidarity

It was just exciting to see this [the WMA] opening and to
be a part of that excitement—of the opening up of this new
space, as an observant [Jewish] woman who had decided not
to be Orthodox because of some of the feminist issues, but
also being connected to the modern Orthodox community
and knowing what some of the issues were, and to see the
similarities. It was just fascinating for me to hear the language
around broaching this new project, and seeing similarities between what the Women's Mosque was doing and . . . women
in the modern Orthodox community who are also breaking new ground. . . . We were already having most of those
conversations—we're still dealing with sexism in our communities but not in terms of ritual life to the same degree.
—Shira, white, Jewish, in her fifties

Throughout 2015, around twenty non-Muslim women were in regular attendance at the WMA's monthly Jummah services.[1] During the
summer of 2017, I observed anywhere between five and eight interfaith
congregants each month. Since then, these numbers have almost certainly shifted back and forth, as has the total number of congregants
in general. Whichever direction these numbers flow in future years, it
is worth noting that the steady presence of interfaith members at the
WMA sets it apart from other American religious congregations, Muslim or otherwise. To be sure, many US mosques conduct interfaith
outreach through special programming and community service. In this
regard, the WMA's embrace of interfaith engagement is aligned with the
post-9/11 trend in faith communities to promote interreligious dialogue.[2]
Yet the WMA attracts a small but loyal cadre of congregants from other

faiths at its actual prayer services, which is not the norm at other houses of worship, even those with robust interfaith programming.

Why do non-Muslim women come? And why does the WMA lead initiatives to build alliances with them? By exploring a set of dynamics around interfaith work unfolding at the WMA, we can situate its relationship to interfaith community building within broader trends in American religious history that have limited women's access to public religious life. Shira, one of the WMA's Jewish supporters, alludes to this shared history of women's marginalization across religious communities in her reflections above. The WMA's aims resonated with her own struggles as an observant Jewish woman. Witnessing the WMA's inaugural Jummah was a powerful and meaningful experience to Shira, and her eyes began to tear as she described why. "It was such an honor, really an honor just to see the power of voice that was coming out, and the power of the community really drawing together . . . it was a real privilege to be there," she shared.[3] Her emotional and spiritual motivations for supporting the WMA were rooted in the parallels she identified with her past issues with Orthodox Judaism.[4] Shira felt deeply connected to the WMA because of her own familiarity with issues of women's marginalization in religious spaces. Having experienced similar struggles with access and representation in Jewish communities, she explained that she understood WMA organizers' aims to build a new type of community.

At the same time, even as she was energized by her familiarity with the sorts of issues the WMA was addressing, Shira drew immediate distinctions between its aims and Jewish women's comparable struggles. To her, there were key differences in rhetoric between Muslim organizers of the WMA on the one hand and both Conservative and Reform Jewish women on the other. She shared that, to her, "the language around 'This is not coming to take the place of—this is in addition to' and 'this is not challenging—this is creating a space for women, a special space for women,'" did not feel strong enough. She explained: "The language wasn't a language of challenge in the same way it is in the Reform movement or the Conservative movement."[5] Shira viewed the WMA as placating in its role relative to mainstream mosques, which stood in sharp contrast with her experiences with Conservative and Reform Jewish women alike, who in her view were more explicit about challenging the status quo in their communities. Shira also readily identified as "feminist,"[6] a term that WMA leaders have carefully avoided. Her sentiments here signal the rich connections, as well as key divergences, among Muslim, Jewish, and also Christian women's struggles for increased visibility and leadership within their faith communities.

Most of the WMA's interfaith congregants I encountered in 2017 were Jewish or Christian, though occasionally they also included women from other religious backgrounds. Cultivating Abrahamic religion as an interfaith category that emphasizes connections among Judaism, Christianity, and Islam, which all trace their lineage to the Prophet and patriarch Abraham, has been politically expedient in the post-9/11 US context. Yet the category of "Abrahamic religions" is problematic for a myriad of reasons, including its exclusion of other religious groups in the US, and for the way this category is mobilized in the service of curtailing LGBTQ and women's rights. Though the WMA does not single out the "Abrahamic traditions" anywhere in its messaging, it tended to be (white) Jewish and Christian women who took on roles as interfaith allies.

The WMA's commitment to interfaith solidarity and community building is especially noteworthy in the sociopolitical climate of the US in the 2010s, in which religious minorities in general and American Muslims in particular were increasingly marked as national others. This trend has persisted in the 2020s. In other words, since Muslims are stigmatized in the broader context of the US as intolerant, insular, and un-American, what does it mean for a multiracial US mosque to act as a site of ongoing interfaith solidarity even as Islamophobia may undermine their efforts? What is the role of Islamophobia in motivating these alliances in the first place? What can we learn from the interfaith model of the WMA that centers lay religious women across traditions rather than male members of clergy, as other models of interfaith engagement do? And within Muslim communities, what does it mean to build an inclusive space across sectarian identities?

In this chapter, we explore how the WMA is part of a trend of intersectional interfaith activism that prioritizes solidarity across religious identities against a US sociopolitical climate that threatens minority religious communities. The women of the WMA develop relationships at the locus of shared historical and contemporary experiences of gendered marginalization in US religious communities and a joint commitment to combatting religious bigotry. In addition to its interfaith work, the WMA also provides opportunities for members to normalize intra-Muslim inclusivity across Shi'i, Sunni, and other sectarian identities. Interfaith and intrafaith solidarity are both central to the WMA's constructions of Islamic authority and Muslim community. Moreover, since the WMA is just one of a number of experiments with alternative Muslim worship spaces in the US, attending to its dynamics of interfaith inclusivity and sectarian pluralism allows us to understand shifting ideas in the US Muslim landscape about what the mosque is and who it is for, and more broadly what religious community should look like.

Muslim Belonging in the US

[Fatima's] actions are a stark reminder for you and me that it really doesn't matter how much space we might be taking up in the world, that we have the right to demand equal rights and protections for ourselves and for everyone around us. . . . No longer is the earth considered safe for all to walk on because it's easier for those in power to tell us that we deserve less than those around us. That the pie is not meant for everyone to eat. So time is spent convincing vulnerable humans that they deserve just a small piece of the pie.[7]
—Laila Alawa, from her January 2018 pre-khutbah bayan, "We All Deserve to Be Here, No Matter What the World Says"

In her bayan, Laila Alawa drew on the example of the Prophet Muhammad's daughter Fatima to encourage WMA congregants to stand up for themselves in the face of discrimination. Speaking broadly about the prevalence of anti-Muslim hostility in the US, Alawa, founder and CEO of the Tempest, a global media tech company that celebrates women's storytelling, recalled a few of her own experiences of prejudice. As a Syrian-Danish American woman who wore a hijab, Alawa recalled for the congregation how as a young child, many of her friends stopped associating with her after learning about her Muslim identity. She cited this as why she and her siblings were homeschooled, an experience she described as lonely and isolating. Throughout her childhood, learning about prominent Islamic historical figures like Fatima became a coping mechanism for her. Fatima inspired her as a role model because of how she is said to have stood up to her father's enemies. Even when she was just a young girl, Fatima used her words to defend him and herself against those who harassed and persecuted Muhammad and the early Muslim community. Learning stories about the Prophet's daughter gave Alawa resolve to stand up for herself too. Her invocation of Fatima is consistent with other khateebahs' references to prominent female figures in Islamic history as role models and moral exemplars for themselves.

Alawa's experiences with anti-Muslim discrimination did not end with childhood, but continued when she was a student at Wellesley, the elite liberal arts college in the Northeast, in the early 2010s. Based on her stellar academic record, she was accepted into a competitive psychology program that involved a service trip to a South Carolina school. However, the professor leading this program called her in for a meeting, stating that she had felt compelled to inform the South Carolina school's principal of Alawa's headscarf, and that he was uncomfortable at the prospect of her visit. Her professor then stated, "Sometimes, certain precautions must be taken [on these academic trips]," before suggesting that Alawa remove her headscarf in order to participate. Alawa described her acceptance in the program as being rescinded on the basis of her religious identity. What is striking in Alawa's narrative is that her professor seemed to have given no indication that the situation was unjust in any way, instead speaking awkwardly and inarticulately about necessary "precautions."

Sharing her vulnerabilities with the WMA congregation, as khateebahs are encouraged to do by mosque leaders, Alawa reported feeling morally deflated:

> I'd heard countless accounts of discrimination happening to women wearing the head covering even here at Wellesley, but this couldn't be one of them. It wouldn't be one of them. "Can we do anything about this?" I asked. I remember the moment she suggested that I take off the head covering in order to participate in the program. The numbness that crept over me as I saw my ambitions crumble in one fell swoop. I left her office in a state of shock.[8]

Alawa described how she was caught off-guard by the situation and ultimately left her professor's office "in a state of shock." She also left feeling unsure of herself and whether she should have pushed back more than she did in the moment. Part of her felt resigned to the fact that her religious identity would stand in the way of her academic and future professional success. Her uncertainty and initial acquiescence had to do with the fact that her professor, while speaking in polite and uncomfortable tones, did not seem to understand her own role in the situation.

"I remember her reluctant handshake, saying 'I'm so sorry' when I refused to take off my scarf," Alawa said. "Her apology was full of sorrow not at the circumstances but at my failure to give in."[9] That Alawa's professor may not have held openly anti-Muslim views like the South Carolina school principal does not matter here because she nevertheless accepted these views as legitimate. By asking Alawa to remove her headscarf, she validated the principal's "concerns" about Muslims.

With encouragement from a non-Muslim friend and her mother, who were both outraged at the incident, Alawa stood up for herself. After getting in touch with the college president, she was promptly reinstated in the program and received apologies from various college leaders after she threatened to publicize the religious discrimination she experienced. The incident engendered a keen sense of defiance and the fire to defend herself and understand that "to thrive would be an act of survival."[10] In her bayan, she brought this incident back to the example of Fatima, who as a young woman in Mecca, where the powerful Quraysh tribe routinely persecuted Muhammad and his early followers, spoke up against injustice and fought back against her oppressors. Just as Fatima took up space in the world when she defended herself and her father, so too should WMA congregants, Alawa said, remember that they had "the right to demand equal rights and protections for ourselves and for everyone around us."[11]

Alawa's bayan speaks to the sociopolitical climate of the US throughout the 2010s and 2020s, where Muslims and other minority groups are treated as second-class citizens, even on liberal college campuses that purport to value religious diversity and pluralism.[12] This is a period during which communities of color have become exponentially more vulnerable to diverse forms of violence based on the resurgence of white supremacy in the public sphere. To be sure, the logic of white supremacy has always been embedded within the US national project of settler colonialism and the enduring legacies of African slavery. And yet there has been an uptick in public expressions and endorsements of white nationalism by elected officials and the general public since Barack Obama's first presidential term. The 2011 birther movement, which pushed a conspiracy that Obama was born in Kenya and therefore could not legitimately be president, is one example of how mainstream xenophobic attitudes had become over the course of the 2010s. For instance, Donald Trump was one of the most vocal proponents of the birther conspiracy. That he never formally apologized for his part in it and still won the presidency in 2016 demonstrates how, just over the course of four to five years, xenophobic views that were once considered fringe conspiracies were no longer alienating, and indeed appealing, to broad cross-sections of the voting public.[13]

The acceleration of white nationalism in the late 2010s and early 2020s has coincided, unsurprisingly, with the rise of anti-Muslim racism. For example, accusations about his country of birth went hand in hand with charges that Obama was a "secret Muslim." As a practicing Christian, Obama repeatedly rebuffed these false allegations throughout his presidency. But in the process, he never publicly called attention to the Islamophobia inherent in the accusations themselves, and appeared to distance himself from US Muslims (who for their part, had enthusiastically rallied behind his campaign in 2008). For example, Obama had not set foot in a US mosque until February 2016, during the final months of his presidency. Even then, his speech primarily promoted Countering Violent Extremism (CVE) policing, which not only causes further harm to Black and brown Muslim communities, but is also rooted in Orientalist tropes about Muslims as inherently prone to violence.[14] CVE programming is predicated on mobilizing various community members to identify and report individuals who they consider might be susceptible to violent extremism based on so-called "suspicious" factors like levels of religiosity and political activism. CVE programs largely target Muslims and, while framed as a way to empower communities, have the adverse effect of stigmatizing and dividing them. They are also ineffective at foiling terrorism plots.[15]

Based on how he continued Bush-era domestic policies that curtailed Muslims' civil liberties, Obama seemed unwilling to see Muslims as full US citizens who have the right to learn, work, and pray without being treated with suspicion and extensively surveilled. In Alawa's encounter with anti-Muslim discrimination, she confronts an academic culture at an elite liberal institution in US that asks her to accept second-class status. It is a climate that attempts to normalize her headscarf as a barrier to professional achievement. Beyond the Obama years during which Alawa's incident at Wellesley College took place, Islamophobia in the US has only further escalated. Indeed, anti-Muslim racism and xenophobia reached new though not unprecedented peaks under the Trump administration through discriminatory policies including the "Muslim Ban," which barred entry to foreign nationals from seven Muslim-majority countries, and the expansion of the authority of Homeland Security's Immigration and Customs Enforcement (ICE).[16] When Alawa references the lack of safety that members of so many vulnerable populations feel when walking down the street, this is the broader context to which she refers. When she spoke to the WMA congregation in 2018, she and her audience were acutely aware of how little they were valued as Muslims, and as racial and ethnic minorities, by substantial portions of the American populace.

As we have seen, Alawa was certainly not the first to use her platform at the WMA to speak on Islamophobia. However, what is worth noting here is how she responded to experiences of anti-Muslim discrimination: she founded her own media company, the Tempest, in 2016, centering the diverse voices of women across religious, racial, and ethnic identities.[17] The Tempest features stories from diverse millennial and Gen Z writers on a wide range of topics from religion, social justice, and politics to fashion, beauty, and music. Explaining her motivations for starting this media company, Alawa shared with the congregation:

> I made a vow to myself as a teenager if I ever had the power the ability to do something about it, that I would make sure that no woman or girl ever felt silence-censored or othered. It was a vow that I carried close to my heart throughout my time growing up and it's the reason that I founded the Tempest, fighting against the current political social and cultural climates both here and abroad: to build a global media company with more than a thousand women sharing their stories and taking up their space in the world, no apologies attached.

Alawa created the Tempest to provide a global platform for women who had ever felt silenced or discouraged from arguing for their place in a hostile world. With a team of thirty people and over fifteen hundred writers around the globe, Alawa has accomplished her goal and was even featured in the *Forbes* 30 Under 30 media list in 2018 for the Tempest's achievement of garnering millions of visitors each month.[18]

Online platforms like Alawa's, aimed at Muslims and others who do not easily conform to the white majority based on their religious, racial, gender, or sexual identity, provide space for those with marginalized identities to belong. While the Tempest does not have a specific focus on interfaith community, it nevertheless achieves diverse faith representation on its site and hosts rich interfaith discussions as the inevitable result of championing diverse women's experiences. Muslim, Sikh, Hindu, Jewish, and Christian women writers focus on issues of misrepresentation and stereotyping, or how to balance their queer and religious identities in a culture that treats these identities as mutually exclusive. Others highlight women's struggles with religion, questioning the teachings they grew up with and in some cases documenting their processes of leaving their faith. Still others focus on managing multifaith identities and navigating interfaith and intrafaith marriages.[19] A few contributions address interfaith relations more broadly beyond individual relationships, specifically an article on anti-Semitism in Muslim communities and another on the importance of solidarity across faiths.[20]

To be clear, cultivating interfaith solidarity among groups that are vulnerable to racially motivated violence and discrimination is one of multiple options available to American Muslims as they negotiate what it means to belong in America. For example, prominent American Muslim preacher Hamza Yusuf has allied with the conservative Christian right, joining the Trump administration's Commission on Unalienable Rights in 2019, which sought to restrain human rights discourse to facilitate the creation of restrictive laws around abortion, LGBTQ rights, and immigration. Yusuf has also described the United States as "one of the least racist societies in the world" and discouraged American Muslims from supporting the Black Lives Matter movement, citing the racist trope of "black on black crime" as the central issue plaguing Black communities.[21] In other words, Muslims like Yusuf, a white American, have opted to cultivate interfaith alliances not with fellow marginalized groups, but with the Republican Party and conservative Christian leaders in the US, as well as with authoritarian regimes like the UAE.[22] Such alliances have been detrimental to many US Muslim communities.

Likewise many American Coptic Christians, despite their own racialization as Arabs who are subjected to Islamophobia, have also forged alliances with white Evangelicals, who incorporate Coptic persecution by Muslims in Egypt into their own Islamophobic agendas.[23] Sikh Americans similarly have complex relationships to Islamophobia and Muslims. As fellow targets of War on Terror policies, Sikh communities in the US have had to negotiate the need to differentiate themselves from Muslims and contend with being incorporated into Islamophobic Hindu nationalist narratives.[24] Since any given religious minority group in the US has its own distinct relationship to American whiteness, it is not inevitable that a group will opt to cultivate solidarity within and across religious difference. Alawa's and the WMA's commitment to solidarity among marginalized groups is a conscious choice, one configuration of interfaith relationships among many.

Moreover, Alawa's mission to lift up diverse women's storytelling through the Tempest makes her a natural fit at the WMA, which has a similar goal of elevating Muslim women and their varied, enriching stories. In the WMA's emphasis on providing the khateebah platform to lay women, they often choose professionally accomplished women like Alawa, who are entrepreneurs, activists, doctors, community leaders, or professors, as we have seen. Being attentive to the Muslim women to whom the WMA extends a platform sheds light on a set of emergent values in the community. These values at the WMA grow increasingly coherent each year, as we can see from the overlapping themes and connections between different khutbahs. Both Alawa's bayan and her media site indicate that building solidarity among women across religious, racial, and ethnic difference is one of the WMA's values. It also illustrates the context of Islamophobia in which American Muslims, and institutions like the WMA, enter interfaith conversations and initiatives, which in turn helps us understand the limits of religious inclusivity in the US.

Islamophobia and the Limits of Religious Pluralism

The other thing I'd like to address today is to start the conversation on how we can build a more pluralistic ummah, Muslim ummah and society in general in America, and open up our hearts to the beauty of our community and its

differences. . . . How many times do we stop and think "why are we really here? What are we really doing with our lives? What is the higher purpose in life that we should strive for?" What I suggest, and this is merely a suggestion, is that we engage in intense *muhasaba al-nafs*, or accounting of the self, and work on purifying our souls to better engage with a Muslim and greater American community.[25]
—Rose Aslan, from her February 2015 khutbah, "Taking Account of Ourselves to Give Back"

In the WMA's second khutbah, in February 2015, Rose Aslan, a religious studies professor at California Lutheran University, called for Muslims to engage in interfaith outreach. The fact that interfaith relations appeared in a khutbah so early in the WMA's tenure indicates its commitment to building interfaith community beyond welcoming women from other religious traditions to Jummah. Indeed, the WMA's commitment to interfaith coalition building in US Muslim communities is part of a broader post-9/11 trend. Religious studies scholar Rosemary Corbett shows that since the beginning of the Obama years, through the creation of the White House Office of Faith-Based and Neighborhood Partnerships, there has been a federal call for interfaith coalitions to engage in service projects together. Many Muslim organizations have taken up this call, not only because their faith encourages this type of outreach, but also in the hope that these measures will help to curtail prejudice against Muslims and present a favorable impression of them as dedicated American citizens.[26] A similar logic underpins Aslan's khutbah, which posits that uplifting community, both Muslim and non-Muslim, is a part of worship and would also help create ties with American society in general. Drawing on Qur'anic verses to support her point, Aslan argues for the importance of cultivating *taqwa*, God-consciousness, so that Muslims can better engage those both inside and outside of their communities.[27]

While in the first half of her khutbah, Aslan shared her theological reflections on God's attributes, focusing particularly on *Rahman* and *Rahim* (the Most Merciful and the Most Gracious) and the number of times these epithets appears in the Qur'an, the second half highlighted her suggestions for building a pluralistic community. Differentiating it from religious tolerance and diversity, Aslan argued for the merits of pluralism, stating, "In a pluralistic society everyone is welcome at the table and there is active and real engagement across differences. This is the best but certainly the most challenging option, although it leads to the greatest rewards and most successful society."[28] Citing religious studies scholar Diana Eck, the architect of the Pluralism Project at Harvard University, Aslan argued that, in a pluralistic society, people of diverse backgrounds could engage each other in meaningful ways and form real relationships. Part of the appeal of the WMA, she continued, was precisely that, in many US mosques, women were only tolerated rather than considered an active part of a community that met their needs. To this end, she stated, "A truly pluralistic community will include the active seeking of understanding across the lines of difference and would ensure that everyone's voices are heard despite disagreement."[29] Aslan considered the WMA a pluralistic space not only due to its inclusion of interfaith women but also because it made room for Muslim women with diverse opinions. She called for congregants to "seek out allies through various means both from within and without the Muslim community."[30]

Aslan's promotion of "pluralism" over "mere tolerance" at the WMA is worth considering in light of broader academic debates. The Diana Eck model of pluralism that Aslan promoted in her khutbah characterizes the religious condition of the United States as "post-Protestant," due to the diversity of religious life after 1965 following the mass influx of immigrants into the country. Eck argues that religious pluralism involves not only diversity but, as Aslan states in her khutbah, engagement, involvement, and participation.[31] Underpinning Eck's study, which was published in 2001, is the claim that America is no longer a Christian nation. Eck's analysis of American Muslims appears to celebrate the relinquishing of particular ethnic and cultural practices and customs in favor of a "universal" American Islam. American Muslim communities have certainly negotiated and legitimized their American Muslim identities by creating distance between religion and various immigrant cultures. However, calling for the separation of religion and "foreign" cultures can promote an American exceptionalist narrative that implies the inferiority of other Muslim contexts, particularly when thinking about religious pluralism and interfaith relationships.

Moreover, characterizing the US as "post-Protestant" fails to account for the Christian hegemony that pervades the treatment of other religious traditions. As Corbett shows, American Muslim engagement with interfaith community building and service projects does not guarantee their acceptance by a wider US public.[32] So while many American Muslim communities around the country have already taken up the suggestions that Aslan lays out in her khutbah—"to make room for one another drawing upon the *rahma*, the mercy, of Allah to listen and offer a space to anyone who wants to join us"[33]—misunderstandings about Islam, Muslims, and especially Muslim women prevail in the US. Here, anthropologist Shabana Mir's ethnography of Muslim American women at elite liberal arts colleges in the US provides useful context to understand the uneven dynamics. Specifically, Mir problematizes the success narratives of liberal pluralism by highlighting the ways that markers of Islamic religiosity marginalize Muslim students on liberal arts college campuses that in principle celebrate religious diversity and pluralism. Her work draws attention to how the optimistic rhetoric of pluralism often masks Christian hegemony and the ways that religious minorities continue to be marginalized in subtle and overt ways across racial, ethnic, and gendered lines. For example, social leisure culture and professional networking opportunities that are often centered on alcohol consumption can be alienating for Muslims who do not partake in drinking. Muslims also experience both overt discrimination and discreet microaggressions based upon the visibility of their religious identity by race, ethnicity, clothing, and social behaviors.[34]

Academic debates on American religious pluralism have set important groundwork for understanding how particular Muslim institutions and the people within them, including the WMA, choose to navigate the difficult terrain of interfaith politics. The WMA, for example, through Aslan's khutbah, extends an embrace of interfaith and pluralist outreach, irrespective of whether some groups, both Muslim and non-Muslim, choose to respond in kind. To this end, Aslan stated, "For those who don't want to join us, we can reach out in other ways. Despite our disagreements let's open ourselves to others to offer a spark of the divine that resides in all of us."[35] Here, Aslan emphasizes that Muslims need to reflect inward, taking account of their own lives and "opening themselves up to others." Yet even as she attests to the possibility of a religiously plural ideal, her khutbah does not preclude the fact that other faith groups may not reciprocate.

Aamna, a Pakistani American congregant in her thirties, was very drawn to Aslan's messaging that the WMA could be "a potential catalyst for Muslim pluralism."[36] Aamna was in attendance at the WMA the day of Aslan's khutbah, and she brought it up in our conversation more than two years after hearing it, describing how it differentiated between diversity, tolerance, and pluralism in interesting ways. She was particularly moved by the idea that Muslims should work toward achieving a pluralistic society.[37] Aamna explained that she especially appreciated how Aslan connected Islamic texts with secular scholarship, stating: "I appreciated so much the fact that the individual giving the khutbah was not only bringing in Islamic texts, but also academic texts to supplement it."[38] This reflection gestures at the value that Aamna and other congregants at the WMA ascribe to pluralism and multiple forms of knowledge.

When Aamna was growing up, she never heard any imam in her mosque speak on such topics.[39] That observation also came up with other women I interviewed. Aamna's and other WMA congregants' descriptions of their other mosque-going experiences are by no means an empirical confirmation of what is and is not discussed in other US mosques. Yet their constant comparisons of the WMA to other Muslim communities help us understand their particular values and concerns, and by extension the values and concerns of a growing number of diverse American Muslims who believe their religious needs are not met in their existing communities. To this end, it is noteworthy that despite the climate of Islamophobia that curtails Muslim acceptance into a so-called religiously plural America, the WMA continues to value and celebrate the ideal of interfaith community. This is demonstrated at the community level by the interfaith congregants who show up each month and also on the level of discourse, as Aslan's khutbah highlights.

Aslan explicitly credited her interfaith allies for making it possible for her to give a khutbah at the WMA. She explained to the congregation that her Christian male colleague agreed to cover her morning class, which enabled her to make the drive to LA from Thousand Oaks on a Friday afternoon. Her female Christian colleague, an ordained Methodist who was in the WMA congregation that day, gave her valuable advice about how to preach a sermon. It is noteworthy here that Aslan credits a Methodist woman ally for providing counsel on the art of preaching rather than a male counterpart. The fact that Aslan turned to an ordained Christian woman for advice on preaching, over a Muslim or even a Christian man, speaks to the connections that American Muslim women can feel toward their interfaith counterparts. This is explicitly evidenced in Aslan's khutbah as she mentions that although she had only ever witnessed one Muslim woman serve as a khateebah in her life— Edina Lekovic, a month prior—she had plenty of inspiration from her interfaith sisters. She credits her Christian and Jewish friends who serve as ordained ministers and rabbis for normalizing female religious leaders for her.[40] Aslan's acknowledgement of interfaith influences allows us to consider how relationships among religious women of different faith backgrounds, based in common experiences of patriarchal marginalization, can open up opportunities to offset the general climate of Islamophobia that otherwise limits Muslim inclusion.

The WMA's American Antecedents

Christians also went through that—when it was questionable whether or not there could be female pastors. And Catholics are going through whether or not there can be female priests. Because it was already established in the church that women can lead as pastors, I already believed that men and women can be spiritual leaders and so praying behind a female imam is acceptable to me. . . . I definitely believe that women can be spiritual leaders.[41]
—Cynthia, East Asian, in her thirties

Cynthia, an East Asian WMA congregant in her thirties who had grown up in the Presbyterian Church, shared with me the above reflections on female-led Jummah. To her, women holding leadership roles in other religious communities normalized the idea of Muslim women as ritual authority figures. Cynthia, who had recently become Muslim, explained that female religious leadership was something that she had long considered legitimate because she grew up in a church where women could be pastors. This, she stated, made her comfortable as a Muslim praying

Jummah behind a female imam. Her reflections demonstrate how women in other American religious communities have set up meaningful precedents through which to make sense of the WMA. This is especially true for Muslims with strong interfaith community networks through their activism and professional relationships, as Aslan highlighted in her khutbah, or through family ties for converts like Cynthia.

Understanding its interfaith precedents allows us to situate the WMA within broader trends of American religious history whereby women have argued for their increased participation in public religious life in creative ways. For instance, some have created their own spaces, much like the WMA, and others have negotiated their positions within their existing communities. In the WMA's own narrative, its leaders have been keen to emphasize how women-only mosques have existed across the world in both Muslim-majority and -minority contexts in Syria, India, and China.[42] Yet paying attention to the WMA's situatedness in the US context also illuminates the interfaith dynamics between American Muslim women and their counterparts from other faiths. The legacies of women's active participation in their religious communities throughout US history provide another way to contextualize the WMA in addition to framing it within the global Muslim context of women's authority. The challenges that contemporary American Muslim women face in their religious communities closely resemble the same issues that women of other faiths have dealt with in the past or continue to confront today.

In thinking about the broader role of American women in religious history, Ann Braude shows that women have been key players within religious institutions. They have served as audiences and ritual participants, passed on their faith traditions to their children, and provided material resources for their religious institutions.[43] Braude argues: "There could be no lone man in the pulpit without the mass of women who fill the pews. There would be no clergy, no seminaries to train them, no theology to teach them, and no hierarchies to ordain them, unless women supported all of these institutions from which they historically have been excluded—and still are by Catholics, conservative Protestants, and Orthodox Jews."[44] In other words, women have been integral to preserving the vitality of religious life, even as they have been marginalized by the very same structures and institutions that would cease to exist without their support.

Furthermore, just as the American religious landscape is character-ized by the ubiquity of women's presence in religious institutions, it is equally characterized by their exclusion from leadership roles. Due to this systematic exclusion, Braude argues that women have always contested gender norms that limit their public participation.[45] While women's ordination is possible within some Protestant and independent Catholic communities,[46] ordained women as congregation leaders are far from the norm. For example, while three-quarters of the mainline Protestant churches in a 2018 study permitted women to serve as pas-tors, fewer than one in five actually had a woman pastor.[47] Cynthia at-tested to as much while drawing comparisons between the WMA and the Presbyterian Church to which her family belonged. She stated that her family's congregation mostly had male pastors, despite the fact that women pastors were considered legitimate there. Cynthia identified a stark discrepancy between what was theoretically "allowed" and what actually happens in practice. For example, male pastors most often acted in the larger leadership roles, while female clergy were less visible. Ad-ditionally, she explained that although she knew Christian women were permitted to "read the Sunday scripture and give the sermon," she had rarely witnessed this herself. Nevertheless, noting that change takes time, Cynthia believed women religious leaders, like those at the WMA, would become increasingly common across different faith traditions.[48]

In thinking about how gender norms in American religious commu-nities have changed over time, it is worth noting that, by the nineteenth century, women were increasingly visible in public worship. By this pe-riod, Protestant women's active involvement in institutional church life, though not in leadership roles, was commonplace. Protestant Ameri-cans no longer considered women to be seductive temptresses who threatened male virtue, but moral agents in their own right.[49] Women's church attendance therefore became an indicator of white middle-class piety that members of other religious groups, such as American Jews, would aspire to and emulate to gain acceptance in mainstream culture.[50] Throughout the nineteenth and twentieth centuries, American Jewish communities renegotiated strict gender barriers in synagogues, because women's visibility could represent Jews' acculturation into American so-ciety and affirm the religious legitimacy of the American synagogue.[51] Women's lack of attendance in synagogues was perceived as antithetical to Protestant culture; accordingly, American Jews sought to cultivate a new idea of female Jewish identity that could be seen as compatible with Protestant values.

The American synagogue served as the primary space for the renegotiations of gender identity within Judaism because it was, as historian Karla Goldman has explained, "an edifice that presented a public face for Judaism to the non-Jewish community."[52] It was not only Reformists who were interested in reconciling Jewish practices that precluded women's participation in public worship with new standards of visibility for women, but traditionalists as well.[53] These reforms included the eventual introduction of mixed-gender choirs and family pews wherein men and women would sit together rather than separately. But even as the structure of the synagogue evolved to be more physically inclusive of women, these reforms did not necessarily reflect the particular concerns of Jewish women. Rather, they illustrated the broader Jewish quest for respectability in a white middle-class America that had been shaped by Protestant values. Goldman highlights how despite the fact that the introduction of mixed choirs and pews to the American synagogue did not alter or expand the religious responsibilities of Jewish women, it still held remarkable symbolic weight. Women's inclusion in choirs and the inception of family pews redefined women's overall status as legitimate congregants and challenged the male monopoly over Jewish religious services.[54]

The nineteenth-century internal Jewish debates over the legitimacy of women's voices in synagogue choirs for worship services mirror contemporary Muslim debates over female-led Jummah. For example, Rabbi Isaac Mayer Wise, one of the nineteenth-century advocates for including women's voices in synagogue choirs, argued that the Talmud's prohibition of women's participation was not meant to be taken as law, but rather as the particular opinion of the rabbis who authored the text. He further argued that the Talmudic judgments were not applicable to contemporary society.[55] Similarly, as we saw earlier, twenty-first-century Muslims who advocate for gender-egalitarian mosques and for women's increased roles in worship services also argue that classical Islamic legal opinions reflect the interpretations of the specific jurists rather than the intent of the sacred texts themselves. Mixed pews in synagogues eventually came to be understood as "a requirement of American religion" rather than as a violation of Jewish law, but their introduction formed a dividing line between traditional and progressive Judaism by the twentieth century.[56] For example, in some Jewish communities, mixed choirs were initially only used for nonreligious ceremonies rather than in traditional worship services because of heated debates over the Talmudic legitimacy of women's voices in prayer.

While American mosques did not undergo an identical process to synagogues in acculturating to Protestant norms, those run by immigrant Muslims resemble synagogues in being sites for integration into US culture.[57] As such, American Muslim women share similar concerns to their Jewish counterparts about their lack of visibility in worship spaces. For example, Yasmin, a WMA congregant in her twenties whom we met earlier, interpreted the relegation of women to the back of the mosque as disrespectful. To Yasmin, women were not regarded as spiritual equals in mainstream mosques, but rather treated as potential distractions. Notably, around the same time that Yasmin began attending the WMA, she had also started attending a Korean church with a friend. She explained that while she had no interest in converting to Christianity, and did not agree with the theology that Jesus was the son of God, she enjoyed learning from the sermons and experiencing the community.[58] To Yasmin, both the church and WMA communities were enriching and valuable, in large part because she felt visible in both. In her friend's church, congregants were not separated by gender and she felt they were all there to learn. She believed the women-only nature of the WMA created space for women to be fully visible and respected.

The emergence of the WMA continues twentieth-century trends in Christian and Jewish communities in which women both contested and worked within the ideological confinements that limited their public participation. By introducing new liturgical norms through women-led Jummah and its khateebahs' Qur'an interpretations based on personal experiences, the WMA represents how American Muslim women, like Christian and Jewish women before them, negotiate increased authoritative roles in their religious communities. From the twentieth century onward, there has been an increase in female clergy as well as new expressions of liturgical and theological doctrines in American Protestantism that incorporate women. Earlier we discussed the Pentecostal Women's Aglow Fellowship, a global organization of Christian women who engage in Bible studies, charismatic healing, and the cultivation of religious community.[59] Similarly, women's prayer groups began to emerge in Orthodox Jewish communities across the US by the end of the twentieth century. This was a result of educated and pious Jewish women seeking fulfillment in communal prayer while also respecting the constraints of Halakhic law, which precluded their full participation.[60] During this same period, Reformist and Reconstructionist Jews first ordained female rabbis.[61] Evangelical women have also since formed nationwide networks of women's groups wherein female congregants cultivate charismatic authority.[62]

There are also parallels between the WMA and *tefillah* groups (women-only prayer groups) in Orthodox Jewish communities in the US. These tefillah groups began taking shape in the 1970s, as a growing number of educated Jewish women held both secular and religious degrees, and were able to challenge specific customs in Halakhic law. Ailene Nusbacher argues that tefillah groups represent a broader movement among American Jewish women who wished to stay consistent with the requirements of the Orthodox tradition while also arguing for their increased role in worship.[63] Like many WMA congregants dissatisfied by the status quo at mainstream mosques, Nusbacher's interlocutors from various tefillah groups in New York City felt marginalized at regular Shabbat services. As such, they desired "an intense, spiritually gratifying religious experience, which they believed could best be achieved in a framework where women lead services, pray together and read from the Torah."[64] Many of my interlocutors expressed similar sentiments when discussing what drew them to the WMA. They desired to participate in a space where they could engage with the Qur'an, be spiritually moved, and feel like an active part of the congregation. Just like Nusbacher's tefillah participants, WMA members believed that an all-women's space lent itself well to cultivating a spiritually intense and moving environment.

Notably, Orthodox women-only prayer groups and the WMA both appear to accommodate the parameters set by mainstream Jewish and Muslim worship spaces—to the frustration of some of their supporters. Among Nusbacher's interlocutors from seven different women's prayer groups in New York City, certain women did not feel the prayer groups were a radical enough challenge to patriarchal norms. They wanted to openly advocate for women to perform full liturgical services, and eventually entered into other Jewish egalitarian spaces that did not have the same constraints as Orthodox women's prayer groups. Likewise, some of my interlocutors, including Celeste and Kenyatta, both African American, felt at least to some degree that the WMA would better serve the needs of gender equality if it were a mixed-gender space. For these critics, along with Shira who opened this chapter with the sentiment that the WMA was not posing enough of a challenge to existing mosque structures, women's so-called accommodating attitudes toward their religious traditions' rendered them inadequate in some way— either not feminist or not progressive enough. Yet even religious women who overtly challenge male monopoly on clerical roles face comparable backlash. For example, women from independent Catholic communities (that are not affiliated with the Roman Catholic pope) who seek ordination face criticism from progressive Roman Catholics for not "doing away with a sacerdotal priesthood altogether."[65] These progressives contend that ordaining women "changes nothing . . . if the resulting clericalism just perpetuates hierarchies."[66] However, as Catholic studies specialist Julie Byrne shows, independent Catholics find ways to challenge hierarchies even as they uphold the importance of ordination, for example by simultaneously affirming lay power: "instead of ordaining no one, ordain everyone."[67] Religious women who explore their various options for equality within their communities are bound to have critics on all sides who accuse them of deviating too far from their traditions, or otherwise not deviating far enough to pose a serious threat to male power. Yet fixating on these criticisms might mask our understanding of the ways that religious women in the US have negotiated their authority through simultaneously challenging and acquiescing to male structures of power. Whether by carving out new spaces for new roles or taking up established roles that are not available to them in conventional religious spaces, women have cultivated religious authority in a number of ways, irrespective of outsiders' arbitrary benchmarks for what constitutes radical, progressive, or feminist advances.

Moreover, many US religious women have been intentionally cautious about how they negotiate change, and may not want to be perceived as radical as some of their critics may wish for them. For example, tefillah group members, much like WMA leaders, carefully represented themselves as motivated by faith rather than by secular feminism. This is because many members of both Orthodox Jewish and mainstream Muslim communities in the US may perceive feminism to be antithetical to religious values. As we saw earlier, WMA leaders have actively avoided the "feminist" label precisely because it would alienate mainstream American Muslim communities, though some individual congregants do adopt the label for themselves. Moreover, just like participants in Jewish prayer groups, those who are a part of the WMA do not see themselves—and more importantly, do not want others to perceive them—as competing with mainstream prayer services. Like many Orthodox women's prayer groups, the WMA meets just once a month, clearly indicating that they are not trying to replace regular prayer services. For these women, their co-religionists' perceptions of them are integral to the efficacy of their respective projects; insisting on how they are not threatening allows them, in principle at least, to more easily reach their goals. Furthermore, both WMA and tefillah group members exemplify how women create separate communities when the existing ones do not serve their needs, rather than stand by waiting for structural change.

There is a shared sense between American Jewish and Muslim women who seek reform that male authorities, rather than scripture or even legal doctrine, pose barriers to their progress. For example, Nusbacher's Orthodox Jewish interviewees characterized rabbinic resistance to their queries as not rooted in Halakhic law, but rather based in the vague claim that there were no precedents. Moreover, rabbis' resistance to their various queries prompted the women to study the law for themselves.[68] The Orthodox Jewish women in Nusbacher's study did not believe that the foundations of Jewish law constrained their participation, but rather that male rabbis did not understand how to read the Halakhic tradition properly. This motivated them to seek traditional religious education to argue for their increased rights under Jewish law. Similarly, many Muslim feminist thinkers, whose works we examined earlier, argue that the Qur'an is essentially gender-egalitarian and that patriarchal readings originate from male interpreters.[69] WMA leaders also share the belief that the Qur'an advances women's rights and therefore they promote Qur'anic literacy as the ultimate form of women's empowerment.[70] The logic here is that if Muslim women become intimately familiar with scripture, they will be better positioned to articulate their religious rights. Orthodox Jewish women similarly seek to understand and communicate their rights, though they emphasize the Jewish legal tradition while Muslim feminists tend to focus on the Qur'an rather than the Islamic legal tradition.

The WMA does not exist in a vacuum, but has historical antecedents in other American religious communities, particularly Jewish and Christian ones. Understanding the WMA as a parallel development for American Muslims in the twenty-first century to women's reforms in Christian and Jewish communities at the end of the twentieth century provides historical context to the solidarity expressed among Jewish and Christian members of the WMA. Cynthia's perspectives demonstrate the importance of the historical continuities among different American religious communities. Her receptive attitude toward woman-led prayer at the WMA was largely informed by her family's religious background and involvement in a church community. Her mother was trained in Christian theology, so Cynthia was raised in a household that took seriously women's capacity to serve as spiritual leaders. As she became Muslim, she continued to cultivate the values of women's equal spiritual status with which she had grown up.[71] Having been raised in an observant Christian family, Cynthia explains that Islamic doctrines were already familiar to her, and she had considered Islam to be "one of the Abrahamic faiths."[72] Yet she held certain preconceptions about the status of Muslim women before she attended the WMA. "The common misperception is that Muslim women are oppressed and so when I saw everybody, I was like, OK, these are just women. You know? They're not oppressed women, these are just normal women [laughs]. You know, with careers, mothers, et cetera."[73] Attending the WMA and seeing women in leadership roles clarified for her that common tropes about the oppression of Muslim women were false. Moreover, interfaith connections also featured centrally in the discussion that Cynthia and I had about how she had come to be a part of the WMA. She became interested in learning more about Islam after first meeting her now husband, who is Muslim. He was not able to answer many of the questions that she had about "women's roles and rights in Islam," because as a man who had grown up Muslim, he had never had to contend with them himself.[74] In a quest for more information about Islam and its attitude toward women, Cynthia reached out to several local Muslim organizations over email but never heard back from any. She then happened upon a media article on a woman-led mosque in Denmark (the Mariam Mosque in Copenhagen referenced earlier), which briefly mentioned the WMA in Los Angeles. Cynthia reached out to the WMA and went on to attend a Jummah, where she had a welcoming experience and was greeted immediately by other congregants.

Furthermore, Cynthia described the WMA as a space that was beneficial for all women irrespective of whether they identified as religious. She brought her sister, who is not religious, to the WMA because she believed it was a "good space for all women." She sees it as providing "a positive message or conversation that any woman can really relate to or be a part of. . . . I would say that it's not just for Muslims, it's really just a positive community."[75] To Cynthia, the WMA has a universal appeal that is inclusive of not only women from different traditions but also those who do not belong to a faith.[76] Her experiences demonstrate how the WMA often acts as an initial point of contact for religious community for many congregants. She also shared with me that the gender segregation in mainstream mosques was initially a turnoff for her as she was accustomed to attending church with her entire family. She felt nervous about attending Jummah at her husband's mosque knowing that she would be separated from him and on her own.

Yet participating in the WMA allowed her to gain confidence to attend the regular Jummah services she had previously found intimidating. Cynthia has become a regular mosque-goer who attends Jummah at one of three mosques in the LA area every week, in addition to being at the WMA once a month. Moreover, her experiences with women pastors in her family's Presbyterian Church community imbue her with the confidence as a Muslim to accept and receive women as authority figures at the WMA. For example, while her husband did not feel certain about the legitimacy of woman-led prayer at the WMA, Cynthia did not share his discomfort based on her own knowledge of the parallel conditions in Christian communities. She felt certain in her faith that women were legitimate religious authority figures in Islam and could confidently cultivate her own Islamic values separate from her husband, even as a newer Muslim.

Additionally, for Cynthia, the WMA functioned as a space where she felt spiritually nurtured by the warmth of community members who made her less self-conscious about being a new Muslim. Being a member of the WMA enabled Cynthia to become more at ease in mainstream mosques that were previously out of her comfort zone. Other congregants cite the WMA as their reason for still being Muslim, and some have even converted and taken their *shahadah*, or testimony of faith, there. By creating an inclusive atmosphere, the WMA promotes interfaith relationships within newer Muslims' mixed religious families and also offers opportunities for intra-Muslim solidarity across sectarian identities and degrees of religiosity.

Toward Intra-Muslim Inclusivity

When meeting a new Muslim, be patient. Do not be judgmental and do not overwhelm the new convert with multiple rules. Remember that the Prophet Muhammad did not introduce rules as a priority. He taught for thirteen years the belief in one God. Offer your help one on one on how to perform the prayer, how to do the ablution. Have the person learn the wording of the prayer in their language and later in Arabic.[77]

—Marta Khadija Galedary, from her December 2015 khutbah, "Healing Racial Conflict: The Latino Community"

The WMA prioritizes interfaith engagements on multiple levels, and in her December 2015 khutbah Marta Khadija Galedary addressed interfaith relations on the intimate level of family. Galedary's khutbah, "Healing Racial Conflict: The Latino Community," discussed the relationships between Muslim converts and their non-Muslim families. Galedary founded LALMA, La Asociación Latina Musulmana de América, in Los Angeles in 1999 as a study group at the Islamic Center of Southern California for Latino Muslims to learn more about Islam and specifically to transition from Catholicism to Islam. Under Galedary's leadership, the organization has since expanded to include formal Spanish-language classes on the Qur'an, *sirah* (biographical information about Muhammad), and Arabic, as well as interfaith events.

A Mexican immigrant to the US, Galedary was raised in a household with strong Catholic values, which she herself embodied before turning away from religion after being introduced to Marxism in college.[78] After studying English in the UK and meeting Muslim classmates from Brunei, Galedary eventually became Muslim herself. Her family of devout Catholics had difficulty accepting her decision to become a Muslim. Her mother felt relief after consulting with her Catholic priest at Galedary's suggestion, who assured her that Islam was a "legitimate ancient religion" and that her daughter was still on the right path.[79] Other family members, including her sister who is a nun, continued to struggle with Galedary's decision but eventually came to terms with it. She now only speaks to her family about Islam when they ask specific questions, but her fifteen-year-old son, with her Iranian American husband, has a much easier time "traversing the cultural boundaries of [being] Latino-Iranian and the multicultural Muslim communities of Southern California as a native-born American Muslim."[80]

In her khutbah, Galedary draws attention to the harmful, often racist treatment that Latino Muslim converts experience from their fellow Muslims in their new religious communities, and calls on the WMA congregation to be more supportive. Specifically, she emphasized the importance for new converts to preserve relationships with their non-Muslim family members. She advised:

> Encourage converts to remain close to their non-Muslim family members, and to participate in their celebrations. Remember . . . Islam does not intend to take you away from your family. . . . Many of us, we were told by good-intentioned Muslims that we cannot participate in festivities like Christmas or any other festivities with family. . . . You must participate with your families . . . there's nothing wrong with having dinner on Christmas or Thanksgiving or other festivities. Of course we follow the rules of no pork and no alcohol, but otherwise we should participate with our families. And we Latina Muslims . . . the majority of our family are still Christians and Catholics.[81]

Galedary urged Muslims to support better interfaith relations within the intimate settings of family by offering a powerful critique of Muslims who discourage new converts from participating in family festivities. Her khutbah calls attention to the destructive patterns of advice that new converts often receive from other Muslims, even as she generously categorizes these Muslims as "good-intentioned." Given that the vast majority of WMA congregants are neither Latina/x nor are most of them new converts, though some members belong to these categories, Galedary's khutbah seems aimed at the very Muslims who might engage in the kinds of behaviors that make life for Latino and other Muslim converts difficult. Indeed, she speaks directly to these Muslims in her khutbah by offering them directives to "be patient" and nonjudgmental. In other words, Galedary not only affirmed for new Latina Muslims that they should celebrate holidays and maintain ties with their non-Muslim family members, but she also provided a corrective to non-converts about the proper relationship between Islamic teachings and family ties: "Islam does not intend to take you away from your family." Her advice also speaks to broader ways that Muslims can maintain ties to mainstream nonreligious American culture, for example by participating in Thanksgiving. Her khutbah demonstrates how the WMA addresses interfaith relations from a variety of angles, including at the interpersonal level of relationships between new Muslims and their non-Muslim families.

In her khutbah, Galedary also addressed the overt racial and ethnic discrimination that Latino Muslims routinely face in their religious communities. She shared that when new Muslims first enter into Islam, they often idealize their new faith communities. This was the case for her, and she explained that based on the Prophet Muhammad's final sermon delivered before his death, which upholds the principle of racial equality, she used to think that all Muslims embodied this ideal. However, she quickly learned that this was not the case. She explained, "After I converted, I started awakening to a reality that Muslims are not really different from any other human beings, having the same weaknesses and challenges to overcome [with] racial or ethnic discrimination."[82] In coming to terms with racism in Muslim communities, Galedary highlights the extent to which both intra- and interfaith relations are always racialized. For example, over the course of her khutbah, she made clear that while Latino Muslims are encouraged by other Muslims not to participate in holidays with their Catholic families, they are simultaneously seen as "less than" by these same Arab and South Asian Muslims.

Latino Muslims' "less than" status in the eyes of Arab and South Asian Muslims plays out in several ways, including being overlooked and discriminated against as suitable marriage partners. Galedary addressed this in her khutbah, stating:

> Often in our community several Latina Muslims have informed me that they have been told by Muslims from Arabic-speaking countries that a Latina Muslim is not considered a true Muslim because he or she is not from a Muslim-majority country nor born in a Muslim household. Male and female Latino Muslims have been rejected by the families of those born into the faith as husbands or wives simply because of their ethnicity.[83]

The discrimination against Latina Muslims by Muslims from Arabic-speaking and Muslim-majority countries demonstrates the reality of racial dynamics in American Muslim communities. Latinx American Muslim experiences with intra-Muslim racism mirror the experiences of Black American Muslims, described earlier. These dynamics of intra-Muslim racism reveal the limits of American Muslim unity. Galedary's khutbah highlights the ways non-Black or -Latinx Muslims will impose harmful standards on new converts, such as discouraging them from celebrating Christian holidays with their family members, but still continue to view them as outsiders, further contributing to their alienation. These intra-Muslim dynamics revolve around notions of Islamic authenticity and authority, and highlight the endogamous tendencies within Muslim ethnic groups that preclude the possibility of a more unified and cohesive American Muslim identity.[84] The concerns that Galedary raised in her khutbah highlight the challenges of interfaith and intrafaith community building across racial and ethnic differences.

In thinking about intrafaith community, it is worth considering how Muslims from minority sects fit in at the WMA. WMA khateebahs and congregants have come from a range of backgrounds, including Sunni, Shi'i, Sufi, Ahmadi, NOI (and Sunnis from W. D. Mohammed's communities), reflecting intra-Muslim diversity. By branding itself as a space that accommodates multiple perspectives, the WMA cultivates an intrafaith community on an institutional level, by for example providing clay tablets, or *turbah*, for Shi'a women to pray with. Aamna, an Ahmadi

Muslim, shared with me her experiences at the WMA as a Muslim minority. Aamna appreciated that the WMA "doesn't subscribe to any sect" and therefore helped her feel more comfortable being herself, adding that, at the WMA, "you're free to come as you are and there's no judgment. That to me is a beautiful thing."[85]

For Aamna, being an Ahmadi Muslim meant that she had to exercise caution and guard her identity from others, especially during visits to Pakistan, her family's country of origin. She explained, "we grew up [knowing] Ahmadis are marginalized, you'd have to be really cautious of what you say in Pakistan. When I was in Pakistan I couldn't go around telling people that I was Ahmadi. Here [at the WMA] it's like, we don't care."[86] The Ahmadi sect emerged in late nineteenth-century India and has been controversial among other Muslims ever since on the basis of their theological beliefs. Ahmadi Muslims believe that their leader Mirza Ghulam Ahmad (d. 1908) was a recipient of divine revelation and the Messiah, beliefs that do not conform to Sunni doctrine, which holds that the Prophet Muhammad was the final messenger. Aamna's remarks allude to the persecution that Ahmadi Muslims face in Pakistan, where in 1974, the Constitution declared them apostates, sanctioning legal discrimination as well as vigilante violence against them.[87] However, the level of caution that Aamna was accustomed to exercising regarding her identity was not only relevant in the Pakistani context, but also applied to some Muslim spaces in the US. For example, while an undergraduate student at a university in California, she refrained from joining the Muslim Student Association (MSA) because she worried about the potential consequences of her Ahmadi identity. She worried that, if she did not fit in, word might spread that she was Ahmadi to other Muslim students' parents who might not be "open-minded about it." Reflecting on her experiences in college, she explained that she probably could have joined the MSA and challenged any pushback that came her way, but that at the time she did not feel as if she had enough knowledge.[88] While Aamna retrospectively thought that perhaps she was overly cautious in isolating herself from other Muslims when she was younger, it is worth noting that the WMA's messaging about welcoming all sects made her feel safe and seen.

Legal debates still on my mind, I asked Aamna about the technicalities of praying in an intrafaith setting, curious about how she felt about the validity of praying behind a non-Ahmadi Muslim. For Aamna, praying in a non-Ahmadi mosque was not an issue. She explained that while she had heard from the elders in her community that Ahmadi Muslims were only allowed to pray behind other Ahmadis, she disagreed with this:

> You're typically not supposed to read [perform] prayers behind a non-Ahmadi, but to me that is ridiculous. If somebody is leading prayer, I'm going to read behind them because I believe in the power of ummah, the power through congregation. A lot of people do too. . . . It's kind of one of those things that's up to you whether or not you want to do that. In regards to the way that the prayer is read, it's almost identical. We kind of mirror a lot of Sunni rituals so it's very, very similar. . . . The older generation may be a little bit more hesitant perhaps, but for the most part I would say young [Ahmadi] women would be 100 percent open to it.[89]

Aamna highlights a generational difference in the Ahmadi community regarding attitudes toward praying in intrafaith settings. Her attitude that individuals can decide for themselves what is appropriate aligns with both WMA and Protestant values of individual relationships to faith. Moreover, Aamna asserts that she believes in the power of ummah, indicating that she feels camaraderie with her fellow American Muslims across sectarian identity.

Additionally, khateebahs from different Islamic backgrounds also provide a way for the WMA congregation to meaningfully discuss intra-Muslim diversity in the congregation. For example, in her khutbah from August 2016, Nayawiyyah Muhammad spoke about her personal experiences as a former member of the NOI. She articulated the merits of being a part of a movement that uplifted Black Americans. Speaking from her experiences, Muhammad corrected misperceptions about the NOI and credited it for empowering many Black Muslims.[90] Likewise, Noor-Malika Chisti spoke to the WMA congregation from the perspective of Sufism, the Islamic mystical tradition. Additionally, there have been a number of Shi'a khateebahs, including Soheyla Aryan, a *hafidhah* (a woman who has memorized the Qur'an) who teaches classes on the Qur'an and Imam Ali's sermons at a Shi'i mosque in LA. Ali, the cousin and son-in-law of the Prophet Muhammad, is the central authority figure in Shi'i Islam, and accounts of his family members have featured in a handful of WMA khutbahs from Shi'a khateebahs. This includes Shabnam Dewji, who delivered her first khutbah in 2015 on the central role of Fatima, the daughter of the Prophet Muhammad and Ali's wife, in the Shi'i tradition.[91]

WMA khutbahs from Shi'a Muslims like Dewji that provide context about prominent historical figures like Fatima or Ali are significant because large segments of Sunni Muslims in the US are often unfamiliar with these narratives. Dewji's second WMA khutbah, in September 2017, also focused on sharing the stories of prominent Shi'a figures and events, this time focusing on Zaynab, the granddaughter of the Prophet Muhammad, and the Battle of Karbala in 680 CE that resulted in the brutal massacre of Husayn, the grandson of Muhammad, and his army. Filling in these historical gaps for a majority-Sunni congregation lays the groundwork for greater intrafaith understanding and respect at the WMA.

In fact, Dewji's khutbah on the Battle of Karbala was explicitly framed by a broader call for Sunni-Shi'a understanding and respect for each other's customs and religious lessons. She delivered it on the day of Ashura, the tenth day of the month of Muharram, when Shi'a Muslims mourn Karbala. Preceding Dewji's khutbah was a bayan by Anne Myers, a white Sunni convert, which addressed the different meanings of Ashura to Shi'a and Sunni Muslims. In her bayan, Myers called on congregants to take lessons from both perspectives on the holy day. Starting with the Sunni perspective, Myers explained that Sunnis fasted on Ashura to commemorate the day that Moses and the children of Israel were freed from slavery in Egypt. To Sunnis, Myers went on, Ashura was a celebration and a continuation of the Prophetic practices of both Muhammad and Moses, who according to some hadith traditions, also fasted on this day. Moreover, Myers explained that this practice felt like "a kind of Islamic Passover, a holiday that I had grown up celebrating with my Jewish mother."[92] It was not until she met her Iraqi American Shi'a friend that she learned that not all Muslims fast on Ashura. For Shi'a Muslims, Ashura was observed through "a solemn day of mourning."

Myers shared that, in her own observance of Ashura, she aspired to "combine these various lessons to create a different way of looking at the day." Sharing her plan with the congregation, Myers explained that she would fast on Ashura, just as Moses and Muhammad did, and also "take time to reflect on the story of Karbala and the bravery that Imam Husain and his family showed in the midst of injustice. . . . I will remember that such injustice still occurs today." Additionally, she planned to donate to causes that aid against people's suffering in Husayn's honor while renewing her "commitment to enjoin justice and what is right and condemn what is wrong." For Myers, this included reflecting on the injustices in the world, from the massacre and treatment of the descendants of Muhammad at Karbala, to present-day systemic oppression of racial, gender, and sexual minorities and the economic exploitation of the working classes.[93]

In August 2020, Dewji and Myers participated in a livestreamed discussion on Facebook, facilitated by Maznavi and Samia Bano, the WMA's then director of operations, where they reflected together on the Shi'a-Sunni divide in Muslim history and in contemporary communities. Dewji and Myers drew on their respective reflections on Ashura as a point of departure for this conversation, taking the time to address the feedback they received from congregants about their remarks in 2017. Dewji explained that her 2017 khutbah on Karbala was educational for many congregants, with many stating that they had never previously learned about the Prophet Muhammad's granddaughter and the events at Karbala. Dewji and Myers reflected on the importance of Shi'a-Sunni unity and the lessons that Karbala offered to understanding racial injustice and the Black Lives Matter movement in the contemporary US.[94] By creating space for these types of conversations, the WMA cultivates an inclusive atmosphere through which to promote intrafaith solidarity among American Muslims. Also, in drawing comparisons between the lessons of oppression at Karbala and within the movement for Black lives, the WMA places social justice activism at the forefront of its calls for solidarity.

Intersectional Interfaith Activism

Immigration, it is something that has unified us, doesn't matter if you're a Muslim, Catholic, Evangelical, and you even meet Mormon Latinos.[95]
—Marta Khadija Galedary, 2017 interview with author

I first met Galedary at an iftar event at Masjid Omar Ibn Al-Khattab, where LALMA is now based. I learned that she has had extensive experiences in multicultural and multiracial interfaith work, not only through

LALMA but also through other organizations like LA Voice. LA Voice is a multifaith organization comprising a network of fifty-seven church, synagogue, and mosque communities in LA, including LALMA and the Muslim Anti-Racism Collaborative (MuslimARC), a human rights educational organization. Galedary explained that interfaith collaborations that are issue-centered rather than focused on the specifics of faith tend to be the most effective. Her decision to involve LALMA with LA Voice in 2014 was a result of learning about the group's aims and realizing that other religious communities faced similar social injustices to those experienced by Latino Muslims in Los Angeles. LA Voice focuses on immigrant rights, criminal justice reform, voter participation, and access to affordable housing in LA.[96] Her involvement in LA Voice opened her eyes to the long-term changes that could be fostered through targeting policy makers.[97] Galedary's experiences in multiple interfaith settings demonstrate how intersectional interfaith activism is critical in engendering long-term change.

Galedary believed in the importance of forging intersectional ties. She explained to me that the issue of immigration under the Trump administration had unified Latino communities across religious lines.[98] It is critical to keep in mind that, during my fieldwork in the summer of 2017, Latino communities in LA felt very deeply the traumas inflicted by the Trump administration as their families were being torn apart by ICE raids and DACA (Deferred Action for Childhood Arrivals) was under threat of removal. Interfaith organizations such as LALMA, LA Voice, and MuslimARC represent the spectrum of the multicultural faith-based work that members of the WMA community are involved in. These organizations all take seriously the racialized nature of the issues that plague faith communities in LA and how immigrant communities of color face challenges relating to immigration policy, criminal justice reform, and affordable housing.

When describing her collaborations with MuslimARC, Galedary explained that one of her goals was to increase awareness among immigrant groups and racial minorities of how and why they should become more civically engaged. The attitude she sought to convey to Muslims was the importance of solidarity across different identities: "Be concerned about your [non-Muslim] neighbors, about the community where you are. Don't say, 'That's not me, I don't care.'"[99] To her, it was important that Muslim immigrant communities felt like they were a part of the community around them and did not exile themselves.

Galedary's leadership roles in various interfaith organizations in LA are part of a broader pattern of WMA congregants' and khateebahs' involvement in interfaith activism. Aamna, Shira, and Rose Aslan, all discussed in this chapter, as well as Mariyah, Sufiya, and Rana, mentioned in earlier chapters, are similarly part of the robust interfaith networks in Los Angeles. Upon my arrival in Los Angeles, I quickly learned how interconnected members of the WMA were within larger interfaith activist networks. I attended the annual fundraising and awards ceremony of CLUE (Clergy and Laity United for Economic Justice), a large network of religious leaders from Jewish, Christian, and Muslim congregations who work toward economic justice for low-wage workers.[100] The board members of CLUE, which operates in LA and Orange County, represent a range of Latino, Korean, African American, white, Jewish, South Asian, and Arab backgrounds. At this ceremony that featured prayers from different faith leaders, Najeeba Syeed, a recurring WMA khateebah, delivered the Muslim prayer.

I would later learn that Elaine, one of my Jewish interlocutors from the WMA, was also a member of CLUE. Elaine participated in CLUE as a Jewish woman, but explained that she was not affiliated with any Jewish congregation because of the racism she experienced following her interfaith, interracial marriage with her husband, a Black Christian. Elaine, who was in her eighties, explained that she and her husband, who was born into the Baptist tradition, had together joined the Presbyterian Church after Jewish officials refused to marry them because they were an interracial couple. Accordingly, when their son was young, they chose to enroll him in a Presbyterian preschool rather than a Jewish one. However, while the church community was kind to her family, she ultimately wanted her son to learn about Judaism so that he could feel connected to that aspect of his background. Through her own research she identified a Jewish temple with a rabbi who was a prominent civil rights activist and sent her son there. Elaine and her husband then joined a family group at the temple when they were discriminated against by one of its facilitators who stated that they did not want "their kind of people" there, meaning racially mixed families. While the rabbis at that temple did not agree with the group facilitator's discriminatory views, Elaine and her family ultimately left the community due to repeated incidents of bigotry. These experiences led Elaine to dissociate herself from the Jewish temple communities, although she shared how she still identified strongly as Jewish: "I consider myself very much a Jewish person of Jewish heritage, but because of the horrendous experience I had, I just couldn't belong to Temple again."[101] The discrimination faced by Elaine and her family faced reveals the harsh realities of racial prejudice in religious communities, even those led by prominent civil rights supporters.

A final example of an LA interfaith organization connected to the WMA through mutual members is NewGround: A Muslim-Jewish Partnership for Change, mentioned earlier. A number of WMA khateebahs and congregants including Edina Lekovic are key members of NewGround, which engages religious difference in forging interfaith alliances between Jews and Muslims. NewGround is a community-building organization that aims to connect American Jews and Muslims by empowering them to advance social change. It was jointly created by MPAC, the Muslim Public Affairs Council, and the Progressive Jewish Alliance in 2007. NewGround cultivates a space for Muslim-Jewish dialogue through its yearlong fellowship program for young Jewish and Muslim professionals. During this fellowship program, a cohort of twenty individuals meet twice a month in each other's worship spaces to learn more about each other, including their religious convictions, customs, and rituals, and they engage in service projects. They also learn communication and organizational tools that equip them to become leaders. During this period, not only do they engage in each other's worship, they also attend two weekend retreats, with one devoted solely to discussing the Palestinian-Israeli conflict, the proverbial elephant in the room in many Jewish-Muslim alliances. Based on my interviews with NewGround fellows and facilitators who have been through this program, their experiences of the weekend retreats were typically very intense, uncomfortable, and heated. However, because it is held toward the end of the fellowship year, participants have already gotten to know each other by then. By that point they have cultivated a sense of mutual respect and friendship, so they are able to work together despite the discomfort of often having diametrically opposed views on Israel-Palestine.

Beyond the year-long fellowship, NewGround offers grants for former fellows to actualize projects in community building, civic engagement, or policy advocacy that encompass the skills and values that are taught over the course of the fellowship. For example, some recent projects included starting an interfaith podcast about everyday struggles of Muslims and Jews, providing access to computer hardware and programming to middle schoolers in South Central LA, and developing workshops at local colleges to provide an alternative to criminal activity for youth. Other projects included interfaith Shabbat dinners to raise funds for refugees, and a program that combined Sunday school sessions of a Jewish Community Center and a mosque to connect and learn about each other's faiths, while engaging in community service projects like assembling hygiene kits and lunches. While NewGround in its mission statement does not focus on gender and is not exclusively for women or racial minorities, it is worth noting that in 2020 the executive director, Aziza Hasan, as well as the two co-directors of the fellowship, Andrea Hodos and Tasneem Noor, were women. Notably, Hasan and Noor have both served as WMA khateebahs, and Hodos has also been a part of the WMA interfaith community. Additionally, half of the advisory council were also women, lending credence to the idea that women-led interfaith initiatives tend to center on developing and sustaining relationships.

There are clear challenges to sustaining meaningful interreligious relationships such as those forged at NewGround. For example, Hodos, in her capacity as a co-director for the NewGround fellowship, explained to me that one of the key aims of their fellowship program was to enable their Jewish and Muslim participants to honestly engage with each other not only on the level of community, but on the more intimate levels of scripture and politics. To this end, she described posing the following question about the NewGround fellows: "Will they now be able to face the fact that their texts, and their operations, and their interpretations, and their political self-interests hurt the other?"[102] Here Jerusha Lamptey's work, which generates new conceptions of what theological pluralism might look like, provides a helpful framework to understand the challenges of deep and meaningful interreligious community. Lamptey's approach requires an honest engagement with Qur'anic depictions of rejecting other faith traditions and affirming continuity instead. She achieves this by emphasizing lateral relationships between different religious communities and privileging Qur'anic suggestions of individual agency in achieving God-consciousness. Interreligious and interfaith dialogues in the US tend to flatten differences, an approach Lamptey rejects as ultimately limiting, as it does not allow participants to seriously and honestly engage significant differences.[103]

Islamic studies scholar Aysha Hidayatullah refers to a related concern about opposing political agendas in her engagement with Muslim feminists' reluctance to emphasize their shared concerns with Jewish and Christian feminists. This reluctance is rooted in the risk of being co-opted by an imperialist narrative that demonizes Islam. She notes, "In drawing attention to the concerns they share with Jewish and Christian women, Muslim women run the risk of being roped into neoconservative state platforms aimed at promoting the spread of so-called moderate forms of Islam deemed least likely to challenge the United States' global ascendency and branding all other forms of Islam as 'fundamentalist' and dangerous."[104] Hidayatullah describes how Muslim feminist discourses can be weaponized against Muslim communities in the US by contributing to anti-Muslim narratives about the incompatibility of Islam and modern societies. For this reason, interfaith connections, particularly on the theological level, can delegitimize Muslim feminist exegeses in mainstream US Muslim communities and detract from claims of Islamic authenticity.

Despite the challenges that interfaith engagements pose on a theological and interpersonal level, they are integral to the WMA's mission statement.[105] Analyzing how the WMA integrates interfaith activism into its mission statement allows us to gain a fuller picture of how it approaches community building across different US religious traditions. It also provides a window to understanding how the WMA addresses the challenges associated with interfaith coalition building. WMA members' various reflections on interfaith work, including with organizations like LA Voice, CLUE, and NewGround, demonstrate how alliances forged between women who are part of racial and religious minorities are effective in addressing religious bigotry. Moreover, these interfaith organizations take race and ethnic identity seriously. Though representation remains an issue—Muslim involvement in CLUE is sparse compared to its Christian and Jewish affiliates—these groups thrive in part because they acknowledge intersectionality. That is, they understand how racial, ethnic, economic, gender, and sexual identities function to create specific vulnerabilities within religious groups.

Although the WMA is not an interfaith organization with an explicit policy agenda, it overlaps with these nonprofits in its commitment to equality. As we have seen, the WMA stands within a longer American religious history that has limited women's public roles in congregational communities. Like the Christian and Jewish American women before them, WMA members have cultivated authority outside of, or alongside, their religious communities. Like women's prayer groups in Orthodox Jewish communities, the WMA demonstrates how women respect the constraints posed by religious law and carve out their own worship spaces that do not overtly challenge the structure of mainstream congregations. Despite the challenges of interfaith alliances, including rendering Muslim women susceptible to co-option by imperialist narratives that advance anti-Muslim political agendas, the WMA embraces interfaith advocacy as central to its aims. In fact, some WMA members see interfaith relationships as a model for combating anti-religious bigotry in post-2016 America.

On the other hand, the centrality of interfaith engagement to the WMA community and its larger project poses its own set of challenges and is likely not appealing to all of its congregants. In the same way that many congregants appreciate that the WMA is a safe space exclusively for women, away from their regular mosque communities and inaccessible to men, it is not hard to imagine there would be a similar appeal in having an exclusively Muslim space that was not open to all. As we have seen, the presence of interfaith members of the WMA opens them up to subtle judgments and criticisms, like Shira's comment that its leaders were not as bold as Jewish women in challenging patriarchal norms. There is also the sense that the Muslim women at the WMA are constantly operating under the gaze of their often white interfaith counterparts, who do not occupy the same minority religious or racial status as them, and tacitly vying for their approval. Just as optimistic rhetoric that the US is a religiously plural nation masks Protestant hegemony, so too does the WMA's focus on cultivating interfaith ties as a central objective mask the white Judeo-Christian hegemony unfolding in its space.

The power dynamics of interfaith relationships in the US are always uneven based on race, gender, class, and sexual orientation.[106] At the WMA, most if not all of the interfaith congregants are white, and while there are white Muslim converts in the congregation, they do not play prominent leadership roles over brown and Black Muslim women. Whiteness operates in different ways at the WMA, whether through subtle judgments like Shira's or the mere fact that interfaith members are invited and welcomed to every prayer service. This open invitation to join the WMA congregation would not necessarily be reciprocated in these interfaith women's own religious communities, at least not with the same level of regularity. Ultimately, white Jewish and Christian women in the US do not need validation from their mostly non-white Muslim counterparts, and therefore do not need to open their doors to the same extent. For US Muslims, on the other hand, as religious-racial minorities in a political climate that is increasingly hostile to them, external validation from their white Christian and Jewish counterparts is critical for their larger sense of national belonging. This is not to downplay the merits of the WMA as a multiracial mosque operating as a site of ongoing interfaith solidarity or what it can teach us about combating anti-religious bigotry, as this chapter has shown. Nevertheless, it is worth reflecting on how Islamophobia and its racialized dimensions compel US Muslims into prioritizing interfaith engagement.

Conclusion

American Muslim Women from the Margins to the Center

In the closing remarks of Gail Kennard's 2015 khutbah on the Prophet Muhammad's twelve wives as his disciples, she included a message for Muslim men. "Shout out to the brothers," she stated. "Several brothers came to me when they heard that I was doing the khutbah, [saying] that they would love to be here today and *insha'Allah* [God willing] they will listen to this at a later date on the audio (online recording). But they, and all the men, need to hear what women have to say and insha'Allah there will come a day when the voices of Muslim women will be heard."[1] Her voice then broke with emotion as she thanked WMA leaders for creating a space for Muslim women to "grow stronger" so they could speak up like Muhammad's wives and serve as religious authorities in their communities.[2]

Kennard's remarks suggest that, to her, the WMA is not only an alternative physical worship space but also an important platform for Muslim women to speak authoritatively. Indeed, this book has shown that the WMA is far more than an alternative worship space; it is also a discursive project that produces and disseminates women's khutbahs, providing opportunities for Muslim women to engage scripture and cultivate interpretive authority through the role of khateebah. By publishing them online, the WMA signals its intent for these khutbahs to reach an audience beyond the women who physically gather at the monthly Jummah services in Los Angeles. Khateebahs like Kennard embrace this wider reach.

Furthermore, congregants are receptive to the WMA's discursive goal. Many are interested in hearing women preach, and their appreciation for the WMA deepens in light of the fact that their other religious communities do not provide this opportunity, even if they might otherwise be welcoming or inclusive of women. To many congregants, the WMA fills a specific need: it not only provide access to women's voices but also addresses topics they believe to be more meaningful from a female perspective. Some are also drawn to seeing women in positions of ritual authority, and they perceive the WMA as affirming their progressive feminist values. For others, the WMA is simply a refreshing departure from the male-dominated spaces in their lives. They appreciate having a safe environment where they feel nurtured and revived, but do not necessarily see themselves as challenging particular religious norms. Lastly, for some, the WMA provides a sense of belonging to a religious community, a remedy to their negative and sometimes traumatic experiences in other mosques. For those previously "unmosqued" Muslim women, the WMA provides a religious home. For others, it actually motivates them to leave their home mosques after realizing what they are not receiving from those communities. Yet others engage the WMA as a supplementary space to their home mosques.

Clearly, the women in this book have multiple motivations for being a part of the WMA as congregants, volunteers, khateebahs, and board members—motivations that do not always align with each other. Some voice their critiques of certain aspects of the WMA even as they speak to its importance. This diversity of views indicates that individuals are committed to the WMA's broader aims but not overly concerned with forging uniform positions within it.

When the WMA was founded, Muslim critics asserted that there was no historical precedent from the time of the Prophet Muhammad to support woman-led Jummah, and that the WMA was divisive to American Muslim communities. To the latter critique, its leaders continue to emphasize that the WMA is not in competition with mainstream US mosques, but complementary to them. Yet at the same time, the WMA as an institution clearly advocates for women's increased representation in, and access to, roles of religious authority, inherently critiquing the patriarchal status quo of many mosques in America. In so doing, WMA members participate in twenty-first-century global contests over Islamic authority. As religion is increasingly individualized and Islamic authority fragmented, lay Muslims claim authority for themselves and debate the criteria that enable them to make such claims.

American Muslims' participation in these global debates over the criteria for Islamic authority is informed by white Protestant hegemony in the US, which dictates the norms through which religions are considered legitimately American. At the WMA, various women adopt Protestant understandings of scripture in their approaches to the Qur'an, adhering to the notion that any individual can cultivate a relationship to sacred texts. Moreover, the WMA as an institution promotes Qur'anic literacy as a source of women's empowerment, which it furthers by employing English-language translations of the Qur'an and instructing individual khateebahs to read scripture through the lens of their values and experiences. By inviting Muslim women with a range of backgrounds and credentials to serve as khateebahs, WMA leaders expand the criteria for exercising roles of religious authority and legitimize multiple understandings of the Islamic tradition and individuals' relationships to it.

These fluid attitudes toward the Islamic tradition show that using a binary rubric to understand the WMA—in other words, seeing it as either claiming tradition or abandoning it—is not useful. Instead, understanding the WMA on its own terms enables us to situate it at the intersection of global developments in Islamic authority and the racialized trends of acculturation in US religions. The WMA claims continuity with women's mosques in other parts of the world, including in Syria, India, and China. It is also deeply informed by its US context and by the Protestant secular tradition that has defined that context, particularly in its emphases on the central role of English-language translations of the Qur'an, the right of individual khateebahs to read and interpret scripture through the lens of their values and experiences, and the authority of congregants to read scripture for themselves.

WMA congregants confer religious authority on khateebahs through their insistence that women have insights on particular subjects—including sexual violence, marriage, divorce, and grief—that men lack. The WMA's *Khateebah Guidebook*, which enumerates requirements and suggested practices for delivering a khutbah, encourages khateebahs to cultivate a feminine form of religious authority predicated on showing vulnerability and sharing personal experiences. By discussing topics such as sexual violence and domestic abuse, the WMA treats women's bodies as important sites of religious knowledge and suggests that women's experiences can be used as valid bases to interpret Qur'anic verses. As such, the WMA shares elements in common with Black feminist and womanist frameworks that emphasize women's experiences to challenge established forms of deriving knowledge, and promotes distinctly gendered views of female authorities as nurturing and supportive.

WMA khateebahs also respond to American social justice concerns in their Qur'anic interpretations. By drawing attention to issues like anti-Black racism, mass incarceration, and environmental degradation, the WMA demonstrates an American branding of Islamic authority. It also attempts to create a shared sense of morality and Muslim identity across racial and ethnic lines, which stands in contrast to patterns of racial segregation in other mosques. There are, however, clear challenges to cultivating such a shared Muslim identity given the anti-Black racism that pervades US society, as we saw with congregants' mixed reactions to the WMA's Black Lives Matter discussion series. Congregants' disparate reactions demonstrate the challenges of cultivating meaningful dialogue about anti-Black racism in a racially diverse congregation.

Finally, the WMA fosters intrafaith inclusivity across Muslim sects and schools of law, while also developing interfaith relationships. Its emphasis on interfaith collaborations and civic engagement, both requirements of American civil religion, further evidences the tensions it experiences in navigating its US context. It stands within the history of American Jewish and Christian women who have advocated for greater visibility and increased authority within their religious traditions, and in fact has some Jewish and Christian women who regularly attend. The WMA, in its promotion of religious pluralism, participates in an emergent trend of interfaith activism that centers the voices of women and ethnic minorities as a means to combat religious bigotry in a hostile US political climate. Analyzing the WMA therefore sheds light on debates over pluralism and national belonging in the US, demonstrating how religious minorities are in some ways coerced into prioritizing interfaith relationships. In other words, the WMA brings to the fore the question of whether Islam has a legitimate place in the broader fabric of a so-called religiously plural America.

Members of the WMA negotiate their marginalization in their patriarchal religious communities while also navigating the racialized and gendered Islamophobia that questions their national belonging. The prevalence of Islamophobia in the US imposes a double burden on Muslim women as they bear the brunt of anti-Muslim hostility in the broader American cultural context while also experiencing censure from within their own communities. Fellow Muslims pressure them to avoid making internal critiques of any marginalizing trends that take place within their own communities, for fear that being public about women's treatment will fuel anti-Muslim hate in an already fraught political climate.

Yet no degree of self-censorship in Muslim communities could conceivably reverse the Islamophobia that is entrenched within American culture and diffused globally. The growth of religious and racialized forms of nationalism has magnified anti-Muslim sentiment around the world, including in Europe and South Asia. For example, the rise of right-wing populism across Europe has resulted in exclusionary asylum and immigration policies, as well as hostility toward European Muslims. In India, the spread of Hindu nationalism under Prime Minister Narendra Modi and his attempts to strip Muslims of citizenship has invigorated transnational Islamophobia between India and the US. Additionally, the US framework of the War on Terror and the securitization of Islam have shaped a number of countries' security policies toward Muslims worldwide, including China's cultural genocide and mass internment of Uyghurs, the majority of whom are Muslim.[3]

Islamophobia also prevails within Muslim-majority states, notably in the United Arab Emirates, Saudi Arabia, and Egypt. These states have increasingly clamped down on groups like the Muslim Brotherhood, designating them as terrorist organizations. Such designations find support among US Republican leaders and prominent US Muslim leaders alike, imperiling a number of major American Muslim civil society organizations founded by members of the Brotherhood in the 1960s.[4] In other words, the diffusion of global Islamophobia catalyzed by Muslim actors abroad contributes to stifling American Muslims' political and social activism and generally vilifying them in the process.

Understanding the contours of global Islamophobia helps us to think about how developments within American Islam reverberate throughout the rest of the so-called "Muslim world" and vice versa. Muslims in the US should therefore not be treated as peripheral religious actors who exist on the outskirts of the study of Islam, but instead recognized as players who contribute to global and geopolitical conversations about Islam and Muslims. American Muslim interventions in Islamic law, exegesis, or politics have implications for communities and societies beyond their own. Moreover, recent debates over the state of Islamic studies have brought to bear the issues with limiting the field to the Middle East, Arabic sources, or medieval texts. Ultimately, Arab-centric trends in Islamic studies can reify Orientalist and Islamophobic frameworks about what Islam *is*, which has repercussions within the academy and in lived religious communities.[5]

This book on the WMA contributes to the growing body of literature that challenges the notion that "real Muslims" doing "Islam" occurs only outside of the US, in the realm of male scholars interpreting and reinterpreting medieval legal texts. The American Muslim women showcased here exemplify how significant developments in Islamic authority come from actors who are often overlooked in the study of Islam. Drawing on existing methods of Qur'anic exegesis, these American Muslim women cultivate Islamic authority that simultaneously contends with issues like gender inequality, anti-Blackness, and global Islamophobia. Their contributions are also very much rooted in their national context, including in gendered trends in American religious history, demonstrating that Islam is indeed a US religion.

I have insisted in this book that the American Muslim women at the WMA are worthy of our attention as legitimate Muslim actors who intervene in critical debates over authority, religious community, and national belonging. Scholarship in the growing subfield of American Islam, with which this book is in conversation, offers a corrective to the erasure of so-called peripheral Muslims. The US hosts significant populations of Black and Latinx Muslim communities, along with African, South Asian, Arab, Bosnian, Iranian, and other ethnic communities, each of which make distinct and valuable contributions to religious life, which could suitably be incorporated into understandings of global Islam, not just Islam in the US. The rich insights that these studies yield should be included in new theorizations of contemporary Islam. Doing so would lead to richer conversations that more accurately depict the diversity of Muslim life and complex interconnected histories of Islam in a global context.

ACKNOWLEDGMENTS

A number of individuals and institutions have lent their support to this project. At the Women's Mosque of America, I thank everyone who generously shared their time with me. While this does not imply their endorsement of the book's content, I am grateful for their assistance and this book is indebted to them. Grants from Boston University's Department of Religious Studies, Center for the Humanities, and Institute for the Study of Muslim Societies and Civilizations, as well as the Woodrow Wilson Women's Studies Fellowship, have supported this research.

At Boston University, I am grateful to Kecia Ali, who has been an invaluable conversation partner throughout the various stages of this work, and whose insights have shaped my goals as a scholar. I am also thankful to Anthony Petro for all of his counsel and support over the years and for his enthusiasm for this project in its nascent stages. At the University of Edinburgh, a special thank you to Hugh Goddard and Tom Lea for their support. At Washington University in St. Louis, I thank my wonderful colleagues at the John C. Danforth Center on Religion and Politics, Fannie Bialek, R. Marie Griffith, John Inazu, Debra Kennard, Laurie Maffly-Kipp, Lerone Martin, Sheri Peña, Leigh Schmidt, and Mark Valeri, for providing a welcoming academic home. A longtime admirer of her work, I am especially thankful for R. Marie Griffith's careful and thoughtful readings of the manuscript. I also thank Jean Allman and Ignacio Infante for their leadership at the Center for the Humanities at Washington University, where I finished the manuscript as a junior faculty fellow.

This book has also been strengthened by generative comments from a number of interlocutors. I am grateful to Zareena Grewal for her review and feedback on the full manuscript. I also thank the members of the colloquiums hosted by the Danforth Center on Religion and Politics and by the Department of Women, Gender, and Sexuality Studies at Washington University, to Joseph Stuart and the Rocky Mountain

American Religion Seminar, as well as to my colleagues Samba Diallo, Garrett Kiriakos-Fugate, Candace Lukasik, Aria Nakissa, and David H. Warren, who have all offered their comments on various chapter drafts. My sincere thanks also to Penny Edgell, Jonathan Walton, and my Young Scholars of American Religion cohort for their support. At NYU Press, I thank my editor, Jennifer Hammer, who read through multiple iterations of these chapters; her suggestions have vastly improved my writing. I am additionally grateful to the anonymous reviewers whose meticulous feedback alongside their enthusiasm for the project were critical sources of guidance. I thank Jana Riess for working with me through the early stages of this manuscript, providing both encouragement and writing momentum. I am also deeply grateful to Arvid H. Choudhury and Zafir H. Choudhury for lending their creative expertise in the final stages and for always modeling engaged listening.

Most importantly, I thank my family. I am grateful to Sultana Y. Ali and Mir M. Ali for their love, guidance, and faith (matched only by their high expectations!), and also to Simon F. Warren and Annie Maddison for their love and support. A special thank you to Adiba and Ishraq, my role models and confidantes in all matters, and to Rafat, Sarah, Leila, and Ayah for all that they bring to their lives and mine. And of course, to David: his care (and scholarly expertise) have seen me through the duration of this project, though I am most moved by the advanced juicing skills he has acquired during its completion, creating antioxidant-rich green concoctions that would humble even the smuggest of wellness warriors (that is, me). I thank him for his reassurance that lugging our juicer, along with half of our kitchen, around the country during our many pandemic road trips still makes us light packers and savvy travelers.

NOTES

INTRODUCTION

Epigraph. Gail Kennard, *The 12 Wives as Disciples of the Prophet*, audio recording, Women's Mosque of America, August 28, 2015, https://soundcloud.com.

1 Susie Ling, "Monrovian Superstar, Architect Robert Kennard," *Monrovia Weekly*, February 7, 2019, www.monroviaweekly.com.

2 Kennard, *The 12 Wives as Disciples*.

3 Ibid.

4 Here Kennard categorizes Mariyya the Copt as one of Muhammad's wives rather than a concubine. Mariyya was sent as a gift to Muhammad from a Byzantine Christian leader and he took her as his concubine, later freeing her. See Kecia Ali, *Sexual Ethics and Islam: Feminist Reflections on Qur'an, Hadith, and Jurisprudence*, exp. and rev. ed. (London: Oneworld, 2016), 39.

5 Kennard, *The 12 Wives as Disciples*.

6 Ibid.

7 Nick Street, "First All-Female Mosque Opens in Los Angeles," *AlJazeera America*, February 3, 2015, http://america.aljazeera.com.

8 "FAQ," Women's Mosque of America, 2015, http://womensmosque.com.

9 Street, "First All-Female Mosque."

10 Sarah Sayeed, Aisha Aa-Adawiya, and Ihsan Bagby, "The American Mosque 2011, Report 3: Women and the American Mosque" (Islamic Society of North America, 2013), www.hartfordinstitute.org; Jamillah Karim, *American Muslim Women: Negotiating Race, Class, and Gender within the Ummah* (New York: New York University Press, 2009), 173.

11 Sayeed, al-Adawiya, and Bagby, "Women and the American Mosque."

12 Margot Badran, *Feminism in Islam: Secular and Religious Convergences* (London: Oneworld, 2009), 336.

13 Simonetta Calderini, *Women as Imams: Classical Islamic Sources and Modern Debates on Leading Prayer* (London: I.B. Tauris, 2020), 29.

14 Ibid., 31.

15 See Dale Eickelman and James Piscatori, *Muslim Politics* (Princeton, NJ: Princeton University Press, 2004); Zareena Grewal, *Islam Is a Foreign Country* (New York: New York University Press, 2014).

16 See Rosemary Corbett, *Making Moderate Islam: Sufism, Service, and the "Ground Zero Mosque" Controversy* (Stanford, CA: Stanford University Press, 2016);

Edward E. Curtis IV, *Muslims in America: A Short History* (New York: Oxford University Press, 2009); William Hutchison, *Religious Pluralism in America: The Contentious History of a Founding Ideal* (New Haven, CT: Yale University Press, 2003).

17 Here Kennard refers to and paraphrases parts of Qur'an 33:32–34, which reads: "O wives of the Prophet, you are not like anyone among women. If you fear Allah, then do not be soft in speech [to men], lest he in whose heart is disease should covet, but speak with appropriate speech. / And abide in your houses and do not display yourselves as [was] the display of the former times of ignorance. And establish prayer and give *zakah* [alms] and obey Allah and His Messenger. Allah intends only to remove from you the impurity [of sin], O people of the [Prophet's] household, and to purify you with [extensive] purification. / And remember what is recited in your houses of the verses of Allah and wisdom. Indeed, Allah is ever Subtle and Acquainted [with all things]" (https://quran.com/33/32-42?translations=20).

18 For studies that have analyzed Muslim communities in Los Angeles, see Pamela Prickett, *Believing in South Central: Everyday Islam in the City of Angels* (Chicago: University of Chicago Press, 2021); Carolyn Rouse, *Engaged Surrender: African American Women and Islam* (Los Angeles: University of California Press, 2004); John O'Brien, *Keeping It Halal: The Everyday Lives of Muslim American Teenage Boys* (Princeton, NJ: Princeton University Press, 2017); Harold D. Morales, *Latino and Muslim in America: Race, Religion, and the Making of a New Minority* (New York: Oxford University Press, 2018).

19 WMA director of operations, email communication with author, March 17, 2021.

20 Ihsan Bagby, "The American Mosque 2020: Growing and Evolving—Report 1 of the US Mosque Survey 2020: Basic Characteristics of the American Mosque," July 1, 2021, www.ispu.org.

21 Mucahit Bilici, *Finding Mecca in America: How Islam Is Becoming an American Religion* (Chicago: University of Chicago Press, 2012); Justine Howe, *Suburban Islam* (New York: Oxford University Press, 2018); Timur Yuskaev, *Speaking Qur'an: An American Scripture* (Columbia: University of South Carolina Press, 2017).

22 Bruce Lincoln, *Authority: Construction and Corrosion* (Chicago: University of Chicago Press, 1994), 11.

23 Ibid.

24 Anthea Butler, *Women in the Church of God in Christ Making a Sanctified World* (Chapel Hill: University of North Carolina Press, 2007), 35.

25 Judith Weisenfeld, *African American Women and Christian Activism: New York's Black YWCA, 1905–1945* (Cambridge, MA: Harvard University Press, 1997).

26 Ibid., 41.

27 Donna Auston, "Prayer, Protest, and Police Brutality: Black Muslim Spiritual Resistance in the Ferguson Era," *Transforming Anthropology* 25, no. 1 (2017): 11–22.

28 Asma Sayeed, *Women and the Transmission of Religious Knowledge in Islam* (New York: Cambridge University Press, 2013), 62.

29 By contrast, the female hadith transmitters during the tenth and eleventh centuries rose to prominence based on their intellectual capacities, so the criteria for Islamic authority have evolved throughout history (ibid., 21).

30 Given that the canonization of the Hadith and Sunnah arose to meet legal needs, scholars debate whether these criteria for authority were indeed accurate reflections of norms in the Prophetic era or later reimagined as such. See chapter 1 in Kecia Ali, *The Lives of Muhammad* (Cambridge, MA: Harvard University Press, 2014).

31 Sayeed, *Women and Religious Knowledge*.

32 Hilary Kalmbach, "Social and Religious Change in Damascus: One Case of Female Islamic Religious Authority," *British Journal of Middle Eastern Studies* 35, no. 1 (April 2008): 37–57, 38.

33 Ibid., 44.

34 Hilary Kalmbach, "Introduction: Islamic Authority and the Study of Female Religious Leaders," in *Women, Leadership, and Mosques*, ed. Masooda Bano and Hilary Kalmbach (Abingdon: Brill, 2012), 11.

35 M. Hasna Maznavi, *The Women's Mosque of America Khateebah Guidebook* (internal WMA document, 2017).

36 Debra Majeed, "Womanism Encounters Islam: A Muslim Scholar Considers the Efficacy of a Method Rooted in the Academy and the Church," in *Deeper Shades of Purple: Womanism in Religion and Society*, ed. Stacey M. Floyd-Thomas (New York: New York University Press, 2006), 46.

37 See Talal Asad, "The Idea of an Anthropology of Islam," *Center for Contemporary Arab Studies at Georgetown University*, Occasional Paper Series, 1986.

38 See Eickelman and Piscatori, *Muslim Politics*; Grewal, *Islam Is a Foreign Country*.

39 Grewal, *Islam Is a Foreign Country*, 35.

40 Aysha Hidayatullah, *Feminist Edges of the Qur'an* (New York: Oxford University Press, 2014), 3.

41 For more on the debates on Islam and feminism, the politics of naming, and the limitations of the label "Islamic feminism," see Fatima Seedat, "Islam, Feminism, and Islamic Feminism: Between Inadequacy and Inevitability," *Journal of Feminist Studies in Religion* 29, no. 2 (2013).

42 Saba Mahmood, *Politics of Piety: The Islamic Revival and the Feminist Subject* (Princeton, NJ: Princeton University Press, 2004); Carolyn Rouse, *Engaged Surrender: African American Women and Islam* (Los Angeles: University of California Press, 2004); Garbi Schmidt, *Islam in Urban America: Sunni Muslims in Chicago* (Philadelphia: Temple University Press, 2004).

43 Juliane Hammer, *American Muslim Women, Religious Authority, and Activism: More than a Prayer* (Austin: University of Texas Press, 2012); Debra Majeed, *Polygyny: What It Means When African American Muslim Women Share Their Husbands* (Gainesville: University Press of Florida, 2015).

44 Grewal, *Islam Is a Foreign Country*; Bano and Kalmbach, *Women, Leadership, and Mosques*; Amina Jamal, *Jamaat-e-Islami Women in Pakistan: Vanguard of*

a New Modernity? (Syracuse, NY: Syracuse University Press, 2013); Su'ad Abdul Khabeer, *Muslim Cool: Race, Religion, and Hip Hop in the United States* (New York: New York University Press, 2016); Kambiz GhaneaBassiri, *A History of Islam in America from the New World to the New World Order* (New York: Cambridge University Press, 2010).

45 Sa'diyya Shaikh, "Feminism, Epistemology and Experience: Critically (En)Gendering the Study of Islam," *Journal for Islamic Studies* 33 (2013): 14–47; Kimberlé Crenshaw, "Mapping the Margins: Intersectionality, Identity Politics, and Violence against Women of Color," *Stanford Law Review* 43, no. 6 (1991): 1241–99.

46 Crenshaw, "Mapping the Margins"; Karim, *American Muslim Women.*

47 For more on third-space theory, see Edward Soja, *Thirdspace: Journeys to Los Angeles and Other Real-and-Imagined Places* (Oxford: Blackwell, 1996).

48 Justine Howe, *Suburban Islam* (New York: Oxford University Press, 2018), 11.

49 Abdul Khabeer, *Muslim Cool,* 12.

50 See Sherman Jackson, *Islam and the Blackamerican: Looking Toward the Third Resurrection* (Oxford: Oxford University Press, 2005); amina wadud, "American Muslim Identity: Race and Ethnicity in Progressive Islam," in *Progressive Muslims: On Justice, Gender, and Pluralism,* ed. Omid Safi (Oxford: Oneworld, 2003).

51 Abdul Khabeer, *Muslim Cool.*

52 See Judith Butler, *Gender Trouble: Feminism and the Subversion of Identity* (Abingdon: Routledge, 1990); Joan Scott, "Gender: A Useful Category of Historical Analysis," *American Historical Review* 91, no. 5 (1986): 1053–75; Bruce Dorsey, *Reforming Men and Women: Gender in the Antebellum City* (Ithaca, NY: Cornell University Press, 2002).

53 See Scott, "Gender."

54 See Jerusha Lamptey, *Never Wholly Other: A Muslima Theology of Religious Pluralism* (New York: Oxford University Press, 2014).

CHAPTER 1. RITUAL AUTHORITY

Epigraph. Amal, interview with author, August 10, 2017.

1 Antonia Blumberg, "Women's Mosque Opens in LA with a Vision for the Future of Muslim-American Leadership," *Huffington Post,* January 30, 2015, www.huffpost.com; Tamara Audi, "Feeling Unwelcome at Mosques, 2 Women Start Their Own in LA," *Wall Street Journal,* January 30, 2015, www.wsj.com.

2 Juliane Hammer, "A (Friday) Prayer of Their Own: American Muslim Women, Religious Space, and Equal Rights," *Religious Studies News* (AAR), March 24, 2015, 2, http://rsn.aarweb.org.

3 Furhan Zubairi, "Thoughts on the Women's Mosque of America," *MuslimMatters. Org* (blog), January 30, 2015, https://muslimmatters.org.

4 Staff, "USA: All Women Mosque Opened in Los Angeles," *Muslim Times* (blog), February 11, 2015, https://themuslimtimes.info.

5 For an in-depth analysis of this event, see chapter 1 in Hammer, *American Muslim Women.*

6   M. Hasna Maznavi, "9 Things You Should Know about the Women's Mosque of America—and Muslim Women in General," *Huffington Post*, May 20, 2015, www.huffingtonpost.com.

7   M. Hasna Maznavi, interview with author, August 23, 2017.

8   Salma ElKhaoudi, "Women's Mosque of America: In the Founder's Own Words," *Muslim Girl* (blog), 2015, https://muslimgirl.com.

9   Mariyah, interview with author, July 11, 2017.

10 Tamara Audi, "New Mosque Sparks Discussion on Role of Women in Islam," *Wall Street Journal*, February 5, 2015, www.wsj.com.

11 M. Hasna Maznavi, status update, Facebook, July 25, 2014, www.facebook.com.

12 Seher, interview with author, July 27, 2017.

13 Ibid.

14 Ibid.

15 Ibid.

16 Ibid.

17 Maznavi, interview.

18 "Our Vision," Pico Union Project, accessed December 20, 2017, www.picounion-project.org.

19 Shayna Rose Arnold, "How a Church in Pico-Union Became a Symbol of Religious Peace," *Los Angeles Magazine*, May 27, 2015, www.lamag.com.

20 Maznavi, "9 Things."

21 Edina Lekovic, *Stepping Up*, Women's Mosque of America, January 30, 2015, www.youtube.com/watch?v=4g26wK-VYVo&t=224s.

22 Street, "First All-Female Mosque."

23 Maznavi, interview.

24 I am using the label "neo-traditional" to signify a commitment to the methodologies of traditional Sunni jurisprudential schools. Notably, even beyond neo-traditional US institutes, some of the instructors at the Salafi-leaning AlMaghrib Institute have training in Islamic jurisprudence.

25 For more information, refer to www.zaytuna.edu.

26 For more information, refer to http://almadinainstitute.org.

27 For more information, refer to http://almaghrib.org.

28 The currency placed on obtaining *ijazas* at these American Muslim educational institutions demonstrates the value of formal credentials, such as emphasis on scholarly chains of authority, oral transmission, and memorization.

29 For more information, refer to http://rawiyacollege.org.

30 Enith Morillo, "Shaykha Fest: Celebrating Female Scholarship in Islam," *The American Muslim (TAM)* (blog), February 28, 2013, http://theamericanmuslim.org.

31 For more information, refer to www.alrawiya.org.

32 *Can Women Lead Salah?*, Alrawiya, 2015, www.youtube.com/watch?v=OkHPOtp7GNo.

33 Ibid.

34 Ibid.
35 The hadith of Umm Waraqa is a Prophetic narration in which Muhammad is observed to have appointed one of his female Companions, Umm Waraqa, to lead her household/community in prayer. This hadith is often cited by supporters of woman-led mixed-gender prayer as evidence of its legal validity.
36 Maznavi, interview.
37 Muslema Purmul, status update, Facebook, January 29, 2015, www.facebook.com.
38 Muslema Purmul, "Guarding the Validity of the Prayer: Women's Mosque of America," *MuslimMatters.Org* (blog), January 30, 2015, https://muslimmatters.org.
39 Maznavi, interview.
40 Hammer, *American Muslim Women*, 82.
41 Ibid.
42 Ibid.
43 Maznavi, *Khateebah Guidebook*.
44 Krista Riley, "'You Don't Need a Fatwa': Muslim Feminist Blogging as Religious Interpretation" (PhD diss., Concordia University, 2016), 178.
45 Ibid., 193.
46 Maznavi, *Khateebah Guidebook*.
47 Ali, *Sexual Ethics and Islam*, 194.
48 Edina Lekovic, interview with author, August 9, 2017.
49 Hammer, *American Muslim Women*, 34; amina wadud, *Inside the Gender Jihad: Women's Reform in Islam* (Oxford: Oneworld, 2006), 208.
50 Alburujpress, *Role of Men vs Women by Shaykh Yasir Qadhi (USA)*, YouTube, 2014, www.youtube.com/watch?v=yNgIOGucPlo.
51 Yasir Qadhi, status update, Facebook, February 2, 2015, www.facebook.com.
52 Ibid.
53 See Mahmood Mamdani, *Good Muslim, Bad Muslim: America, the Cold War, and the Roots of Terror* (New York: Three Leaves Press/Doubleday, 2004); Evelyn Al-sultany, *Arabs and Muslims in the Media: Race and Representation after 9/11* (New York: New York University Press, 2012).
54 Qadhi, "Status Update."
55 See, for example, http://sideentrance.tumblr.com.
56 Qadhi, "Status Update."
57 Ibid.
58 Ibid.
59 Hammer, *American Muslim Women*, 15.
60 Examples include Qalbu Maryam Mosque in Berkeley, Mariam Mosque in Copenhagen, Ibn Rushd-Goethe Mosque in Berlin, and the women-led mosque in Bradford, UK.
61 See Jesper Petersen, "Pop-up Mosques, Social Media Adhan, and the Making of Female and LGBTQ-Inclusive Imams," *Journal of Muslims in Europe* 8 (2019): 178–96.
62 Zaid Shakir, "An Examination of the Issue of Female Prayer Leadership," *Lamp Post Productions*, March 23, 2005, 1–12.

63 Ibid., 1.

64 Ibid., 2.

65 Ibid., 3.

66 Ibid., 5.

67 Ingrid Mattson, "Can a Woman Be an Imam? Debating Form and Function in Muslim Women's Leadership," in *The Columbia Sourcebook of Muslims in the United States*, ed. Edward E. Curtis IV (New York: Columbia University Press, 2008), 252–63.

68 Ibid., 258.

69 Laury Silvers, "Islamic Jurisprudence, 'Civil' Disobedience, and Woman-Led Prayer," in Curtis, *Columbia Sourcebook of Muslims*, 247.

70 Ibid., 248.

71 Ibid., 252.

72 Ahmed Elewa and Laury Silvers, "'I Am One of the People': A Survey and Analysis of Legal Arguments on Woman-Led Prayer in Islam," *Journal of Law and Religion* 26, no. 1 (2010–2011): 142.

73 Ibid., 161.

74 "FAQ," Women's Mosque of America.

75 Comments section in Audi, "Feeling Unwelcome at Mosques."

76 Ibid.

77 "Fritz" in comments section in Purmul, "Guarding the Validity."

78 Yasmin Mogahed, "Female-Led Prayers: A Step Forward for Women?," *AboutIslam*, April 24, 2017, http://aboutislam.net.

79 Ibid.

80 Ibid.

81 Ibid.

82 This blog no longer exists but the post has been moved to her official website: Yasmin Mogahed, "A Woman's Reflection on Leading Prayer," *Yasmin Mogahed* (blog), December 19, 2010, www.yasminmogahed.com.

83 Yasmin Mogahed, status update, Facebook, December 11, 2011, www.facebook.com.

84 Mogahed has since clarified on her public Facebook page that she was not referring to all female congregations, which she apparently takes no issue with. She also denied authoring the section of the online response that falsely claimed that amina wadud was remorseful about her role in the 2005 mixed-gender prayer, though she notably included no public apology to wadud.

85 "Juma Circle: Our Story," May 2009, www.jumacircle.com; "Inclusive Mosque Initiative: Our Vision," 2012, http://inclusivemosque.org.

86 Mogahed, "Female-Led Prayers."

87 Yasmin Mogahed, "Official Statement," Facebook, April 28, 2017, www.facebook.com.

88 Mogahed reaffirmed her 2005 position on female-led mixed-gender prayer, clarifying only that she has no issue with female-only congregations or with women in other leadership roles besides leading men in prayer.

89 As of January 2022, there were only female experts listed under counseling services but none under the title of "scholar."

90 See wadud, *Inside the Gender Jihad*, chapter 4.

91 amina wadud, "American by Force, Muslim by Choice," *Political Theology* 12, no. 5 (2011): 699–705. Additionally, Mogahed's erasure of African American Muslims here calls to mind Sherman Jackson's critique of revivalist movements in Islam that influenced American Muslims to develop an anti-culture stance in their definitions of authoritative Islam. Jackson argues that Black culture suffered as a result of these developments as black cultural productions were excluded and shunned by rigid and regionally demarcated barriers to what constituted authentic Islam.

92 Ali, *Sexual Ethics and Islam*, 197–98.

93 Yasmin, interview with author, July 13, 2017.

94 Ibid.

95 Tina, interview with author, August 15, 2017.

96 Ibid.

97 Mariyah, interview with author, July 11, 2017.

98 Bagby, "American Mosque 2011."

99 Tina, interview.

100 Rana, Skype interview with author, September 9, 2017.

101 Seher, interview.

102 Sarah, interview with author, July 28, 2017.

103 Mariyah, interview.

104 Sarah, interview.

105 Leila, interview with author, August 3, 2017.

106 Yasmin, interview.

107 Ibid.

108 Ibid.

109 Rana, interview.

110 Ibid.

111 Leila, interview.

112 Tina, interview.

113 Celeste, phone interview with author, October 12, 2017.

114 Krista Riley, "Documenting, Changing, and Reimagining Women's Mosque Spaces Online," in *The Rowman & Littlefield Handbook of Women's Studies in Religion*, ed. Helen Boursier (Lanham, MD: Rowman & Littlefield, 2021), 319.

115 Ibid., 322.

116 Robert Rozehnal, *Cyber Sufis: Virtual Expressions of the American Muslim Experience* (London: Oneworld, 2019), 37.

CHAPTER 2. INTERPRETIVE AUTHORITY

Epigraph. Zahara, interview with author, July 12, 2017.

1 Johanna Pink shows that, for most premodern Muslims, the Qur'an was "not necessarily the main source of guidance" but central in ritual and healing practices.

See Johanna Pink, *Muslim Qur'anic Interpretation Today: Media, Genealogies and Interpretive Communities* (Sheffield: Equinox Publishing, 2019), 17.

2 Zahara, interview.

3 Kenyatta, interview with author, August 1, 2017.

4 Black Muslims in the US are not a homogenous group; some examples of communities whose experiences would not conform to Zahara's characterizations are Salafi African American Muslim organizations like the Brooklyn-based Darul Islam and African immigrant Sufi communities, as well as for example groups of African American Muslims who seek classical Islamic education in places like Senegal. See Aminah McCloud, *African American Islam* (New York: Routledge, 1995); Cheikh Anta Babou, *The Muridiyya on the Move: Islam, Migration, and Place Making* (Athens: Ohio University Press, 2021); Samiha Rahman, "Black Muslim Freedom Dreams: Islamic Education, Transnational Migration, and Mobility" (PhD diss., University of Pennsylvania, 2020).

5 Kenyatta, interview.

6 Maznavi, *Khateebah Guidebook.*

7 Salma ElKhaoudi, "Women's Mosque of America: In the Founder's Own Words," *Muslim Girl* (blog), 2015, https://muslimgirl.com.

8 Zahara, interview.

9 Pink, *Muslim Qur'anic Interpretation Today, 17.*

10 Ibid., *26.*

11 Ibid., *26–27.*

12 Ibid., *28.*

13 For more on this point in the context of early enslaved Muslims in the US, see chapter 4 in Diouf, *Servants of Allah* (1998); in the context of the post-1965 wave of Muslim immigrants, see chapter 2 in Bilici, *Finding Mecca in America*, and pp. 139–144 in Grewal, *Islam Is a Foreign Country.*

14 Maznavi, *Khateebah Guidebook.*

15 Edina Lekovic, *Stepping Up*, Women's Mosque of America, January 30, 2015, www.youtube.com/watch?v=4g26wK-VYV0&t=224s.

16 Ibid.

17 Ibid.

18 Maznavi, "9 Things."

19 Grewal, *Islam Is a Foreign Country*, 200.

20 ElKhaoudi, "Women's Mosque of America"; Lekovic, *Stepping Up.*

21 Ali, *Sexual Ethics and Islam*, 170.

22 Grewal, *Islam Is a Foreign Country*, 42.

23 Ibid., 47.

24 Ibid., 49.

25 Alexander Thurston, "Polyvalent, Transnational Religious Authority: The Tijaniyya Sufi Order and Al-Azhar University," *Journal of the American Academy of Religion* 86, no. 3 (August 23, 2018): 789–820.

26 Ibid., 790.

27 "FAQ," Women's Mosque of America.

28 "Description of Our Services," Women's Mosque of America, 2015, http://womensmosque.com.

29 Mohamed Nimer, *The North American Muslim Resource Guide: Community Life in the United States and Canada* (New York: Routledge, 2002), 50.

30 See Jackson, *Islam and the Blackamerican.*

31 Karim, *American Muslim Women*, 152–53.

32 GhaneaBassiri, *History of Islam in America*, 286.

33 Karim, *American Muslim Women*, 192; Abdul Khabeer, *Muslim Cool*, 146.

34 Abdul Khabeer, *Muslim Cool*, 146.

35 Ibid., 147.

36 Ingrid Mattson, "Women, Islam, and Mosques," in *Encyclopedia of Women and Religion in North America*, ed. Rosemary Keller and Rosemary Ruether (Bloomington: Indiana University Press, 2006), 617.

37 Grewal, *Islam Is a Foreign Country*, 42.

38 Abdul Khabeer, *Muslim Cool*, 96–97.

39 Ibid.

40 Kalmbach, "Social and Religious Change," 38.

41 Grewal, *Islam Is a Foreign Country*, 251.

42 Ibid., 246.

43 Khaled Abou El Fadl, *Speaking in God's Name: Islamic Law, Authority and Women* (Oxford: Oneworld, 2001), 163.

44 Ibid., 265–67.

45 Ingrid Mattson, whose ideas on female religious leadership I explored in chapter 1, is an exception here as she marshals Islamic authority and holds only secular credentials.

46 Zahra Ayubi, "Owning Terms of Leadership and Authority: Toward a Gender-Inclusive Framework of American Muslim Religious Authority," in *A Jihad for Justice: Honoring the Work and Life of Amina Wadud*, ed. Kecia Ali, Juliane Hammer, and Laury Silvers (Akron, OH: 48 Hour Books, 2012), 50.

47 I follow Hidayatullah's extension of the label "feminist" to scholars whose works challenge "male power and interpretive privilege—which vitally links them, for better or for worse, to feminist thought regardless of authorial intention or self-identification" (*Feminist Edges of the Qur'an*, 4). For more on the politics of naming and the limitations of the label "Islamic feminism," see Seedat, "Islam, Feminism, and Islamic Feminism."

48 These women include Riffat Hassan, Azizah al-Hibri, amina wadud, Asma Barlas, Kecia Ali, Sa'diyya Shaikh, Aysha Hidayatullah, and Ayesha Chaudhry.

49 Hammer, *American Muslim Women*, 63.

50 Feminist interpretations of the Qur'an are rooted in the modern exegetical methods promoted by nineteenth- and twentieth-century reformers like Muhammad Abduh and Fazlur Rahman. Notable among these methods are the historical contextualization method and the *tawhidic* paradigm. The historical contextualiza-

tion method emphasizes *asbab al-nuzul*, or the occasions of revelation, as central to understanding the full meaning of particular Qur'anic verses. For example, according to wadud, understanding the historical circumstances surrounding the Qur'anic conceptions of polygyny and male guardianship would significantly curtail their contemporary implementation. The *tawhidic* paradigm uses the concept of God's oneness to reject gender hierarchy on the basis that ascribing authority to men over women is a form of idolatry. This is a central interpretive move for wadud because it renders any designation of men "as the superiors of women or attributing maleness to God" an act of idolatry. The *tawhidic* paradigm allows wadud to reject patriarchal Qur'anic interpretations that equate disobedience of a wife toward her husband with disobedience toward God. For more, see amina wadud, "Towards a Qur'anic Hermeneutics of Social Justice: Race, Class and Gender," *Journal of Law and Religion* 12, no. 1 (1995–1996): 37–50; wadud, *Inside the Gender Jihad*; Hidayatullah, *Feminist Edges of the Qur'an*.

51 Maznavi, *Khateebah Guidebook*.
52 Howe, *Suburban Islam*, 18.
53 Ibid., 140.
54 Ibid., 108.
55 Christopher Pooya Razavian, "Yasir Qadhi and the Development of Reasonable Salafism," in *Modern Islamic Authority and Social Change. Volume 2: Evolving Debates in the West*, ed. Masooda Bano (Edinburgh: University of Edinburgh, 2018), 155.
56 Ibid., 162.
57 Grewal, *Islam Is a Foreign Country*, 331.
58 Ibid., 209.
59 Ibid., 210.
60 Ibid., 209.
61 Maznavi, "9 Things."
62 Grewal, *Islam Is a Foreign Country*, 213.
63 Maznavi, *Khateebah Guidebook*, 3; Maznavi, "9 Things."
64 Lekovic, interview.
65 Samara Yusuf, "The First Women's Mosque: An Interview with Its Founders," *Altmuslimah* (blog), February 11, 2015, www.altmuslimah.com.
66 Lekovic, interview.
67 Yuskaev, *Speaking Qur'an*, 13–15.
68 Lekovic, *Stepping Up*.
69 Lekovic, interview.
70 For more on literature on the Qur'an in translation, see M. Brett Wilson, "Ritual and Rhyme: Alevi-Bektashi Interpretations and Translations of the Qur'an (1953–2007)," *Journal of Qur'anic Studies* 17, no. 3 (2015): 75–99; Bruce Lawrence, *The Qur'an: A Biography* (New York: Atlantic Monthly Press, 2006).
71 The WMA refers its khateebahs to four different resources for Qur'anic translations: the comparison tool at islamawakened.com, the search tool at islamicity.

com, the Muhammad Asad complete translation, and other translations from al-quran.info.

72 Lekovic, *Stepping Up.*

73 Ibid.

74 Bilici, *Finding Mecca in America*, 84.

75 Ibid., 88.

76 Ibid., 84.

77 Lekovic, *Stepping Up.*

78 Ibid.

79 Maznavi, "9 Things."

80 Wallace Best, *Passionately Human, No Less Divine: Religion and Culture in Black Chicago, 1915–1952* (Princeton, NJ: Princeton University Press, 2005), 150.

81 Ibid., 152.

82 Ibid., 175.

83 Asma Barlas, "Still Quarrelling over the Qur'an: Five Theses on Interpretation and Authority," paper presented at Redefining Boundaries: Muslim Women and Religious Authority in Practice Conference at the Institute for the Study of Islam in the Modern World (ISIM), Amsterdam, June 24, 2007, 8.

84 Ibid., 6.

85 Ibid., 5.

86 Ibid.

87 Ibid., 3.

88 Lekovic, interview.

89 Lekovic, *Stepping Up.*

90 Lekovic, interview.

91 Howe, *Suburban Islam*, 160.

92 Lekovic, *Stepping Up.*

93 Ibid.

94 Lekovic, interview.

95 wadud, "American Muslim Identity," 272.

96 wadud, *Inside the Gender Jihad*, 19.

97 Laila Al-Marayati, *Overcoming Struggle during Ramadan*, audio recording, Women's Mosque of America, June 26, 2015, https://soundcloud.com.

98 Ibid.

99 Ibid.

100 Charles McCrary and Jeffrey Wheatley, "The Protestant Secular in the Study of American Religion: Reappraisal and Suggestions," *Religion* 47 (2017): 257. See also Charles McCrary, *Sincerely Held: American Secularism and Its Believers* (Chicago: University of Chicago Press, 2022).

101 Al-Marayati, *Overcoming Struggle during Ramadan.*

102 Ibid.

103 Yuskaev, *Speaking Qur'an*, 76.

104 Ibid., 94.

105 Seher, interview.

106 Ibid.

107 Ibid.

108 Ibid.

109 Ibid.

110 Jennifer Thompson, "'He Wouldn't Know Anything': Rethinking Women's Religious Leadership," *Journal of the American Academy of Religion* 81, no. 3 (2013): 664.

111 Rouse, *Engaged Surrender*, 80.

112 Rouse, *Engaged Surrender*; Pamela Prickett, "Negotiating Gendered Religious Space: The Particularities of Patriarchy in an African American Mosque," *Gender and Society* 29, no. 1 (2015): 51–72.

113 Sufiya, interview with author, July 12, 2017.

114 Seher, interview.

115 Leila, interview.

116 Ibid.

117 Yasmin, interview.

118 See Rudolph Ware, *The Walking Qur'an: Islamic Education, Embodied Knowledge, and History in West Africa* (Chapel Hill: University of North Carolina Press, 2014); Anna Gade, *Perfection Makes Practice: Learning, Emotion, and the Recited Qur'ān in Indonesia* (Honolulu: University of Hawai'i Press, 2004).

119 Yasmin, interview.

120 Ibid.

121 Ana, interview with author, July 27, 2017.

122 Sarah, interview with author, July 28, 2017.

123 Amal, interview with author, August 10, 2017.

124 Lekovic, *Stepping Up*.

125 Maznavi, "9 Things."

126 Street, "First All-Female Mosque."

127 R. Marie Griffith, *God's Daughters: Evangelical Women and the Power of Submission* (Berkeley: University of California Press, 1997), 135.

128 See Saba Mahmood, *Religious Difference in a Secular Age: A Minority Report* (Princeton, NJ: Princeton University Press, 2015); McCrary, *Sincerely Held*.

129 Grewal, *Islam Is a Foreign Country*, 223.

CHAPTER 3. EMBODIED AUTHORITY

Epigraph. Sabrina, interview with author, August 15, 2017.

1 Sabrina, interview.

2 Ibid.

3 Omaima Abou-Bakr, "The Interpretive Legacy of Qiwamah as an Exegetical Construct," in *Men in Charge? Rethinking Authority in Muslim Legal Tradition*, ed.

Ziba Mir-Hosseini, Jana Rumminger, and Mulki Al-Sharmani (London: One-world, 2014).

4 Omaima Abou-Bakr, *The Ethics of Gender Justice*, Women's Mosque of America khutbah, December 2020, www.youtube.com/watch?v=IMNmJACWV1k.

5 wadud, "Towards a Qur'anic Hermeneutics," 48–50.

6 Isabella, interview with author, August 1, 2017.

7 Guest Post, "A Statement Regarding Br. Nouman Ali Khan: A Statement from Sr. Aisha Al-Adawiya, Sr. Salma Abugideiri, Sh. Tamara Gray, Dr. Altaf Husain, Imam Mohamed Magid, and Dr. Ingrid Mattson," *MuslimMatters* (blog), October 3, 2017, https://muslimmatters.org.

8 In 2016, Saleem pled guilty to two counts of sexual abuse, while Khan has not been charged with any crimes, and in fact is back on the lecture circuit with his reputation intact, demonstrating how, despite the initial attention these incidents receive, there has been no sustained efforts in American Muslim communities to address sexual abuse by religious leaders.

9 Shabana Mir, "Nouman Ali Khan Shows Us That We Need More Women Religious Leaders," *Altmuslim* (blog), October 2, 2017, www.patheos.com. Emphasis in original.

10 Ingrid Mattson, Twitter post, September 29, 2017, https://twitter.com/ingridmattson/status/913642479626457088.

11 "FAQ," Women's Mosque of America.

12 Hammer, *American Muslim Women*, 114.

13 Maria Jaschok, "Sources of Authority: Female Ahong and Qingzhen Nüsi (Women's Mosques) in China," in Bano and Kalmbach, *Women, Leadership, and Mosques*, 37–58; Jingjun Shui and Isabella Jaschok, "The Culture of 'Associational Leadership' in the Hui Muslim Women's Mosques of Central China," *Asian Journal of Social Science* 42, no. 5 (2014).

14 Margaret Rausch, "Women Mosque Preachers and Spiritual Guides: Publicizing and Negotiating Women's Religious Authority in Morocco," in Bano and Kalmbach, *Women, Leadership, and Mosques*, 59–83.

15 Mona Hassan, "Reshaping Religious Authority in Contemporary Turkey: State-Sponsored Female Preachers," in Bano and Kalmbach, *Women, Leadership, and Mosques*, 85–104.

16 Sarah Islam, "The Qubaysīyyāt: The Growth of an International Muslim Women's Revivalist Movement from Syria (1960–2008)," in Bano and Kalmbach, *Women, Leadership, and Mosques*, 161–84.

17 Jamal, *Jamaat-e-Islami Women*.

18 Mahmood, *Politics of Piety*, 89.

19 Ibid., 156–58.

20 Ellen McLarney, *Soft Force: Women in Egypt's Islamic Awakening* (Princeton, NJ: Princeton University Press, 2015), 259.

21 Ibid.

22 Maznavi, *Khateebah Guidebook*.

23 Ibid., 5.

24 While the WMA brands itself as a nondenominational middle ground welcoming to all Muslim sects, the *Khateebah Guidebook* specifies that any invocations of the *shahadah* (declaration of faith) during khutbahs or additional du'a after the prayer should read: "There is no god but God, and Muhammad is the messenger of God," which is the Sunni version, implying that for example the Shi'a *shahadah*, which also contains a third part reading "And Ali is the *wali* [friend] of God," would not be permitted.

25 Maznavi, *Khateebah Guidebook*, 7.

26 Ibid., 10.

27 "Description of Our Services," Women's Mosque of America.

28 Maznavi, *Khateebah Guidebook*.

29 Ibid.

30 Ibid.

31 See chapter 2, note 69.

32 Maznavi, *Khateebah Guidebook*, 7.

33 Ibid., 8. Emphasis in original.

34 Mariyah, interview with author, July 11, 2017.

35 Ibid.

36 Sumaya Abubaker, *Sexual Violence and the Necessity of Compassion and Justice*, Women's Mosque of America, April 24, 2015, www.youtube.com/watch?v=CxaLZxb-bcI.

37 Anonymous, interview with author.

38 Ibid.

39 See wadud, "Towards a Qur'anic Hermeneutics," 49–50; wadud, "American Muslim Identity"; Sa'diyya Shaikh, "A Tafsir of Praxis: Gender, Marital Violence, and Resistance in a South African Muslim Community," in *Violence against Women in Contemporary World Religions: Roots and Cures*, ed. Daniel C. Maguire and Sa'Diyya Shaikh (Pilgrim Press, 2007); Majeed, *Polygyny*.

40 Shaikh, "A Tafsir of Praxis," 67.

41 wadud, *Inside the Gender Jihad*, 134.

42 Majeed, *Polygyny*, 20–21.

43 Cheryl Kirk-Duggan, "Womanist Theology as a Corrective to African American Theology," in *The Oxford Handbook of African American Theology*, ed. Anthony B. Pinn and Katie Cannon, 2014, 268.

44 Majeed, *Polygyny*, 17–18; Majeed, "Womanism Encounters Islam."

45 Majeed, *Polygyny*, 20–21.

46 Abubaker, *Sexual Violence* (Qur'an 4:135).

47 Patricia Hill Collins, *Black Feminist Thought: Knowledge, Consciousness, and the Politics of Empowerment* (New York: Routledge, 1991), 257.

48 Ibid.

49 Sufiya, interview.

50 Collins, *Black Feminist Thought*, 269.

51 Ibid., 270.

52 Shaikh, "Feminism, Epistemology and Experience," 20–23. See also Joan Scott, "The Evidence of Experience," *Critical Inquiry* 17, no. 4 (1991): 773–97.

53 Kecia Ali, *Marriage and Slavery in Early Islam* (Cambridge, MA: Harvard University Press, 2010); Ayesha Chaudhry, *Domestic Violence in the Islamic Tradition* (Oxford: Oxford University Press, 2013).

54 Ali, *Marriage and Slavery*, 15.

55 Hina Azam, *Sexual Violation in Islamic Law: Substance, Evidence, and Procedure* (Cambridge: Cambridge University Press, 2015), 19.

56 Qur'an 4:34: "Men are in charge of women by [right of] what Allah has given one over the other and what they spend [for maintenance] from their wealth. So righteous women are devoutly obedient, guarding in [the husband's] absence what Allah would have them guard. But those [wives] from whom you fear arrogance— [first] advise them; [then if they persist], forsake them in bed; and [finally], strike them. But if they obey you [once more], seek no means against them. Indeed, Allah is ever Exalted and Grand," from https://quran.com/4/34-44.

57 Chaudhry, *Domestic Violence*, 85.

58 Ibid., 8.

59 Azam, *Sexual Violation in Islamic Law*, 2–3.

60 Najeeba Syeed, *Restorative Social Justice and Radical Love*, Women's Mosque of America, October 30, 2015, www.youtube.com/watch?v=DEirZjbp-8s.

61 wadud, *Inside the Gender Jihad*, 202.

62 Women's Mosque of America Team, "The Women's Mosque of America— Newsletter #222: The Most Important Khutbah You Will Ever Hear . . . ," July 26, 2021.

63 Khaled Abou El Fadl, "The Ugly Modern and the Modern Ugly: Reclaiming the Beautiful in Islam," in Safi, *Progressive Muslims*, 42.

64 Ibid.

65 Juliane Hammer, *Peaceful Families: American Muslim Efforts against Domestic Violence* (Princeton, NJ: Princeton University Press, 2019), 120–21.

66 Mona Eltahawy, "Muslim Women, Caught Between Islamophobes and 'Our Men,'" *New York Times*, November 19, 2017, www.nytimes.com.

67 See also Virginia Sapiro, "Sexual Harassment: Performances of Gender, Sexuality, and Power," *Perspectives on Politics* 16, no. 4 (December 2018): 1053–66.

68 For more on the layered vulnerabilities of black women, see Nigel Bellis and Astral Finnie, "Black Girls Matter," *Surviving R. Kelly* (Lifetime, January 5, 2019).

69 Ana, interview with author, July 27, 2017.

70 Muslema Purmul, *Mother-Daughter High Tea*, Women's Mosque of America, May 22, 2016, www.youtube.com/watch?v=xlf8do2ijZY.

71 Ibid.

72 Shabnam Dewji, *The Prophet's Daughter Fatimah Al-Zahra*, Women's Mosque of America, November 20, 2015, www.youtube.com/watch?v=wBMbnf95bIQ.

73 Mogahed, "A Woman's Reflection."

74 As with the majority of the WMA khutbahs, with the exception of the ones delivered between May and August 2017 when I was in LA, I listened to audio files of
both Khan-Ibarra's bayan and Nadeem's khutbah online rather than in person.

75 Sabina Khan-Ibarra, *Grief, Loss and Divorce + Interracial Marriage*, audio recording, Women's Mosque of America, April 22, 2016, https://soundcloud.com.

76 Ibid.

77 Ibid.

78 Ibid.

79 Qur'an 49:13: "O mankind, indeed We have created you from male and female and
made you peoples and tribes that you may know one another. Indeed, the most
noble of you in the sight of Allah is the most righteous of you. Indeed, Allah is
Knowing and Acquainted," from https://quran.com/49/13.

80 Sarah Nadeem, *Grief, Loss, and Divorce*, audio recording, Women's Mosque of
America, April 22, 2016, https://soundcloud.com.

81 Ibid.

82 Eman Hassaballa Aly, *The Power and Responsibility of Motherhood*, audio recording, Women's Mosque of America pre-khutbah bayan, May 22, 2015, https://
soundcloud.com.

83 Qur'an 3:36 (https://quran.com/3).

84 See "Muslim Leadership Initiative," Shalom Hartman Institute, 2013, www.hartman.org.

85 Zeena Qureshi, "Ananas Advisor Series: Introducing Eman Hassaballa Aly," January 9, 2018, https://medium.com.

86 Maznavi, *Khateebah Guidebook*, 8.

CHAPTER 4. AUTHORITY THROUGH ACTIVISM

Hajjah Krishna Nunnally Najieb, *The Transformative Power of Hajj*, Women's Mosque
of America, February 28, 2020, www.youtube.com/watch?v=CoCoeHgLp1A.

1 Malcolm X and Alex Haley, *The Autobiography of Malcolm X* (New York: Grove
Press, 1965).

2 Najieb, *Transformative Power of Hajj*.

3 Tina, interview with author, August 15, 2017.

4 Karim, *American Muslim Women*; Jackson, *Islam and the Blackamerican*.

5 Jackson, *Islam and the Blackamerican*, 94.

6 Zain Abdullah, *Black Mecca: The African Muslims of Harlem* (New York: Oxford
University Press, 2010), 56.

7 After the death of his father, Elijah Muhammad, in 1975, Warith Deen Mohammed
became the leader of the Nation of Islam and slowly merged it into the fold of
mainstream Sunni Islam by 1978. Louis Farrakhan later revived the NOI in 1981
and continues to lead it today.

8 Bagby, "American Mosque 2011."

9 By "home mosques," I refer to the particular mosque communities in LA to which
my interlocutors belong, as either members or leaders, outside of their participation at the WMA.

10 Najieb, *Transformative Power of Hajj.*

11 Zahara, interview.

12 For more on the dynamics between Black American and African immigrants, see Abdullah, *Black Mecca.*

13 Ibid., 56–57.

14 Babou, *Muridiyya on the Move,* 181; Abdul Khabeer, *Muslim Cool,* 93–96.

15 Abdullah, *Black Mecca,* 234.

16 Edward Curtis, "The Black Muslim Scare of the Twentieth Century: The History of State Islamophobia and Its Post-9/11 Variations," in *Islamophobia in America: The Anatomy of Intolerance,* ed. Carl Ernst (New York: Palgrave Macmillan, 2013), 75–106.

17 Babou, *Muridiyya on the Move,* 179.

18 See, for example, Noura Erakat, "Geographies of Intimacy: Contemporary Renewals of Black–Palestinian Solidarity," *American Quarterly* 72, no. 2 (June 2020): 482, on the hesitation of Palestinian American mosques to rally behind the Black Lives Matter movement.

19 Sanya Mansoor, "'At the Intersection of Two Criminalized Identities': Black and Non-Black Muslims Confront a Complicated Relationship with Policing and Anti-Blackness," *Time,* September 13, 2020, https://time.com; Amal Ahmed, "Muslim Activists Say It's Time to Join Black Lives Matter Calls to Reform Law Enforcement," *Texas Observer,* July 24, 2020, www.texasobserver.org.

20 Zahra Billoo, *Combatting Islamophobia,* audio recording, Women's Mosque of America, July 24, 2015, https://soundcloud.com.

21 Maznavi, *Khateebah Guidebook,* 5.

22 Curtis, "Black Muslim Scare."

23 Khaled Beydoun, *American Islamophobia: Understanding the Roots and Rise of Fear* (Oakland: University of California Press, 2019), 105.

24 Billoo, "Combatting Islamophobia."

25 Sylvester Johnson, *African American Religions, 1500–2000: Colonialism, Democracy, and Freedom* (New York: Cambridge University Press, 2015), 381.

26 Ibid., 380.

27 Ibid.

28 Ibid., 379.

29 Johnson, *African American Religions,* 383.

30 Ibid., 388.

31 Ibid., 396.

32 Curtis, "Black Muslim Scare," 99.

33 Sylvia Chan-Malik, *Being Muslim: A Cultural History of Women of Color in American Islam* (New York: New York University Press, 2018), 15.

34 Billoo, "Combatting Islamophobia."

35 Ibid.

36 Ibid.

37 Ibid.
38 Qur'anic verses that Billoo refers to in her khutbah include Qur'an 94:5 ("Verily with every difficulty there is relief") and Qur'an 2:155 ("We will test you with a certain amount of fear and hunger and loss of wealth and life").
39 To clarify, here Billoo's supplication asking God for forgiveness for victims of police brutality is part of routine condolence supplications in Islam wherein worshipers ask God to forgive the souls of the departed so that they may enter Paradise; it does *not* imply that these victims bear any responsibility for their murders.
40 Billoo, "Combatting Islamophobia."
41 Aziza Hasan, *Empowering Youth to Respond to Hate with Compassion*, audio recording, Women's Mosque of America, May 22, 2015, https://soundcloud.com.
42 Farrah N. Khan, *Post 11/9, Where Do We Go from Here?*, audio recording, Women's Mosque of America, November 18, 2016, https://soundcloud.com.
43 Ibid.
44 Amani Al-Khatahtbeh, *A Message for Muslim Youth*, audio recording, Women's Mosque of America One-Year Anniversary, January 29, 2016, https://soundcloud.com.
45 Ibid.
46 Ibid.
47 Hammer, "Center Stage," 110.
48 Lila Abu-Lughod, *Do Muslim Women Need Saving?* (Cambridge, MA: Harvard University Press, 2013); Charles Hirschkind and Saba Mahmood, "Feminism, the Taliban, and the Politics of Counter-Insurgency," *Anthropological Quarterly* 75, no. 2 (2002): 339–54.
49 Aima Warriach, "Why I Left Muslim Girl," *Aima Warriach* (blog), May 17, 2019, https://medium.com.
50 Mehar, "MuslimGirl.Com: Exploitation, Abuse, & Hypocrisy," *Spill the Chai* (blog), December 29, 2016, https://spillthechai.com; Marie Solis, "What the Fall of the 'Girlboss' Reveals," *CNN*, July 2, 2020, www.cnn.com.
51 Sarah Jawaid, "Being a Steward of God's People and Planet," audio recording, Women's Mosque of America, March 27, 2015.
52 Omid Safi, "Introduction: The Times They Are a-Changin'—A Muslim Quest for Justice, Gender Equality and Pluralism," in Safi, *Progressive Muslims*, 7–11.
53 Ibid.
54 Jawaid, "Being a Steward."
55 Qur'an 33:72, from M. A. S. Abdel Haleem, *The Qur'an: English Translation and Parallel Arabic Text* (New York: Oxford University Press, 2010).
56 "Meet Our Khateebahs," Women's Mosque of America, last accessed December 9, 2015, http://womensmosque.com.
57 Jawaid, "Being a Steward."
58 Curtis, *Muslims in America*, 69.
59 Ibid.

60 GhaneaBassiri, *History of Islam in America*, 164.
61 Karim, *American Muslim Women*, 9.
62 Grewal, *Islam Is a Foreign Country*, 156.
63 Ibid., 138.
64 Ibid., 137.
65 wadud, "American Muslim Identity," 272.
66 GhaneaBassiri, *History of Islam in America*; Bald, "Overlapping Diasporas," 231.
67 Bald, "Overlapping Diasporas," 229; Vivek Bald, *Bengali Harlem and the Lost Histories of South Asian America* (Cambridge, MA: Harvard University Press, 2013).
68 GhaneaBassiri, *History of Islam in America*, 250.
69 Ibid., 252.
70 Syeed, *Restorative Social Justice*.
71 Ibid.
72 wadud, "American Muslim Identity."
73 Ibid., 274.
74 Ibid. wadud draws the above Qur'anic translation from Muhammad Asad's *The Message of the Qur'an*.
75 wadud, "American Muslim Identity," 275.
76 Ibid., 274.
77 Shaykh Muhammad al-Ghazali, *A Thematic Commentary on the Qur'an* (Herndon, VA: International Institute of Islamic Thought, 1992), 574, 579.
78 Here, Kecia Ali and Aysha Hidayatullah would argue that assumptions about the Qur'an's essentially egalitarian nature ultimately constrict opportunities for reform. Ali contends that reformist arguments for justice and equality in the Qur'anic text make incorrect assumptions about the so-called timelessness of what are particularly modern values. Kecia Ali, "Timeless Texts and Modern Morals: Challenges in Islamic Sexual Ethics," in *New Directions in Islamic Thought: Exploring Reform and Muslim Tradition*, ed. Kari Vogt, Lena Larsen, and Christian Moe (New York: I.B. Tauris, 2011), 92.
79 Jawaid, "Being a Steward."
80 This is emblematic of Robert Orsi's argument that religious practitioners actively negotiate their worldly circumstances rather than rely on a fixed, intransitive understanding of religion. See Robert Orsi, "Everyday Miracles: The Study of Lived Religion," in *Lived Religion in America: Toward a History of Practice*, ed. David D. Hall (Princeton, NJ: Princeton University Press, 1997), 8.
81 Ayubi, "Owning Terms of Leadership," 53.
82 Jawaid, "Being a Steward."
83 an-Nawawi, "Hadith 34, an-Nawawi 40 Hadith," Sunnah.com, https://sunnah.com.
84 I was not present for this discussion series and learned about its content through conversations with my interlocutors who were there. I also listened to audio recordings of the second two sessions posted online, which provided a general sense of their content and form.

85   Kameelah Wilkerson, interview with author, August 16, 2017.

86   Ibid.

87   Zahara, interview.

88   Ibid.

89   Ibid.

90   "Map: Where Critical Race Theory Is Under Attack," EducationWeek, July 15, 2021, www.edweek.org.

91   Zahara, interview.

92   Rana, interview.

93   Ibid.

94   Leila, interview.

95   Ibtihal, interview.

96   Ibid.

97   Sabrina, interview.

98   Kenyatta, interview.

99   Maznavi, interview.

100   Ibid.

101   Ibid.

102   Auston, "Prayer, Protest, and Police Brutality." See also Iman AbdoulKarim, "'Islam Is Black Lives Matter': The Role of Gender and Religion in Muslim Women's BLM Activism," in *Race, Religion, and Black Lives Matter: Essays on a Moment and a Movement*, ed. Christopher Cameron and Phillip Sinitiere (Nashville: Vanderbilt University Press, 2021).

103   Abrafi Sanyika, *Balancing Religion and Culture: From an African-American Muslim*, Women's Mosque of America, May 15, 2020, www.youtube.com/watch?v=G2nut-qxv1U.

104   Evelyn Brooks Higginbotham, *Righteous Discontent: The Women's Movement in the Black Baptist Church, 1880–1920* (Cambridge, MA: Harvard University Press, 1994), 7.

105   Ibid., 1.

106   Curtis, *Muslims in America*, 55.

107   Michael Crowley, "Trump Calls for 'Patriotic Education' to Defend American History from the Left," *New York Times*, September 17, 2020, www.nytimes.com.

108   See Jackson, *Islam and the Blackamerican*.

109   Auston, "Prayer, Protest, and Police Brutality."

110   Abdul Khabeer, *Muslim Cool*, 83.

111   wadud, "American by Force," 703.

112   Ibid.

113   Sanyika, *Balancing Religion and Culture*.

114   She quotes the verse as "O humankind behold! We have created you all out of male and a female and have made you into nations and tribes so that you might come to know one another. Verily the noblest of you in the sight of God is the one who is most deeply conscious of God. Behold God is all-knowing, all aware."

115 Sanyika, *Balancing Religion and Culture*.
116 Ibid.
117 *"A Conversation on Hajj, Women & Race" w/Krishna Nunnally Najieb & the Hajjah Project*, 2020, www.youtube.com/watch?v=PtRnJBBtH40. "A Conversation on Hajj, Women, and Race" took place July 3, 2020, and mostly focused on the Hajjah Project.

CHAPTER 5. THE POLITICS OF COMMUNITY BUILDING

Epigraph. Shira, interview with author, August 10, 2017.

1 "The Women's Mosque of America," Pluralism Project Archive, October 22, 2015, https://hwpi.harvard.edu.
2 Lamptey, *Never Wholly Other*, 1–2; Corbett, *Making Moderate Islam*.
3 Shira, interview.
4 Ibid.
5 Ibid.
6 Ibid.
7 Laila Alawa, *We All Deserve to Be Here, No Matter What the World Says*, Women's Mosque of America, January 26, 2018, www.youtube.com/watch?v=3hTUFSFaGho.
8 Ibid.
9 Ibid.
10 Ibid.
11 Ibid.
12 See Mir, *Muslim American Women on Campus*.
13 See Christopher Bail, *Terrified: How Anti-Muslim Fringe Organizations Became Mainstream* (Princeton, NJ: Princeton University Press, 2014).
14 Beydoun, *American Islamophobia*, 55.
15 Faiza Patel and Michael German, "Countering Violent Extremism: Myths and Fact," Brennan Center, October 29, 2015, www.brennancenter.org.
16 "Timeline of the Muslim Ban," ACLU Washington, February 2020, www.aclu-wa.org; Burnett, "Immigrant Detention for Profit Faces Resistance after Big Expansion under Trump," NPR, April 20, 2021, www.npr.org.
17 "Laila Alawa," accessed January 11, 2021, www.lailaalawa.com.
18 "2018 30 under 30: Media," *Forbes*, November 14, 2017.
19 Tova Gold, "Like It or Not, I'm Jewish and Muslim," *Tempest* (blog), September 18, 2015, https://thetempest.co/; Bushra Bajwa, "Larycia Hawkins Is an Interfaith Pioneer," *Tempest* (blog), January 11, 2016, https://thetempest.co.
20 Ayesha Mirza, "Is Anti-Semitism Still Prevalent in Muslim Communities?," *Tempest* (blog), November 23, 2020, https://thetempest.co; Bajwa, "Larycia Hawkins."
21 Emma Green, "Muslim Americans Are United by Trump—and Divided by Race," *Atlantic*, March 11, 2017, www.theatlantic.com.
22 David H. Warren, *Rivals in the Gulf: Yusuf al-Qaradawi, Abdullah Bin Bayyah, and the Qatar-UAE Contest over the Arab Spring and the Gulf Crisis* (London: Routledge, 2021), 108.

23 Candace Lukasik, "Economy of Blood: The Persecuted Church and the Racialization of American Copts," *American Anthropologist*, May 16, 2021.

24 Jasbir K. Puar, *Terrorist Assemblages: Homonationalism in Queer Times* (Durham, NC: Duke University Press, 2017), 166–71.

25 Rose Aslan, *Taking Account of Ourselves to Give Back*, Women's Mosque of America, February 20, 2015, www.youtube.com/watch?v=GvsUH8bxHok.

26 Corbett, *Making Moderate Islam*, 188–90.

27 Aslan, *Taking Account of Ourselves*.

28 Ibid.

29 Ibid.

30 Ibid.

31 Diana Eck, *A New Religious America: How a "Christian Country" Has Become the World's Most Religiously Diverse Nation* (San Francisco: HarperCollins, 2001), 288.

32 Corbett, *Making Moderate Islam*.

33 Aslan, *Taking Account of Ourselves*.

34 Mir, *Muslim American Women on Campus*.

35 Aslan, *Taking Account of Ourselves*.

36 Ibid.

37 Ibid.

38 Aamna, phone interview with author, September 16, 2017.

39 Ibid.

40 Aslan, *Taking Account of Ourselves*.

41 Cynthia, interview with author, August 26, 2017.

42 Lekovic, *Stepping Up*; Maznavi, "9 Things"; Nick Street, "First All-Female Mosque." References to women's mosques around the globe also feature into the public narratives of other projects like the WMA including the Qal'bu Maryam Mosque in Berkeley, California, and the Mariam Mosque in Copenhagen, Denmark.

43 Ann Braude, "Women's History Is American Religious History," in *Retelling US Religious History*, ed. Thomas A. Tweed (Berkeley: University of California Press, 1997), 89.

44 Ibid.

45 Ibid., 90.

46 Julie Byrne, *The Other Catholics Remaking America's Largest Religion* (New York: Columbia University Press, 2016).

47 See Benjamin R. Knoll and Cammie Jo Bolin, *She Preached the Word: Women's Ordination in Modern America* (Oxford: Oxford University Press, 2018).

48 Cynthia, interview.

49 Braude, "Women's History," 99.

50 Karla Goldman, *Beyond the Synagogue Gallery: Finding a Place for Women in American Judaism* (Cambridge, MA: Harvard University Press, 2001), 3.

51 Ibid., 15.

52 Ibid., 49.

53 Ibid., 80.

54 Ibid., 88.

55 Ibid., 90.

56 Ibid., 205.

57 Curtis, *Muslims in America*, 57. As we saw earlier, African American mosques, much like the institutional Black church, served as sites for to strengthen and construct Black autonomous identity, rather than as a vehicle to enter into the white Protestant mainstream culture.

58 Yasmin, interview with author, July 13, 2017.

59 See R. Marie Griffith, *God's Daughters: Evangelical Women and the Power of Submission* (Berkeley: University of California Press, 1997).

60 Aileen Cohen Nusbacher, "Efforts at Change in a Traditional Denomination: The Case of Orthodox Women's Prayer Groups," *Nashim: A Journal of Jewish Women's Studies and Gender*, no. 2 (1999): 95–113; Avraham Weiss, *Women at Prayer: A Halakhic Analysis of Women's Prayer Groups* (Hoboken, NJ: KTAV Publishing House, 2001); Goldman, *Beyond the Synagogue Gallery*.

61 Nusbacher, "Efforts at Change."

62 Griffith, *God's Daughters*.

63 Nusbacher, "Efforts at Change," 101.

64 Ibid.

65 Byrne, *The Other Catholics*, 41.

66 Ibid.

67 Ibid., 43.

68 Nusbacher, "Efforts at Change," 109.

69 Leila Ahmed, *Women and Gender in Islam: Historical Roots of a Modern Debate* (New Haven, CT: Yale University Press, 1992); amina wadud, *Qur'an and Woman: Rereading the Sacred Text from a Woman's Perspective* (New York: Oxford University Press, 1999); Asma Barlas, *Believing Women in Islam: Unreading Patriarchal Interpretations of the Qur'an* (Austin: University of Texas Press, 2002).

70 Maznavi, *Khateebah Guidebook*.

71 Cynthia, interview.

72 Ibid.

73 Ibid.

74 Ibid.

75 Ibid.

76 Ibid.

77 Marta Khadija, *Healing Racial Conflict: Special Focus on the Latino Community*, Women's Mosque of America, December 18, 2015, www.youtube.com/watch?v=YZwk-pca9ws.

78 Ibid.

79 Ibid.

80 Ibid.

81 Ibid.

82 Ibid.

83 Ibid.

84 For more on Latino Muslims' conversion experiences and their struggles as religious and racial minorities in the so-called religiously diverse and plural US, see Morales, *Latino and Muslim in America*.

85 Aamna, interview.

86 Ibid.

87 See Antonio Gualtieri, *Conscience and Coercion: Ahmadi Muslims and Orthodoxy in Pakistan* (Montreal: Guernica Editions, 1989).

88 Aamna, interview.

89 Ibid.

90 Nayawiyyah Muhammad, *History of Women in the Mosque & How to Nurture Our Souls*, Women's Mosque of America, August 26, 2016, youtube.com.

91 Dewji, *The Prophet's Daughter*.

92 Anne Myers, *Shi'a & Sunni Perspectives on Ashura*, Women's Mosque of America pre-khutbah bayan, September 29, 2017, www.youtube.com/watch?v=1rPaRr4iZCc.

93 Ibid.

94 Shabnam Dewji and Anne Myers, *Understanding Shia & Sunni Perspectives on Ashura*, Women's Mosque of America, 2020, www.youtube.com/watch?v=1VhGlmZ3Xxw.

95 Marta Khadija, interview with author, August 1, 2017.

96 "What We Do," LA Voice, accessed December 20, 2020, www.lavoice.org.

97 Khadija, interview.

98 Ibid.

99 Ibid.

100 "About," CLUE Justice, accessed December 20, 2020, www.cluejustice.org.

101 Elaine, interview with author, August 9, 2017.

102 Andrea Hodos, interview with author, August 9, 2017.

103 Lamptey, *Never Wholly Other*, 69–70.

104 Hidayatullah, *Feminist Edges of the Qur'an*, 60.

105 Close engagement with interfaith communities also characterizes other female-led Muslim spaces such as the Qal'bu Maryam Mosque (QMM) in Berkeley. For example, when I attended a Jummah at the QMM in June 2017, the khateebah was actually a female Buddhist nun. The QMM's engagement with interfaith communities therefore differs in important ways from that of the WMA, where self-identifying as Muslim is a prerequisite for serving as a khateebah.

106 Omid Safi, "The Asymmetry of Interfaith Dialogue," *On Being* (blog), October 29, 2015, https://onbeing.org.

CONCLUSION

1 Kennard, *The 12 Wives as Disciples*.

2 Ibid.

3 Sean Roberts, *The War on the Uyghurs: China's Internal Campaign against a Muslim Minority* (Princeton, NJ: Princeton University Press, 2020).

4 See David H. Warren, "When Promoting Religious Freedom Abroad Threatens Minority Communities Back Home," *Religion & Politics*, April 6, 2021, https://religionandpolitics.org.

5 See Ilyse Morgenstein Fuerst, "Job Ads Don't Add Up: Arabic + Middle East + Texts ≠ Islam," *Journal of the American Academy of Religion* 88, no. 4 (2020): 915–46.

INDEX

Aamna, 204, 218–220
Abdullah, Zain, 154, 157
Abou-Bakr, Omaima, 109, 110
Abou El Fadl, Khaled, 79–80, 134
aboutislam.net, 50–51
Abrahamic religions, 24, 193, 213
Abubaker, Sumaya, 124–125, 126, 127–128, 136
activism: authority through, 151–153, 170; of Black church, 186–187; Black Lives Matter (BLM), 153, 177–185, 190, 199, 234; community, 17; intersectional interfaith, 193, 222–229; social justice, 18, 158, 187; WMA and, 13, 157, 189; of women, 10, 185
African American mosques, 157, 262n57
African American Muslim women: Arabic language use by, 68–69; framework regarding, 13; history of, 174, 180–181; identity of, 152; immigrant Muslim women and, 154–155, 156–157; Islamophobia and, 160–161; leadership roles of, 55; marginalization of, 173; polygynous marriages of, 126–127; Qur'an learning by, 69, 70–71, 94; racism of, 136; repression of, 159–160; within WMA, 8, 155–158. *See also* anti-Black racism
African Americans, police brutality to, 161
African American women, 10–11
Ahmadi Muslims, 218–219, 220
ahong (religious leaders), 115
ahsan at-taqweem (best of stature), 131, 132, 133

Aisha, 137, 138
Al-Asqalani, Ibn Hajar, 33
Alawa, Laila, 194, 195–196, 197–199, 200
Al-Azhar, 78
alcohol, alienation of, 203
Al-Ghazali, Abu Hamid (d. 1111), 175
Al-Ghazali, Muhammad (d. 1996), 176
Ali, Kecia, 52–53, 74, 130, 258n79
Ali, Noble Drew, 188
Al-Khatahtbeh, Amani, 166–167, 168
Al-Madina Institute, 32
AlMaghrib Institute, 32, 42, 81
Al-Marayati, Laila, 90–91, 92–93, 114
Al-Shati', Bint, 115
Al-Shatibi, Imam, 175
Aly, Eman Hassaballa, 137, 144–146
Amal, 103–104
American Coptic Christians, 200
American Muslims: anti-culture stance of, 246n91; belonging of, 194–200; collective consciousness of, 171–174; discrimination of, 162; division within, 113; identity of, 152–153, 168; as immigrants, 156; labels regarding, 43; marginalization of, 158, 160; racializing, 158–163; as religious actors, 14–15; religious debates of, 232–233; space significance regarding, 59; stifling of, 235; suspicions of, 22, 27; tradition of, 73; undermining of, 13; whiteness and, 173; WMA criticism by, 25, 37, 49
Ana, 101–102, 137

ABOUT THE AUTHOR

TAZEEN M. ALI is Assistant Professor in the John C. Danforth Center on Religion and Politics at Washington University in St. Louis. She earned her PhD in Religious Studies from Boston University. Her research and teaching focus on Islam in America, Islam and gender, and race and religion in the United States.